Y0-AQS-238

The Speculator's Handbook

The Speculator's Handbook

David Smyth
and
Laurance F. Stuntz

Henry Regnery Company • Chicago

Library of Congress Cataloging in Publication Data

Smyth, David.
    The spectulator's handbook.

    1. Speculation—Handbooks, manuals etc.
2. Investments—Handbooks, manuals, etc. I. Stuntz,
Laurance F., joint author. II. Title.
HG60l5.S56   332.6'78   74-6911
ISBN 0-8092-9005-7

Published by Henry Regnery Company
180 North Michigan Avenue, Chicago, Illinois 60601
Manufactured in the United States of America
Library of Congress Catalog Card Number: 74-6911
International Standard Book Number: 0-8092-9005-7

TO HELENE, FARIS, AND DR. JOSEPH RANSOHOFF

Contents

Foreword

Do you have $10 in your pocket that you have no immediate use for? Or $50 that you would be willing to risk on some offbeat investment that gives you a chance for your money to multiply? Perhaps you have an extra $500 or $1,000 in your checking account—money that you could use for some out-of-the-ordinary investment or speculation.

If you do, this book is for you.

It will show you how to invest that money in new, exciting ways, in things you might never have imagined possible for yourself. Some of these investments are conservative; many others are highly speculative. All of them offer you a chance to make your money grow—if you know the secrets. This book will give you a great deal of that "inside information" that will help you become a winner.

Before we begin, we want to make some general statements about the purposes and contents of this book. First, we want to stress that we are not giving advice on how to invest *all* your life savings. If that's the kind of advice you're looking for, put this book down. Put your money in a federally insured savings account. If you have dependents, get adequate life insurance to take care of them in case anything happens to you. Make sure you have sufficient health insurance. Keep a cash reserve to meet any unforeseen emergencies. Make any other safe investments you think you should to take care of your own security and the security of those whom you love and are responsible for.

If you have a few dollars left over after all that, read on. This book will show you how to take those few dollars and turn them into larger and larger amounts. We'll investigate areas of money-making that are open to almost everyone, but that are little known outside certain circles. We'll tell you how to avoid the pitfalls that most investors make, how to interpret market trends and public events that affect them, how to keep from tying up your money unnecessarily. In short—we'll give you all the tools you need to make a success in these exotic investment areas. The rest is up to you.

As you know, or at least should know, there is nobody who can offer you an absolutely foolproof way to make money all the time. The future has an inexhaustible supply of uncertainties and surprises to upset the best-laid plans.

This book makes no pretense of being any exception. All it can do for you is give you the facts and explain the possibilities in commodities, gold coins, whisky, or other out-of-the-way investments. The results you achieve will then depend on your own shrewdness, knowledge, and luck.

In providing you with the facts you need, we have given you the names and addresses of a great many private firms, and have quoted from their sales literature. There are names and addresses of commercial firms in various fields, as well as names and addresses of dealers, brokers, advisers, periodicals, publishers, industry associations, banks, appraisers, and other services in various fields.

By writing to these sources, you can in most cases obtain further information by return post on oil and gas leases, race horses, or whatever particular subject interests you. In fact, if you write to all of them you will probably be swamped by more data than you can handle or absorb in weeks. The flood of booklets, guides, handbooks, and other literature will be enough to keep you busy for months.

In this way we intend to make this book a seedbed of ideas that you can then follow up on your own from other sources of information. But the fact that we mention firms by name does not mean that they are the only ones in their particular field. It does not mean that they are necessarily the best in the field. And it certainly does not mean that we recommend them above any other firm. It simply means that since you have to start somewhere, we are trying to give you a definite starting point for further investigation.

So please note this, here and throughout this book:

We do not endorse any firm we mention in these pages. We do not recommend it. We do not vouch for it in any way. We are unable to check on the competence, honesty or reliability of so many businesses in such a variety of fields as are dealt with in these chapters. Even if we were able to make such checks, there is no way of foreseeing that a firm may be taken over by a different management between the time of writing and the date of going to press.

Consequently, before dealing with any of the firms or other organizations mentioned in these pages you must make your own judgments in every case on their integrity, competence, and reliability.

What we *can* affirm is that we do not knowingly mention firms or other organizations whose reputation has been questioned, to the best of our knowledge and belief.

Similarly, we have quoted the laws and regulations of a great many governments and made statements about political situations that affect each area of speculation. Unfortunately, we live in a world that is constantly changing. This book is written for readers in the United States, Canada, Great Britain, and many other countries. The authors have no way of keeping up with changing legislation in every nation in the world, nor can they alert readers to changes in laws once this book has gone to press.

What we can do — and have done — is to give you some general guidelines for interpreting the news, changes in legislation, and other factors that may affect world prices. Once you understand how to do it, you can apply your own judgment to interpreting various events.

With this book, you are entering whole new areas of investment. Often there is a high degree of risk involved. But for the person with cool judgment, intelligent foresight, and money-making ability, there is also the promise of fast, rich rewards. This book will help make you that kind of investor.

1

Two Chances for Success

$\mathbf{H}$AVE YOU EVER heard of a lottery where you never
lose your money?

Yes, Virginia, there is such a thing. It is run by the government of Her Britannic Majesty Queen Elizabeth II. The
Queen's subjects and others have put nearly $2.5 billion into it
so far. The lottery is currently paying out about 90,000 prizes
a month, worth approximately $8.75 million altogether. The
tickets are called *Premium Savings Bonds,* and they cost one
pound sterling (about $2.50) each.

Instead of paying out interest on these bonds, the British
government calculates the interest the bonds should have
earned (generally about 4½ percent) and then runs a lottery
every month. The interest is paid out in the form of prizes to
the lucky winners, who are selected at random by a computer
called Ernie (Electronic Random Number Indicator Equipment is his full name).

Every month, each bond you buy has a chance to win a

prize of £5,000, £1,000, £500, £250, £100, £50, or £25. Every three months it also has a chance to win a super prize of £25,000 (about $62,500).

Any time you want your money back, you can hand in your bond for redemption, and the British government will pay you back exactly the pound sterling you paid in. You thus cannot ever lose your money, as long as the British government keeps faith with its bondholders.

So how about this idea to start you on your road to riches? Your minimum investment would be one pound sterling. The maximum amount the British government will allow any individual to own is 1,250 one-pound bonds (about $3,125). This money would not earn you any interest. It would be invested in the pound sterling, which is a paper currency like the American dollar, and which is constantly depreciated by inflation, as all paper currencies always have been in the history of the world. But every month you would have a chance with every bond you owned to turn one pound into £5,000, and every three months you could win £25,000 if Ernie favored you.

And, if he did, we could then go on to talk about bigger things.

British Premium Savings Bonds are run by the British government. As such they are 100 percent legal in the United Kingdom. They are also sold to people abroad wherever the British government does not know of any legal impediment to their purchase in any particular foreign country.

In the United States there is a federal law banning any communications about lotteries through the United States mails, and this law creates certain difficulties. In view of the lotteries run by New York, New Jersey, and other states, this law seems increasingly anachronistic, and one day it may be repealed. But, as of 1974, it is still in effect. Other countries have differing legislation.

As far as the authors know, there is no restriction against the actual ownership of British Premium Savings Bonds by United States citizens or residents. But the British government is rather uptight about violating the United States mail laws, and any owner of Premium Savings Bonds with a United States address is liable to get a polite note from Her Britannic Majesty's government asking that the bonds be redeemed at his earliest convenience. The British authorities are worried that if you do win a prize they will have to notify you through the United States mail. If you keep the bonds in England, the problem presumably does not arise.

Consequently, if you live in the United States, the best way to buy the bonds is through a friend who lives in Great Britain or through a British bank. Open an account with any reliable bank in Great Britain and ask the bank to buy the bonds and keep them in safe custody, with each bond registered in your name at the bank's address. You would then be notified of any prizes care of the bank.

The head offices of some of the biggest banks in Great Britain are Barclays Bank Limited, 54 Lombard Street, London EC3; Hambros Limited, 41 Bishopsgate, London EC2; Lloyds Bank Limited, 71 Lombard Street, London EC3; Midland Bank Limited, 27-32 Poultry, London EC2; and National Westminster Bank Limited, 41 Lothbury, London EC2.

Each of these banks has hundreds of branches throughout the United Kingdom. If you live in Great Britain itself or some other country where there are no restrictions against buying the bonds, you can purchase them at any British Post Office. Or, write for further information to the Premium Savings Bond Office, Lytham St. Annes, Lancashire, England.

As regards British banks there is one important thing to watch for if you live outside Great Britain. Make sure your account is an *external sterling* account. Residents of Great Britain are subject to exchange controls, but these are not applied to people who reside abroad. Foreign residents are allowed to hold external sterling accounts, through which they can move their funds in and out of the country as they please. Make a special note of this. As you will see later in this book, your British bank account will come in useful for other purposes.

When you buy Premium Savings Bonds you have an initial waiting period of three months before Ernie includes them in his monthly draws. Once that time is over you are in the running for every prize. Let's hope you hit the jackpot soon. When you do, your prize is free and clear of British taxes. Winners are notified by mail, and most British newspapers also publish the numbers of the prizewinning bonds.

Oil and Gas Leases on United States Public Land

Another kind of lottery is run on the third Monday of each month by the federal government of the United States of America. The government itself says it makes no objection to using the United States mails for this purpose.

In this deal you have to put up $10 and be an American citizen. (Non-citizens, we are sorry, there is apparently no way around this.) You also have to be over twenty-one.

The $10 (nonrefundable) is your filing fee with the United States government to include your name in the monthly drawings of public lands offered by the United States Bureau of Land Management for oil and gas leasing. In addition to the fee, you pay 50 cents an acre for the first year's rental on the parcel for which you are applying. If you are not awarded a lease, the rental fee is returned to you.

Each month the government offers for oil and gas leasing rights several hundred parcels of land, varying in size up to a maximum of 2,560 acres. If there is more than one applicant for any parcel, a public drawing is held and the winner is determined by lot. This ensures that every interested United States citizen has an equal opportunity to participate in these rights over publicly owned lands. The rights entitle you to profit by whatever oil and gas Nature may have placed under your particular parcel of land.

What are the odds against you, and how much money can you make if Lady Luck favors you? According to Federal Oil & Gas Leases Incorporated, a private firm that offers intermediary, advisory, representative, and brokerage services in this field: "Some of the lease-parcels awarded each month provide profit potentials in excess of $1,000,000 under the most ideal production conditions. Your chance of winning one of the more valuable parcels is usually about one out of 2,000 total applicants."

It adds—and we stress this—*"Please remember that all investments in oil and gas must be considered speculative, and no guarantees are made regarding profit potentials."*

What you have here, in fact, is two levels of uncertainty. First, is your name going to be picked out of the hat when the government chooses the successful applicant by lot? The odds would be around 2,000 to one for the more highly esteemed parcels, and perhaps 100 to one or better for the less sought-after parcels. Second, if your name *is* chosen, and you are awarded a lease, are you going to make any money out of it?

Federal Oil & Gas says that "only about 10 percent of the lease parcels posted for public drawing each month is salable for *immediate* substantial profits." Other parcels, of course, may be promising long-term speculations, and the firm says its principals "apply for long term speculative leases and maintain a substantial portfolio of such leases."

Now, what is all this business about, exactly? Let's look at the overall picture. The United States sprawls over a total of 2.2 billion acres of land, of which the federal government owns 755 million acres. According to an official government estimate, more than half the remaining unexploited United States oil and gas resources are on these federal lands, which cover one third of the nation's land area.

The United States is facing a growing energy scarcity. It is using up its known reserves of oil and gas at an accelerating rate, and year by year it is becoming ever more dependent on foreign suppliers. So far it has been well served by two friendly countries—Canada and Venezuela. But future trends indicate an ever-greater reliance on oil-producing nations of the Middle East. These are Arab states, many of which are not noted for their friendliness to the United States. Some have radical, unstable, and unpredictable regimes that have demonstrated their willingness to cut off oil supplies to the West for political reasons. All of them are sworn enemies of Israel, and quite openly exploit any United States dependence on their oil to choke off American support for the Israelis.

In short, in the coming years the United States had better make sure of every drop of oil and each bubble of gas it can squeeze out of its own subsoil. It seems reasonable to expect, therefore, that government policy will spur the development of oil and gas resources of public lands, and that private oil companies will intensify their search for oil and gas within the borders of the United States.

If you are lucky and win a government lease for your $10 filing fee, you will probably stand a growing chance for profit as the years go by, due to these very circumstances.

How do you go about getting in on this opportunity? The first step is to write to the United States Bureau of Land Management, Department of the Interior, Washington, D.C. 20240 and ask for information on their monthly public drawings of oil and gas leases.

You will get back a five-page mimeographed brochure that, for a government document, is a model of clarity in plain, simple English. It explains that if a tract of government land overlies a geological structure that is *known* to produce oil and gas, the lease must be offered on a competitive market. Some of these lands, such as the North Slope of Alaska and offshore Louisiana, have attracted bids in recent years in excess of *one billion* dollars for certain large areas from the giant oil companies.

"All other lands," the government brochure continues, "are available for leasing on a non-competitive basis." If you put in an application, you "are dealing in wildcat land that has an unknown potential for the production of oil and gas. . . the Federal Government makes absolutely no claim regarding the potential of the tract offered."

"Frankly," the government brochure declares, "money invested in a non-competitive oil and gas lease is at best a long-shot gamble. You could make money, but the odds are against it. You should never invest in such a lease any money that you cannot afford to lose. . .In some cases, persons holding non-competitive oil and gas leases have made a substantial profit. A very few have gotten rich."

The brochure gives the addresses of twelve Bureau of Land Management offices where you may file your offer for a non-competitive lease. The offices are located in Alaska, Arizona, California, Colorado, Idaho, Montana, Nevada, New Mexico, Oregon, Utah, Wyoming, and Maryland. These offices will supply you, for a fee, a list of the leases offered each month. You select the parcel you want, mail in your filing card, $10 filing fee, and the first year's rent and then hope for luck to favor you at the monthly drawing.

At this point some difficulties will become apparent to you. The first snag is that the government requires you to mail in your first year's rental, which could go as high as $1,280 for the maximum 2,560-acre allotment. If you do not win the lease, you get your rental payment back, of course, but meanwhile the money is tied up.

The second snag is that if you do win a lease but do not have contacts in the oil industry, you do not know how to go about finding an oil company to exploit your land for you. If you want to drill a wildcat well yourself, the average cost is about $100,000 and could run much higher. However, it is certainly true that, under growing pressure to find new oil and gas resources, the companies will probably come looking for you if you have a hot property.

The third snag is that unless you happen to be an oil geologist and have time to study each parcel, you do not know which of several hundred parcels up for grabs each month is really worth applying for or getting.

This is where a number of firms known as "filing services" step in. They offer to select geologically promising parcels, put up the first year's rental with each application, and later put you in contact with oil companies or lease brokers if you win a lease.

The government brochure says that advertising solicitation of your business by many of these firms "is probably legitimate." It adds, however, that the firms "vary greatly in their reliability and in the actual services they perform for their clients. You should question any that paint an overly optimistic picture. . .or any that pressure you to make a quick decision."

Let's take a look at one of these private filing services (which have no connection with the United States government), Federal Oil & Gas Leases Incorporated, 2995 L.B.J. Freeway, P.O. Box 29119, Dallas, Texas 75229.

This particular firm says it will advance the required rental fee on behalf of its clients. You pay the fee to the firm later only if you win the lease, and your own money is thus not tied up meanwhile. However, instead of mailing in your $10 registration fee to the government, you send Federal Oil & Gas a check for $25.

The extra $15, according to the firm, buys you other services besides the advance rental payment. Federal Oil & Gas says it makes a geological study of the available parcels each month and mails its clients a list of the ones it considers to have the highest profit potential. It handles all the details of filing your entry for the drawing, and if you win a lease it promises to "put you in direct contact with oil companies or lease brokers who are active in the area" without charge to you.

Obviously, the first part of this deal could be highly beneficial to your odds of success in the drawing. If all you have to put up is $25 for each parcel you apply for (instead of $400 or so, the average lease being about 800 acres) you might apply for a number of parcels. (Regulations state that you may enter only one application for each lease available.) Otherwise multiple applications would involve you in an outlay of hundreds of dollars.

Once you do win a parcel you would do well to consult a lawyer, preferably one who is expert in this field, before you sign any contracts with anyone regarding the exploitation of its oil and gas potential. It might be noted, incidentally, that filing services generally enter your application under your name but at their own address. Consequently, should you win a lease, any oil company interested in it would have to approach you through the filing service. If you wanted to act independently you would have to look for your own broker or advertise your lease for sale. It would be pointless to give you names of oil companies or lease brokers here, however, because your parcel might be in any of various states, and different outfits are active in different places.

Supposing you win a lease and get an offer for it. The amount of money involved might well justify the expense of a good independent adviser. Federal Oil & Gas says that in recent months some of its lucky clients have sold, or have been offered, in one case, "$80,000 plus 5% overriding royalty for 800 acres in Eddy County, New Mexico. There were 4,262 applications for this lease. The winner's cost was $400."

In another case, it says, "$1,000,000 of estimated future revenues will be received by a client who farmed his lease out to an oil company and retained half interest in all oil or gas produced. Three oil wells have been completed on the lease which is located in Campbell County, Wyoming. Total applications entered for this lease were 1,525. The winner's cost was $240."

When you win a lease, you try to assign it to an oil company interested in drilling in the area. The usual practice is for the drilling company to pay you an immediate cash bonus while also allowing you to retain an "overriding royalty." This is an interest in oil and gas production, free of expense of production and in addition to the landowner's royalty retained by the government.

Federal Oil & Gas claims that "leases designated as highly recommended on the lists of recommendations mailed to our clients are usually sold for large profits within 90 days."

If no company comes forward to buy your lease immediately, you can keep it merely by paying the government rental punctually each year at 50 cents an acre. You have ten years to do something productive with your lease, which is strictly for oil and gas production. You cannot build on your leased land, cultivate it, or close it to trespassing.

At the end of the tenth year, if there is no oil or gas production from your land, your lease will expire. The government may then put it up for lease by public drawing once again.

If your lease does go into production before the ten years are up, you may keep the lease as long as oil or gas is produced in paying quantities. As soon as it starts producing you no longer have to pay the yearly rental. Your income (under current law) would be 22 percent, tax free under the oil and gas depletion allowance. Even if you don't go into production, your entry fee and first year rental fee are also tax deductible.

It might occur to you at this point that you could bypass this lottery business altogether and make sure of a lease by buying from somebody who had already won a parcel. If that is your intention, beware.

According to Michael Giller, a Bureau of Land Management official, you should especially be wary of purchasing interests from private parties who already own government leases. He says, "Forty-acre leases out of 2,560-acre leases are usually sold for about $100. Since there are 64 forty-acre tracts in one 2,560-acre lease, it becomes obvious that the advertisers could realize $6,400 on an initial outlay of only $1,280. . .this is not a bad deal for the advertisers." You are very probably better off just to try your luck directly with the United States Government in its monthly lottery.

2

The International Portfolio

DID YOU GET CLOBBERED in the New York stock market in 1974? In 1970? In 1962? Maybe even in 1929? Perhaps you should have invested in Hong Kong, or in some other stock market. There are dozens of them around the world, from Tokyo to London to Johannesburg. There is always some stock market boom going on somewhere in the world, even when Wall Street is down in the dumps.

Hong Kong, a tiny British Crown Colony on the bulging coast of Communist China, is one of the most vigorously capitalistic societies on earth. Four million people, jam-packed on a few rocky acres with no natural resources at all, have managed to build up a volume of foreign trade that, incredibly, has at times surpassed that of China itself.

For eighty years the British ran a rather stuffy, clubby stock exchange that reminded some observers of the novels of Somerset Maugham. Then, in 1969, some high-pressure local Chinese businessmen founded a rival institution, the Far East

Stock Exchange, which went out aggressively in search of new business. Trading volume soared and new issues came on the market in a constant stream until they numbered more than 200.

The Hang Seng index, a Dow Jones-type indicator of thirty-three stocks, which had started out at 100 in 1964 and chugged along unspectacularly ever since, began to soar. By 1970 it was up to 213; in 1971 it topped 400; and by the end of 1972 it was nearing 750.

By this time everyone was getting into the act. Foreign money was pouring in from London, Tokyo, and elsewhere, and two more exchanges were founded, making a total of four. The entire population of Hong Kong was now involved in stock dealing. Factory workers carried transistor radios to work and rushed to the telephone every twenty minutes or so to call their brokers with orders. One housemaid raked in such profits that she bought a couple of apartments and a farm.

Early in 1973 the Hang Seng index pushed up through the 800 mark, broke through 900, and rocketed on through the 1,000 barrier, all in a matter of weeks. Speculation reached a frenzied level. Price-earnings ratios had long since been forgotten and all sense of real value was lost. The Hong Kong Land Investment & Agency Company, a major real estate firm, sold at 300 times earnings. Local papers reported the arrest of Lo Fai, a seventy-six-year-old beggar, for panhandling. Police found he was carrying a transistor radio to keep track of his stock holdings.

Foreign newspapers around the world were now running stories on the great Hong Kong stock market boom. In New York, the *Wall Street Journal* reported the case of Dorothy Tsoi, a Hong Kong office girl, who "moved into the stock market a few years back with the then equivalent of $500. She parlayed that up to about $20,000, sold out, and bought a house that today is worth $90,000." Stock market gains were fueling a real estate boom, whose profits were channeled back into the stock market, and the two booms thus fed on each other.

The Hang Seng index continued climbing. By March, 1973, it was up to 1,775. At this point the big professional money managers were already pulling out of the market in a big way. They knew that all good things come to an end and could see the inevitable crash coming soon.

What was left was the wild speculation of the little investors — the cooks, nursemaids, taxi drivers, office clerks, and housewives. Since early in the year, the Hong Kong government had also been taking measures to clamp down on the wild gambling fever that had gripped the colony and emptied the legitimate gambling casinos in Portuguese Macao across the bay.

By April, 1973, the market was beginning to collapse. Declines widened steadily, dropping as much as forty points a day in the Hang Seng index. By June the index was down to 650, barely more than a third of its all-time high only three months before. By May, 1974, it had plunged to 290. The great Hong Kong stock market boom was over.

What are we to make of all this? If you had invested in Hong Kong stock when the Hang Seng index was at 100 in 1964, you could theoretically have multiplied your capital by 17.75 (that is, you could have earned $1,775 for every $100 you put in) by selling out at the 1,775 top in March, 1973.

On the other hand, if you had invested at the 1,775 top in March and then sold out at 650 in June, 1973, you would have lost nearly two-thirds of your money in only three months.

What we have here in fact is a classic stock market boom-and-bust cycle, a manic-depressive swing that soars to ludicrous heights of overoptimism and then plunges into absurd depths of pessimism.

One of the most extreme examples of this was the New York stock market boom and crash of the 1920s and 1930s. All through the Roaring Twenties, American stocks rose to ever dizzier heights as the American public became more and more convinced with every new stock market high that permanent prosperity had been built into the national economy. This bullish sentiment reached a peak on September 3, 1929, when the Dow Jones index of industrial stocks hit a high of 381.17. In October the bubble burst, and the collapse of public confidence did not reach its nadir until July 8, 1932, when the Dow Jones index fell to a rock bottom 41.22.

Billions of dollars worth of paper profits had been wiped out by then and the country was in the grip of a depression from which it did not recover until the late 1930s.

Three obvious conclusions are to be drawn from this. First, it is not prudent to risk everything on the Hong Kong stock exchange, on the New York stock market, or in fact any other individual stock market. Second, it was a ridiculous and calamitous decision to buy stock at the height of the speculative frenzy in New York in September, 1929, or in Hong Kong in March, 1973. Third, it was an equally absurd and ruinous decision to sell stock at the bottom in New York in 1933 or in Hong Kong in 1973-74.

Now let's see if we can turn those three conclusions upside down, so that we make profits while most investors take losses. The problem boils down to this: Is there any way to spread our risks over several stock markets around the world, buying into each market at the bottom and selling at the top?

The answer is yes. On a worldwide scale, you can deal yourself a pretty good chance of getting *somewhere close* to this ideal. Obviously there is no 100 percent foolproof way of buying at the absolute bottom and selling at the absolute top in any market. There are just too many unpredictable factors ahead when you make your buy or sell decision.

In fact, human psychology being what it is, you will find it very hard to avoid being a loser in a Hong Kong-type boom-and-bust cycle. If you are an American, for example, it is very difficult to *avoid* buying United States stocks near the top, when everybody around you is exuding boundless optimism, brokers are pushing perpetual growth stocks, and the economy is booming together with the stock market. It is even more difficult, perhaps, to escape selling stocks near the bottom, when everyone from the experts on down is dripping pessimism, when the economy is in a tailspin, when your firm is on the verge of going out of business, and when your own job seems to be about to go down the drain.

But if you are a foreigner living thousands of miles away in a different country, all such factors will not touch you personally. You will be able to view the situation more dispassionately and you will find it easier to go against the prevailing psychological current. With all this in mind, there *is* a system which will make it easier for you to buy *somewhere near* the bottom and sell *somewhere near* the top in most of the world's stock markets. At the very least, this system will keep you out of a lot of trouble by telling you *not* to invest right before the bust, no matter what the experts are saying to encourage you.

At the same time, this system will alert you to the buying opportunities as one market or another scrapes bottom in Paris, Frankfort, London, Sydney, Tokyo, Zurich, Milan, Toronto, Vienna, Johannesburg, Amsterdam, and other financial centers around the world.

There are only two ways *all* of these markets could plausibly touch bottom at the same time and drag *all* your investments down with them—something that will almost inevitably occur when you are fully invested only in New York, Hong Kong, or some other individual market. One contingency would be a worldwide depression and the other would be a world war. Even in a global depression, however, you would do relatively well in the better-managed countries, and in a world war, at least some of your assets would be safe in neutral nations such as Switzerland. In more normal times—that is, in the absence of these two calamities—you will always have an opportunity open somewhere to buy low or sell high in one country or another around the globe.

Buy Low, Sell High
First of all, ignore all the day-to-day stock market commentaries in your newspaper. When they talk about stocks "plunging" on Thursday or "soaring" on Friday, they mean at the very most a 30-point fluctuation in the Dow Jones index in

one day. What we are looking for is a major swing, such as the 420-point rise in the Dow Jones from 631 in May, 1970, to 1,051 in January, 1973.

Second, pay no attention at all to stories in the paper about stock market booms in foreign lands. By the time United States papers are taking notice of the frenzy of speculation in Hong Kong or Rio de Janeiro (another place you could have made a fortune in a short time in recent years), you can be sure the boom has just about run its course. You will be just in time to be taken for a ride with all the housemaids, taxi drivers, and other living proofs of the theory that "there is always a bigger fool"—which inevitably ends up with the biggest fool taking all the loss.

Third, you can quite safely ignore the predictions of all the "experts." There may have been some pretty good prophets around in biblical times, but they didn't deal in stocks, and they aren't around now. If you want proof that nobody can consistently predict future price levels, consider this: Mutual funds employ hundreds of high-salaried market analysts and portfolio managers to beat the market, and they invariably fail to do so. Studies by the Wharton School of Finance, the Stanford Business School, and the University of Rochester have all found that mutual funds have done just about as well as the market indexes, no better and no worse. They could have achieved practically the same results by firing their experts and buying stocks at random. You can verify this yourself by buying *Barron's* magazine at intervals and checking an item titled "Lipper Mutual Fund Performance Index," which shows that 533 United States mutual funds do a little better in some weeks than the Dow Jones and other market indexes, while in some weeks they do a little worse. In the long run, the mutual funds usually seem to do just a little bit worse. If that is how the "experts" do in the United States stock market, it is a fairly safe bet that foreign "experts" do not do any better in foreign markets. And, most likely, neither will we, either at home or abroad.

But even though you may not be able to beat the markets, you can try to go with them as they swing up or down. The key to each stock market is its stock price index. This tells you with some kind of mathematical certainty and precision whether the present level of prices is near an all-time high, near an all-time low, or somewhere in between.

On the New York Stock Exchange, the Dow Jones index measures the price level of the stocks of thirty major industrial corporations. The Dow Jones index gives an uninterrupted record of price levels since 1897. The New York Stock Exchange index gives the average price level of all common stocks on that exchange; the American Stock Exchange index records the price levels of all stocks quoted on the Amex; and the NASDAQ index covers a representative group of stocks quoted over the counter. Other indexes are published by *Barron's* magazine and Standard & Poor's Corporation. These show price levels in numerous subsections of the market such as utility stocks, transportation issues, airlines, chemical companies, railroads, and many other groups.

In exactly the same way, you can follow the stock exchange indexes of foreign stock markets, which tell you in cold, unemotional figures whether prices are high or low in relation to past years in Tokyo, Paris, Sydney, or other financial centers. How do you keep track of foreign stock market indexes? Quite easily. For a start, you buy *Barron's* magazine. *Barron's* is a United States financial weekly available at your newsstand. Or, you can subscribe by writing to 200 Burnett Road, Chicopee, Massachusetts 01021. On one of the last pages in each issue of *Barron's* you will find a table that looks like the table that follows.

Foreign Stock Indexes

	1974 High	Low	June 28 Close	Week's Change
Australia	536.50	450.57	N.A.	
Austria	2,750.00	2,508.00	2,690.00 —	3.00
Belgium	144.60	119.30	119.30 —	5.50
Canada	228.78	182.05	183.39 —	4.74
France	110.80	82.50	82.50 —	1.60
Italy	8,293.00	6,364.00	6,364.00 —	289.00
Japan	4,782.22	4,151.00	4,602.87 —	63.87

Netherl.	117.30	103.80	105.90 —	3.50
Switzerl.	340.50	302.80	274.80 —	7.90
U.K.	a339.30	246.00	225.10 —	56.90
UK Kaffirs	424.30	207.10	297.30 —	14.70
W. Germany	b93.22	85.00	558.70 —	1.00
A-Pierson 50	124.26	114.15	115.58 +	1.38

N.A.-Not available

In the *New York Times* you will find a similar table in the Business section:

Foreign Stock Index

	Yester- day	Prev. day	——1974—— High	Low
Amsterdam.....124.1	123.8	140.8	121.1
Brussels...........88.44	88.73	102.48	88.44
Frankfurt 109.17	108.50	117.34	103.99
fLondon(30)....261.9	254.4	339.0	246.0
fLondon(500)..109.75	107.79	150.61	104.73
iMilan 115.87	118.54	154.24	115.87
Paris 89.4	92.4	113.5	89.4
Sydney...........331.33	332.36	418.38	331.33
dTokyo(n).......332.71	333.85	342.47	299.22
dTokyo(o)....4,599.51	4,622.15	4,787.54	4,151.00
Toronto 181.32	183.39	227.94	181.32
sZurich...........290.1	287.9	350.8	278.2

The Toronto and Montreal Stock Exchanges were closed Monday, July 1, in observance of Dominion Day.

The *Financial Times* of London (Bracken House, Cannon Street, London EC4, England) runs several tables of stock indexes. This daily, the British equivalent of the *Wall Street Journal*, carries far more information on world stock markets than the *Journal* does. In New York and other United States cities you can buy it the same day it appears in London at news and magazine stores that specialize in foreign publications.

In the *Financial Times* you will find all the major United States stock market indexes, including the Dow Jones Industrials, Transportation and Utilities, the New York and American all-stock Exchange indexes and Standard & Poor's 500-share and 425 industrials indexes. Also included are the daily indexes of stock markets in Toronto, Montreal, Johannesburg, Sydney, Hong Kong, Singapore, Tokyo, Belgium, Denmark, France, Germany, Holland, Italy, Sweden, and Switzerland. The *Financial Times* also runs its own London Stock Exchange indexes, including a 30 industrial stocks index, a 500-stocks index and a gold mines index, and indexes of 48 subsections of the London market, such as oil company, bank, and tea plantation shares.

You can keep track of Canadian stock market indexes in the Toronto *Globe and Mail,* a daily, and the *Financial Post* (P.O. Box 9100, Postal Station A, Toronto, Ontario, Canada), a business weekly. Your own local newspaper may also run some of these foreign indexes.

You will note that nearly all these tables give you the latest index figure plus the high and low for the current year. This is not really a long enough time-span. Remember that the New York boom-and-bust cycle of the 1920s and 1930s took about a decade to run its course from the beginning of the bull market to the bottom of the bear market in 1932.

You really need at least a ten-year period in order to tell whether a given stock market is high or low in relation to its past performance.

Here is a twelve-year table for most of the major stock markets of the world covering the period from 1962 to 1973. You can easily update this table by buying *Barron's*, the *New York Times,* and the *London Financial Times* and *Financial Post* around December 31 of each year and filling in the new high and low for that year.

INDEX	WHERE PUBLISHED	1962-1973 PERIOD	
		HIGH	LOW
(1)			
Australia	Barron's		
Sydney General Index	NY Times		
	Fin. Times	663.48	282.87
(2)			
Austria	Barron's	3661	1743
(3)			
Belgium	Barron's	157.50	93.50
(4)			
Canada			
Toronto Industrials	Barron's		
	NY Times		
	Fin. Times		
	Globe & Mail		
	Fin. Post	229.26	105.77
(5)			
Canadian Oil Companies	Globe & Mail		
Toronto Western Oils	Fin. Post	310.73	64.68
Canada Statistics Petrol-eum Cos.	Fin. Post	373.1	90.8
(6)			
France			
Paris New Index (Base 1961)	Fin. Times	114.3	56.1
(7)			
Germany	Barron's		
Commerzbank Index	Fin. Times	920.5	493.7
Frankfort Index	NY Times	177.24	86.02
(8)			
Great Britain	Fin. Times		
Fin. Times 500 Industrials	NY Times	227.95	84.86
Fin. Times 30 Industrials	Fin. Times		
	Barron's		
	NY Times	543.6	252.8

INDEX	WHERE PUBLISHED	1962-1973 PERIOD	
		HIGH	LOW
(9) British Financial Cos. Fin. Times Financial Group Index	Fin. Times	241.41	69.83
(10) British Investment Trusts Fin. Times Investment Trust Index	Fin. Times	245.79	80.84
(11) British Real Estate Cos. Fin. Times Property Index	Fin. Times	357.40	56.01
(12) British Oil Companies Fin. Times Oil Index	Fin. Times	431.66	87.23
(13) Holland Amsterdam Index (Base 1963=100)	Fin. Times NY Times	171.9	66.0
(14) Hong Kong Hang Seng Index (Base July 31, 1964=100)	Fin. Times	1,775	59.0
(15) Italy Milan Index	Barron's	11,014	5,175
(16) Japan Tokyo Dow Jones Index	NY Times Fin. Times	5,359.74	1,020.49
Tokyo Stock Exchange Index	Barron's NY Times Fin. Times	422.43	81.29

INDEX	WHERE PUBLISHED	1962-1973 PERIOD	
		HIGH	LOW
(17)			
South Africa			
Financial Times Gold Mines Index (mines quoted on the London Exchange)	Fin. Times Barron's	207.1	43.5
Barron's Gold Mining Index (mines quoted on US exchanges)	Barron's	386.36	47.47
Standard & Poor's Gold Mining Index (mines quoted on US exchanges)	S&P Stock Guide	73.77	19.48
(18)			
Switzerland	NY Times		
Zurich Industrial Index	Fin. Times	469.8	176.4
Zurich General Index	Barron's	424.9	160.3

And now, to complete the world picture, we'll follow the same procedure with some of the main United States stock market indexes. (The Standard & Poor's indexes of chemical, oil, real estate, and life insurance companies, which are not usually published by newspapers, may be obtained from Standard & Poor's Security Owner's Stock Guide, 345 Hudson Street, New York, New York 10014. This is a monthly summary of all major American corporations' stock issues, prices, earnings, price-earnings ratios and other data. A yearly subscription costs $30.)

INDEX	WHERE PUBLISHED	HIGH	LOW
(19)			
U.S. Stocks			
Dow Jones 30 Industrials	Most major US daily newspapers	1,051.70	535.76
New York Stock Exchange all-stock Index	Barron's Fin. Times Globe & Mail	65.48	28.2
Standard & Poor's 500 Stock Index	S & P Stock Guide	120.24	52.32

INDEX	WHERE PUBLISHED	1962-1973	PERIOD
(20) U.S. Utility Stocks	Most major US dailies		
Dow Jones Utilities Index	Barron's	163.32	85.28
Standard & Poor's Utility Index	Fin. Times S&P Stock Guide Fin. Post	78.20	46.48
(21) U.S. Oil Companies Standard & Poor's Oil Composite Index	S&P Stock Guide	161.41	71.87
Barron's Oil Companies Index	Barron's	402.73	219.04
(22) U.S. Real Estate Cos. Standard & Poor's Real Estate Co. Index	S&P Stock Guide	52.12	9.00
(23) U. S. Banks Barron's Bank Index	Barron's	392.79	131.21
(24) U.S. Insurance Cos. Barron's Insurance Index	Barron's	1,024.59	414.61
Standard & Poor's Life Insurance Index	S&P Stock Guide	365.24	188.96
(25) U.S. Chemical Companies Standard & Poor's Chemical Companies Index	S&P Stock Guide	76.78	36.93
Barron's Chemicals Index	Barron's	423.17	170.07

You now have the indexes of twenty-five different markets. We will show you how to invest in each of them later on in this chapter. For the present we are interested only in the *timing* of your investment. You want to buy in each market near its bottom and sell somewhere near its top.

The first step is to buy *Barron's,* the *Financial Times,* and the other periodicals mentioned and to check the latest figure for each market index. The job will not take more than ten minutes. Any market that is near its twelve-year low is a possible buying opportunity, while any market that is close to its twelve-year high is one in which you should think about selling any holdings you may have.

You might also develop your own formula for the best moment to buy or sell. For example, you might buy when a market touches a new bottom, when it is within 10 percent of its previous bottom, or when the index is 50 points off its lowest and 200 points down from its highest point. In this last event you could figure that the upside potential is four times better than the downside risk. As long as you make sure to buy low and sell high, it probably does not really matter too much which method you choose.

How To Buy Foreign Stocks

There are three ways to participate in foreign stock markets. One is to build up your own portfolio of foreign stocks by buying the shares of foreign companies quoted in the United States stock markets. Another way is to buy mutual funds or investment trusts that specialize in the stocks of one foreign market or another. This simplifies matters because you do not have to select and manage your own portfolio. Third, you can reach the ultimate in simplification by making one single investment in a mutual fund or trust that has a worldwide spread of investments in its portfolio.

Let's take a look at the individual stocks first. You can buy about four hundred foreign stocks right in the United States from your American broker. Among the stocks available are those from about eighty British firms, fifty South

African firms, and twenty West German firms. Some are quoted on the New York Stock Exchange, others appear on the American Stock Exchange, and many others are sold over the counter. You will find a few of them in a table of quotations titled "Foreign Securities" in the *Wall Street Journal* and in the *New York Times*.

Here are some of the shares you can buy in the United States. Each group is keyed to its corresponding stock market index in the table of indexes on pages 20 to 23. The (1) after Australia, for instance, refers you to the first index in the table, the Sydney General index. Some countries, such as Jamaica and Zambia, have no readily available market index.

Australia (1)
G.J. Coles & Company Limited; Cox Brothers Australia Limited; Custom Credit Corporation Limited; Interstate Oil Limited; Myer Emporium Limited; Ampol Exploration Limited; Ampol Petroleum Limited; Santos Limited; Ultramar Company; Broken Hill Proprietary Company; Peko Wallsend Limited; Union Carbide Australia; Vam Limited; Western Mining Corporation.

Belgium (3)
Gevaert Photo.

Botswana
Botswana RST Limited.

Canada (4) (5)
Canadian Pacific Railway, Alcan Aluminum*, Asamera Oil*, Banff Oil, Bell Telephone Company of Canada, British American Oil, Campbell Red Lake, Canadian Breweries, Canadian Export Gas & Oil*, Canadian Homestead Oils*, Canadian Superior Oil*, Canadianwide Properties, Charter Oil Company, Cominco Limited, Denison Mines, Distillers Corporation Seagrams, Dome Mines*, Dome Petroleum, Dominion Steel & Coal, Dominion Textile, Domtar Limited,

Giant Yellowknife Mines, Golconda Mining, Granby Mining*, Great Plains Development, Home Oil Company, Husky Oil Canada, Imperial Oil Limited*, Imperial Tobacco Company Canada, International Nickel Company of Canada, Lake Ontario Cement, Loblaw Incorporated, Massey Ferguson, Molybdenum Corporation of Canada, National Petroleum Corporation, North Canadian Oils*, Pacific Petroleums*, Power Corporation of Canada, Prairie Oil Royalties, Quebec Lithium Corporation, Rio Algom Mines, St. Lawrence Corporation, Scurry Rainbow Oil, Simpsons Limited, Stanrock Uranium, Steel Company of Canada, Union Gas Company of Canada, United Asbestos Corporation*, Westcoast Transmission.

Many Canadian stocks, including those marked with an asterisk, are exempt from the United States Interest Equalization Tax, which we shall cover later in this chapter.

France (6)

Schneider et Cie., FFSA, Compagnie de Saint Gobain, Compagnie Financiere de Suez, Peugeot S.A., Source Perrier, Simca Industries.

Germany (7)

Allgemeine Elektrizitaets Gesellschaft, August Thyssen Huette A.G., Badische Anilin & Soda Fabrik, Gelsenkirchener Bergwerke A.G., Hoesch A.G., Kloeckner Werke, Mannesman, Rheinische Stahlwerke, Rheinisch Westfaelisches Elektrizitaets, Siemens, Volkswagenwerk, Bayerische Vereinsbank, Commerzbank, Deutsche Bank, Dresdner Bank, Deutsche Lufthansa, Farbenfabriken Bayer, Farbwerke Hoechst.

Great Britain (8-12)

Beecham Group Limited, Fairey Company Limited, International Distillers & Vintners Limited, Sears Holdings, Stewarts & Lloyds, Unigate Limited, Marks & Spencer, Morgan Grampian, Plessey Company, British Leyland Motor Corporation, Burmah Oil Company, Boots Pure Drug Company, British Aluminium Company, Charter Consolidated Limited, Coats Patons Limited, Consolidated Tin Smelters, General Mining & Finance Corporation, Shell Transport & Trading Company, Tate & Lyle Limited, Unilever, Anglo-Ecuadorian Oil Fields, Associated British Foods, Associated Television, Bowater Paper Corporation, British American Tobacco, British Oxygen, British Petroleum, Carreras Limited, Courtaulds Limited, De La Rue Company, Distillers Company Limited, Dunlop Holdings, E.M.I. Limited, Furness Withy, General Electric Limited, Glaxo Group, Great Universal Stores, Hawker Siddely Group, Imperial Chemical Industries, Imperial Tobacco Group Limited, International Computers Limited, Rank Organization, Rio Tinto Zinc, Selection Trust Limited, Tobacco Securities Trust Company, Vickers Limited, F.W. Woolworth & Company.

Holland (13)

KLM Royal Dutch Airlines, N.V. Koninklijke Bijenkorf Beheer, Albert Heijn N.V., Koninklijke Nederlandsche Hoogovens, Unilever N.V., AKU, Philips Gloeilampen, Royal Dutch Petroleum.

Israel

American Israeli Paper Mills, Bank Leumi Le Israel, Rogosin Ind. of Israel, Alliance A, Etz Lavud, Ampal, Israel Discount Bank, Israel Development Corporation, Industrial Development Bank of Israel, Israel Investors Corporation, Isras, PEC Israel Economic Corporation, Rassco.

Italy (15)

Italcementi, Pirelli S.P.A., La Rinascente, Snia Viscosa, Montecatini Edison, Ledoga S.P.A., Societa Finanziaria Siderurgica, Societa Italiana per le Strade Ferrate Meridionali, Olivetti.

Jamaica

Caribbean Cement Corporation, Jamaica Telephone Company.

Japan (16)

Mitsubishi Heavy Industries, Tokyo Shibaura Electric Company, Nomura Securities Company, Ricoh Company, Eisai Company, Tokai Bank, Casio Computer, Canon Incorporated, Dai Nippon Printing, Hitachi, Kansai Electric Power, Komatsu Limited, Marubeni Corporation, Meiji Seika Kaisha, Mitsui & Company, Nagoya Railroad, Nippon Shinpan Company, Sanko Steamship Company, Taisei Construction Company, Taisho Marine & Fire Insurance Company, Toa Harbor Works Company, Tokyo Marine & Fire Insurance, Yasuda Trust & Banking Company, Nippon Electric, Ajinomoto, Asahi Glass, Bank of Yokohama, Calpis Food Industry Company, Dai Ichi Kangyo Bank, Daiwa House Industry Company, Daiwa Securities, Fuji Bank, Fuji Photo, Honda Motor Company, Industrial Bank of Japan, Japan Air Lines, Kajima Corporation, Kao Soap Company, Kawasaki Steel, Kubota Limited, Kyowa Bank, Matsushita Electric, Mitsubishi Bank, Mitsubishi Electric, Mitsubishi Estate Company, Nikko Securities, Nippon Optical, Nissan Motor, Saitama Bank, Sanwa Bank, Sekisui Prefab. Homes, Sony Corporation, Sumitomo Bank, Tokyo Land Corporation, Toray Industries, Toyota Motor Company.

Mexico

Telefonos de Mexico, Tubos de Acero de Mexico.

Philippines

Atlas Consolidated Mining & Development, Benguet Consolidated, Philippine Long Distance Telephone, San Carlos Milling.

Sweden

L.M. Ericsson Telephone Company, Swedish Ballbearing.

South Africa (17)

Free State Geduld Mines, Potgietersrust Platinums Limited, Union Corporation Limited, West Driefontein Gold Mining Company, West Rand Consolidated Mines, Anglo

Alpha Cement, Anglo American Investment Trust, Anglo Transvaal Consolidated Investment Company, Anglo Transvaal Industries, Anglovaal Holdings, Barlow Rand, Bracken Mines, Consolidated Murchison Goldfields, Federale Mynbou, Grootvlei Proprietary Mines, Highveld Steel & Vanadium Corporation, Kinross Mines, Libanon Gold Mining Company, Lydenburg Platinum, Rand Selection Corporation, Southvaal Holdings, Union Platinum, Vereeniging Estates, Anglo American Gold Investment Company, Blyvooruitzicht Gold Mining Company, Daggafontein Mines, De Beers Consolidated Mines, Johannesburg Consolidated Investment Company, Middle Witwatersrand, Virginia Orange Free State Gold Mining Company, Welkom Gold Mining Company, Buffelsfontein Gold Mining Company, Doornfontein Durban Roodepoort Deep Limited, East Driefontein Gold Mining, Gold Fields of South Africa, Harmony Gold Mining, Hartebeestfontein Gold Mining, Kloof Gold Mining Company, Loraine Gold Mines, President Brand Gold Mining, President Steyn Gold Mining, St. Helena Land & Exploration Company, Stilfontein Gold Mining Company, Vaal Reefs Exploration, Western Areas Gold Mining, Western Deep Levels, Western Holdings, O'Okiep Copper, Orange Free State Investment Trust, Palabora Mining Company, Waterval (Rustenburg) Platinum Mining Company.

Zambia

Roan Consolidated Mines, Bancroft Mines.

When you buy these foreign shares in the United States, you are actually buying American Depositary Receipts (ADRs), which certify that the shares you own are deposited in safe custody in the issuing foreign country. Most of the ADRs on the market are issued by four big banks in New York: Morgan Guaranty Trust Company, Chemical Bank, Irving Trust Company, and First National City Bank. Incidentally, in markets like Tokyo it is quite normal for the bluest of blue chips to be quoted at less than $1 a share, so your ADRs may represent 10, 50, or 100 Japanese shares in some cases and will thus be quoted somewhere near the usual price range of American shares.

How much you want to invest each time, and how often, is up to you. You will probably get the best results by setting a fixed sum, say $100, $500, or $1,000 every month, every three months or every six months.

You will note from the stocks listed that in some countries, such as Canada, Great Britain, and Japan, you will be able to build up a fairly diversified portfolio, with companies in many different fields of business. In other countries you will find yourself limited to one or two companies, and in these cases a mutual fund or investment trust may be a better bet.

Canadian readers will have no major problems in buying foreign stocks since they are subject to relatively few government restrictions. British investors have trouble with exchange controls and the investment dollar premium. For United States readers, one potential snag at the time of writing is the United States Interest Equalization Tax, with which Washington has sought in recent years to discourage Americans from sending their money abroad. The tax rate was 11.25 percent on foreign stocks until January 1, 1974, when it was reduced to 3.75 percent. On January 30 it was reduced to zero by order of the President, who has authority to vary the rate at his discretion. The tax was scheduled to expire by law June 30, 1974, but since Congress might extend it beyond that date it is worth noting how the tax works in case it should still be in effect when you buy foreign stocks.

The tax is included in the price you pay. Your broker buys and sells the shares with a certificate of American ownership attached. This shows that the tax was paid. The tax is only paid once, by the first American who buys the share from a foreign owner, so when he sells it to another American citizen or resident, the tax is not collected again. You therefore buy the share with the tax included in the price and you sell it the same way. The only thing that concerns you is that the tax is already built in, making it somewhat more expensive to buy foreign shares.

You may not have the time, inclination, or means to check out the prospects of every foreign company you would like to buy. An alternative is to turn to foreign mutual funds and investment trusts. They will give you a cross-section of each foreign market, and since one fund may include from 20 to 200 different stocks, it will follow the market indexes much more closely than an individual stock, which may fluctuate independently of the general market.

The practical difficulties and opportunities of buying mutual funds and trusts vary greatly, depending on where you live. Canadian readers have the freest hand, since their government has no exchange control restrictions, no investment penalty like the United States Interest Equalization Tax, and minimum regulations on where or how its citizens invest abroad.

Citizens and residents of the United States are more limited. They have a choice of a few mutual funds and trusts issued within the United States that concentrate on foreign stocks. Only funds and trusts issued in developing countries such as Mexico and Israel are exempt from the Interest Equaliation Tax.

The United States Securities and Exchange Commission (SEC), the official watchdog over all stocks sold in the United States, also bars many foreign funds from selling their shares in the United States unless they make a registration statement. The SEC wishes to protect American investors from financial scandals. Recent such scandals have included the multimillion dollar collapse of various "offshore" funds such as those run by International Overseas Services (IOS) and a real estate trust called Gramco. Thousands of foreign investors were badly burned in these funds, which invested mainly in the United States.

Many offshore funds are based in tax havens such as the Bahamas, Curacao, Panama, the Cayman Islands, Bermuda, and Liechtenstein. Regulation of their activities in many of these places is minimal and they should generally be avoided.

However there are solid, reputable funds run by large

Swiss banks and British Unit Trust organizations, as well as in-vestment trusts quoted on the London, Amsterdam, and other exchanges, where the authorities keep a closer watch on possible shady dealings.

While Swiss banks will answer inquiries from Americans saying that they do not sell their funds in the United States, they will in fact usually sell them to any client of any nationality who has a bank account in Switzerland. The sale then takes place in Switzerland, the shares are kept in safe custody in a Swiss bank, and the transaction is subject to Swiss laws. The Swiss consider this a domestic matter. Swiss banks do not feel that they have any responsibility to collect or report the United States Interest Equalization Tax. That is the in-vestor's own responsibility. Generally, what is said here about Swiss banks goes for British banks as well.

Finally, readers who are residents of Great Britain are in a paradoxical position. They are subject to greater restrictions than Canadians or Americans in investing abroad, but they have more opportunities to do so at home through funds of-fered in Great Britain itself, with portfolios of Italian, French, German, and other stocks.

The following is a list of some of the mutual funds and in-vestment trusts—only a small fraction of the total available—through which you can diversify your investments in hundreds of companies in many different nations around the world. In a large number of these funds all that is required is a minimum initial investment of $50 to $100, or perhaps $300 to $400. In some cases, as much as $1,000 may be required. Subsequent investments can be as low as $20 at a time in some funds. The number before each fund refers to its corresponding market index in our table on pages 20 to 23. In buying Pan Australian, for example, you will be guided by the Sydney index.

Australia

(1) Pan Australian Unit Trust, 65 London Wall, London

EC2, England. Has a broad-based portfolio of Australian mining, mineral, manufacturing, and service companies. Minimum investment, about $400; sales charge, 5 percent.

(1) Jessel Australian & General Trust, Jessel Britannia, 155 Fenchurch Street, London EC3, England. Minimum investment, $2,500; sales charge, 5 percent.

(1) Delfin Australian Fund Incorporated, Delfin Investment Services, 16 O'Connell Street, Sydney, Australia. Has a portfolio of about 100 Australian companies and aims to provide long-term capital growth.

(1) Australian Minerals Trust, Manx International Management, 63 Athol Street, Douglas, Isle of Man, Great Britain. Specializes in Australian mining shares and British tax advantages.

Universal Units Limited, 375 George Street, Sydney, Australia. Runs a dozen funds. It finds the optimum size is about four million Australian dollars ($5.5 million in the U.S.), and when it reaches this limit it closes the door to new subscriptions and opens another fund. At the time of writing, only four funds are open to new investors:

(1) Earnings Fund Number 2, oriented toward income. About seventy companies in the portfolio.

(1) Capital Growth Number 2. Oriented toward growth plus dividends. About sixty companies.

(1) Industrial Growth Fund. Growth only, pays no dividends.

(1) Oil & Mining Fund. A specialized mutual fund in a speculative market—oil and mining shares are highly volatile in Australia—but the fund is spread over thirty-five companies.

Austria

(2) The Vienna stock market is rather small, and there are no funds exclusively invested in Austrian shares. The closest thing to it is Selecta, a mutual fund run by the Creditanstalt Bankverein, 1011 Wien, Postfach 72, Austria. It

is usually about 50 percent invested in leading Austrian companies. The other 50 percent embraces a worldwide portfolio of stocks.

Brazil

Brascan Limited, of Toronto. Quoted on the American Stock Exchange in New York. Has a big stake in the Brazilian economy, particularly electric power and financial services, plus holdings in Canada.

Canada

(4) Funds quoted in Canada are too numerous to mention here, as you will find out by checking the column of quotations under the heading "Mutual Funds" in any Canadian newspaper. The *Financial Post Survey of Investment Funds,* Maclean Hunter Publishing Company, 481 University Avenue, Toronto, Ontario, provides a comprehensive listing with many details on each fund. The funds known in Canada as "trust company investment funds" are no-load funds in which you pay no sales charge. They include Canada Permanent Investors, Canada Trust, Guaranty Trust, Investors Trust, Montreal Trust, Royal Trust, and others.

(4) Canadian Fund, Calvin Bullock Limited, 1 Wall Street, New York 10005. A United States-incorporated mutual fund that claims its shares are free of the United States Interest Equalization Tax.

(4) CANAC. A mutual fund of Canadian shares. Offered by the Union Bank of Switzerland, Bahnhofstrasse 45, Zurich, Switzerland.

(5) Growth Oil & Gas Fund and Canadian Gas & Energy Fund. Two Canadian funds that specialize in Canadian oil industry shares.

Denmark

The only fund specializing in Danish shares is Investor. If you want to invest directly in Danish stocks on the Copenhagen Stock Exchange, one Copenhagen brokerage

firm that is able to correspond with you in English is G.I.
Michaelsen & Company, 6-8 Sankt Annae Plads,Copenhagen.
And one stock it can buy for you is Copenhagen Handelsbank,
the largest commercial bank in Denmark, which gets a large
part of its profits from buying and selling Danish shares. You
might almost say that this bank practically *is* the Danish Stock
Exchange, since in recent years it has accounted for about 40
percent of the turnover there.

Europe

Eurit. Invests in the nations of Western Europe. Run by
the Union Bank of Switzerland, Bahnhofstrasse 45, Zurich.It
usually has a portfolio of about sixty companies spread over
about seven countries.

France

(6) Francit, a mutual fund with investments in about forty French companies. Also offered by the Union Bank of
Switzerland.

Germany

(7) Deutsche Investment Trust, 6 Frankfurt am Main, P.O.
Box 3667, Biebergasse 6-10, West Germany. One of the
biggest investment concerns in Germany. It runs two big
funds. Concentra has a portfolio of about sixty companies covering most areas of the German economy. This fund has no
sales charge but has a 4.2 percent redemption fee. The second
fund is Thesaurus, which is more growth oriented — all dividends are plowed back into the fund.

(7) Germac, a mutual fund with a portfolio of about thirty German companies. It is sold by the Union Bank of Switzerland. There is a 4 percent sales charge but no redemption
charge.

Great Britain

There is such a profusion of unit trusts (the British term
for mutual funds), property bonds, equity bonds, and
managed bonds in Britain that you may want to keep abreast

of the field by subscribing to *Fund Investor*, 40 Bow Lane, London EC4, a monthly magazine that keeps track of the latest developments. Further information may be obtained from the Association of Investment Trust Companies, 7 Angel Court, Throgmorton Street, London EC2.

Here are a few of the British trusts:

(8) G.T. Capital Fund, Lloyds Bank, 51-54 Gracechurch Street, London EC3. Specializes in British growth companies. Minimum initial investment about $400. Sales charge 3¼ percent.

(8) Jessel New Issue Units, Jessel Britannia Group, 155 Fenchurch Street, London EC3. Specializes in new issues of companies that come on the London Stock Exchange for the first time. Minimum investment about $400. Sales charge 5 percent.

(8) Giants Unit Trust, Abacus Management, 26 Pall Mall, Manchester 2, England. Concentrates on the biggest British companies.

(8) Hambro Smaller Companies Fund, Hambro House, Rayleigh Road, Brentwood, Essex. A growth-oriented fund that tries to buy the British "blue chips of tomorrow." Minimum investment about $400. Sales charge 3¼ percent.

(9) Unicorn Financial Trust, Unicorn House, 252 Romford Road, London E7. Invests in British banking, insurance, and other financial service companies for which the City of London is world-famous. Minimum investment about $900. Sales charge 5 percent.

(10) Target Investment Trust Fund, 16 Coleman Street, London EC2. Provides huge diversification of your investment with its portfolio of Investment Trusts, each of which in turn invests in scores of individual companies. Minimum holding $250. Sales charge 5 percent.

(11) M & G Property Fund, Three Quays, Tower Hill, London EC3. Has a wide spread of British real estate companies. Minimum investment $250.

(12) Jascot North Sea Unit Trust, 21 Young Street, Edin-

burgh, Scotland. Invests in companies involved in exploring and developing the huge oil resources in the North Sea.

Holland

(13) Holland Fund, Tesselschadestraat, Amsterdam. A mutual fund with a portfolio of about 100 Dutch companies.

Hong Kong

(14) Jardine Securities, Jardine Fleming & Company, 22 Pedder Street, Hong Kong. A closed end trust quoted on the Hong Kong stock exchange and specializing in Hong Kong shares.

(14) Wardley Trust, Wardley Vickers Limited, P.O. Box 64, Hong Kong. Splits its investments between Hong Kong and an international portfolio and aims at well-heeled investors. Minimum investment 100,000 Hong Kong dollars (about $20,000). Sales charge 2 percent.

(14) The Hong Kong and Shanghai Banking Corporation, 1 Queens Road Central, Hong Kong 9. The dominant bank in Hong Kong and also a major international bank, with worldwide interests and $5 billion in assets. Its shares are quoted on the Hong Kong and London stock exchanges and offer a widespread investment in the Hong Kong economy.

Israel

Israel Development Corporation, 30 East 42nd Street, New York 10017. A United States-based closed end investment company specializing in Israeli companies. Quoted on the American Stock Exchange.

Two closed end investment trusts quoted on the Tel Aviv Stock Exchange provide you with a wide diversity of Israeli stocks. One is Bank Leumi Investment Company Limited, which has a portfolio of about forty stocks. The other is Discount Bank Investment Corporation, Limited, of 16 Beth Hashoeva Lane, Tel Aviv, which is somewhat more aggressive in its investment policy and has a portfolio of about thirty Israeli companies. In the United States you can buy both of these trusts through Leumi Securities Corporation, 18 East 48th Street, New York 10017. According to this dealer they are not liable to the United States Interest Equalization Tax, and have been cleared by the SEC. The only Israeli tax is a 25 percent withholding on dividends. Leumi Securities periodically mails out a sheet with the latest prices, price-earnings ratios and other data.

Ireland

Shamrock Unit Fund, National Group House, 3 Norwich Street, Fetter Lane, London EC4, England. Invests in a portfolio of at least 50 companies in business in the Republic of Ireland, Northern Ireland, or internationally. The minimum investment is about $50.

Italy

(15) ITAC. Run by Union Bank of Switzerland, Bahnhofstrasse 45, Zurich, Switzerland. Concentrates its portfolio entirely on about twenty Italian companies. Sales charge 4 percent.

    (15) Interitalia, CADIT S.A., 14 Rue Aldringer, Luxembourg also sold in England by Kleinwort Benson, 20 Fenchurch Street, London EC3). Has a broad Italian portfolio as well as a wide international selection of companies.

Japan

(16) Japan Fund, 25 Broad Street, New York 10004. A closed end investment trust quoted on the New York Stock Exchange with a portfolio of about fifty companies covering most sections of the Japanese economy.

    (16) Japan Growth Fund, Save & Prosper Group, 4 Great St. Helens, London EC3, England. One of several Japanese-stock funds offered in Europe.

Mexico

FIRME Fondo de Inversiones Rentables Mexicanas, Paseo de la Reforma 213, Mexico D.F. Covers about fifty Mexican companies and is exempt from the United States Interest Equalization Tax as well as from Mexican taxes.

New Zealand

Dominion Unit Trust, P.O. Box 1486, Auckland, New Zealand. Invests in New Zealand and Australian companies.

First New Zealand Unit Trust, 296 Lambton Quay, Wellington, New Zealand. Splits its portfolio about 50-50 between Australia and New Zealand, with about thirty New Zealand companies represented.

South Africa

(17) ASA Limited, 46 William Street, New York. A closed-end trust traded on the New York Stock Exchange. It holds about twenty South African shares in its portfolio, mainly gold mines.

(17) International Investors Incorporated, 420 Lexington Avenue, New York 10017. A United States mutual fund concentrating on gold mining shares. Part of its portfolio is in stocks of other nations.

(17) SAFIT. Run by the Union Bank of Switzerland, Bahnhofstrasse 45, Zurich, Switzerland. A portfolio of about sixty South African companies, more than half of them in gold mining.

(17) Jessel Gold & General Trust, Jessel Britannia, 155 Fenchurch Street, London EC3, England. Invests in South African mining stocks and a selection of international issues.

Spain

ESPAC. Run by Union Bank of Switzerland. Has a portfolio of about twenty-five Spanish companies.

Switzerland

(18) Swissvalor. Run by the Swiss Bank Corporation, 6 Paradeplatz, Zurich, Switzerland. A portfolio of more than one hundred Swiss companies.

(18) Fonsa, sold by the Union Bank of Switzerland,

Zurich. A mutual fund spread over about seventy Swiss companies. Sales charge 4 percent.

United States

There are hundreds of mutual funds and scores of investment trusts in the United States Here are a few of them that match up with the market indexes in our table:

(19) Rowe Price New Era Fund, 1 Charles Center, Baltimore, Maryland 21201. A no-load fund concentrating mainly on United States companies rich in natural resources.

(19) Rowe Price Growth Stock Fund. Another no-load fund, concentrating on American growth companies.

(19) Edie Special Growth Fund, 530 Fifth Avenue, New York 10036. No-load, specializes in smaller United States growth companies.

(19) First Multifund of America, 299 Park Avenue, New York 10017. Spreads your money over practically the entire United States economy by investing in about twenty-five other United States mutual funds, whose combined portfolios cover hundreds of individual companies. It is a no-load fund.

(20) Bayrock Utility Securities Incorporated, 200 Park Avenue, New York 10017. A closed-end fund on the American Stock Exchange, which holds shares in about twenty-five United States utility companies.

(21) Petroleum Corporation of America, 522 Fifth Avenue, New York 10036. Covers about forty oil companies. A closed-end fund traded on the New York Stock Exchange.

(22) REIT Income Fund, 225 Franklin Street, Boston, Massachusetts 02110. Provides an enormous spread of investments in the United States real estate field by investing in about thirty other real estate trusts. It is a closed-end trust quoted over the counter.

(24) Century Shares Trust, 111 Devonshire Street, Boston, Massachusetts 02109. Insurance and some bank stocks.

(23) Bank Stock Fund Incorporated, P.O. Box 367, Colorado Springs, Colorado 80901. This is a very small fund

and is not quoted in most newspapers.

(24) Life Insurance Investors Incorporated, 10 LaSalle Street, Chicago, Illinois 60603. A mutual fund.

(25) Chemical Fund Incorporated, 61 Broadway, New York 10006. A mutual fund.

You may wonder why we have mentioned some funds based in third countries. In some cases this is because of language problems. By buying the ESPAC fund of Spanish shares in Switzerland, for example, you will get reports and statements in English from the Swiss management. In other cases you may avoid problems connected with exchange controls. Countries with strong currencies, like Germany and Switzerland in 1973, sometimes try to cut off an unwanted inflow of foreign currencies such as United States dollars by banning investments from abroad. In such cases you are frequently still able to invest there through a third country, by buying shares in Swiss-based Germac, for example. In yet other cases it may be easier to keep track of your investment in a third country. If you receive the *London Financial Times,* you will get daily quotations of the Pan Australian Trust, whereas you may not be able to obtain an Australian paper to check the daily value of Delfin Australian Fund. It may also be cheaper to invest in a third country. British mutual funds usually have a 5 percent sales charge. In Australia the level is around the 8½ percent that United States load funds charge, or even higher.

In listing these foreign investment trusts and mutual funds, we have only included those with which you can communicate in English. If you have a good working knowledge of Spanish, Greek, German, Swedish, French, Dutch, Japanese, or some other language you will find additional investment opportunities open to you. If you know Spanish, for instance, there are funds in Argentina, Colombia, and other Spanish-speaking nations that cater to local investors but are not set up to deal with English-language investors abroad.

Before committing any money to an investment in a

foreign country, first make sure that there will be no restriction on taking your money out again when you want to sell. Most major nations allow foreigners to do this without hindrance in normal times, but others, especially developing countries with weak economies, apply exchange controls from time to time. This could lock you into your investment temporarily.

If some of your holdings should be temporarily immobilized by exchange controls in one country or another, do not let it worry you too much. It is just as possible that this will happen in the United States as anywhere else — gross fiscal mismanagement occurs in every nation in the world at one time or another. And, in such cases, the guilty governments are usually trying to force their own unhappy citizens into keeping their money at home instead of seeking safety abroad. They are certainly not out to antagonize any foreign investors who are bringing money in.

In any event, suppose that every nation in the world slapped on exchange controls at the same time. You still might be ahead of the game. While others are forbidden to spend their own nation's currency abroad, you could still have the freedom to make a world tour, using all or part of your funds in foreign lands to finance your travels in each of them.

Finally we come to the third way to invest in foreign markets, in which you boil your global spread of stocks down into a single investment package. In this case there is only one stock market index you have to watch.

Turn back to the table of *Barron's* stock market indexes at the beginning of this chapter. The very last index on the table, the Amro-Pearson, is an indicator of the average price level of the world's blue chips. About half the component stocks that go into this index are the giant corporations of American industry. The remainder are the biggest of big businesses of other industrial nations, mainly in Europe and Japan.

This index is therefore a barometer of the entire capitalist world's economy. When it hits a high you know that big business is booming all around the globe—or at least that investors think it is about to boom. When this index is low, you know that the world is in an industrial slump or that investors think a slump is on the way. Between 1968 and 1973 the Amro-Pearson index ranged from a low of 100 to a high of 172.79.

It is impossible to predict with any certainty whether a global boom or slump is coming. There may appear to be a boom, when suddenly another Arab-Israeli war breaks out, the Arabs shut off their oil exports, the world faces an energy shortage, and a worldwide slump occurs. Unless you can forecast the outbreak of Arab-Israeli wars, Russian-Chinese confrontations, and other such events, it is better to stick to commonsense principles and buy when the index is low, sell when it is high. All the world's biggest businesses are not going to go bankrupt at the same time, so you are on pretty safe ground. And sooner or later the index will go up again.

So how do you obtain a worldwide spread of investments in one package? Here are a few possibilities, most of which require an initial investment of only a few hundred dollars.

Intervalor. Run by the Swiss Bank Corporation, 6 Paradeplatz, Zurich, Switzerland. Has investments in the blue chips of twelve countries, with the United States and Switzerland most prominently represented.

Robeco, P.O. Box 973, Rotterdam, Holland. An investment trust quoted on the Amsterdam and other stock exchanges. Manages a portfolio of more than $2 billion spread over fifteen stock markets around the world.

Scudder International Investments, 10 Post Office Square, Boston, Massachusetts, 02109. Is invested in about forty companies in a dozen countries. United States residents pay the International Equalization Tax when they buy from the distributors, (if the tax is still in effect when you read this), but not when they buy from previous American owners in the over-the-counter market.

Ebor Universal Growth Fund, 4 Great St. Helens, London EC3, England. Seeks long-term capital growth through investment in leading companies in Britain, the United States, Europe, and the Far East.

Globinvest. Sold by the Union Bank of Switzerland, Bahnhofstrasse 45, Zurich. Has a worldwide portfolio of stocks.

You can also buy worldwide funds that specialize in a particular field, such as companies producing commodities, energy, minerals, or food. Here are a few of them:

Ebor Commodity Share Trust, 4 Great St. Helens, London EC3, England. Has a worldwide portfolio of companies producing or marketing essential commodities.

Ebor Energy Industries Fund. Specializes in international investments in energy and associated industries.

Vavasseur International Mining Fund, 6 Bevis Marks, London EC3, England. Concentrates on mining shares.

DENAC. Run by the Union Bank of Switzerland, Bahnhofstrasse 45, Zurich. A mutual fund with a worldwide portfolio of stocks in the food industry.

Further Investment Opportunities Abroad

Throughout the Roman Empire and for centuries thereafter, the Mediterranean Sea was the center of the western world. Then, in 1492, Columbus discovered the New World and the Atlantic Ocean displaced it as the focus of world power. On the Atlantic shores arose the great colonial powers—Great Britain, Spain, France, Portugal, Germany, Belgium, and Holland. Facing them across the water, as the western world's center of gravity shifted further west, was the rising power of the United States, Canada, and Latin America.

In the twenty-first century, which is now less than thirty years away, it may well be that the Pacific Ocean will be the center of the world stage. Even now it is ringed by four great powers—the United States, Japan, China, and the Soviet Union. In addition, the Pacific Basin has the huge natural resources of Canada, Australia, Indonesia, and Southeast Asia.

There are mutual funds already set up to take advantage of the potential economic growth of the Pacific Basin. One of these is the Greater Pacific Unit Trust, 63 Athol Street, Douglas, Isle of Man, Great Britain. Another is Pacific Invest, a fund run by the Union Bank of Switzerland.

After reading through all these possibilities perhaps you have some further ideas of your own. Perhaps you would like to kick them around with other like-minded investors and pool your resources in a common venture. Once you have decided on your objective — perhaps a global portfolio, a concentration on Pacific-area securities, or United States bank shares — why not form an investment club? Each member undertakes to put $10 or $20 or more a month into the club. You get together with your fellow-members once a month or so and decide what to buy or sell around the world.

You can have a great deal of fun discussing the pros and cons. The members then vote to decide where to put your money. In the United States there are at least 150 clubs that specialize exclusively in Israeli securities. Other clubs have other goals.

If you want further information on how to form and run an investment club, write to the National Association of Investment Clubs, Washington Boulevard Building, Detroit, Michigan 48226.

However you decide to spread your investments around the globe, through individual stocks or mutual funds, once you have done it, sit back and relax. Even a big break in the United States stock market will affect only a part of your assets, and the loss will probably be compensated by a simultaneous boom in Tokyo, Paris, or somewhere else. Besides, by investing when the index is low in each market, you are minimizing the risk of falling from a great height in each case.

And when, over a period of years, you accumulate investments in Japan, Australia, Canada, the United States, Britain, France. Germany, Italy, Switzerland, Holland, South

Africa, and perhaps several other nations, the whole capitalist world will have to come down on top of you before you are ruined.

3

Options

THE TROUBLE with the high-quality glamor stocks is that each share costs too much. In normal times, Polaroid and Xerox have been over $100 a share, and IBM cost three or four times as much. That meant you had to sink at least $10,000 into one of them to get a 100-share block. Even if you bought on margin, borrowing part of the cost from your broker, you would have had to pay more than $6,500 to get a piece of any quick action in these stocks. And the danger of losing a big chunk of money was considerable. By July, 1974, Polaroid was down to $24 a share.

But there is a way you can deal in the glamors with 10 percent or less of that $6,500 entrance fee. You can take a flyer in 100 shares of Polaroid for only a few hundred dollars. The whole profit of any rise is yours, and you can't lose more than your first few hundred dollars. You can even back your judgment that Polaroid will go down and make a profit without the dangers of an open-ended loss. This loss, which can theoretically be any amount, is incurred in ordinary short sales.

The machinery for this limited-loss, high-profit dealing is the option plan. The plan only recently became popular, although it was long used in commodity and stock dealings. Now it is being used on a large scale in stock dealings — some days there are more shares dealt in through options than through outright sales on the New York Stock Exchange.

There are two kinds of options, puts and calls. If you buy a put, you are buying the right to sell stocks in the future at a price fixed in the option. If you buy a call, you are paying for the right to buy stocks in the future at a fixed price. Options are not limited to stocks. You can also buy options to take or deliver silver bullion, silver coins, or foreign exchange.

Option dealings in shares began years ago, but the market has been formalized more recently. Before, you could go to a dealer in options and buy any puts or calls he had on offer if they appealed to you. In general, you actually had to take the stock if you had a profit, and then resell it to cash in on the gain. That meant that you were locked into the option until it expired — it was difficult to take a quick profit and get out.

With the formalization of the market when the Chicago Board Options Exchange was created in 1973, there were daily general dealings in options on twenty-seven major stocks initially. They are expected to total 100 or more by 1975.

Say you paid $1,000 for an option on Polaroid when it was $125, an option giving you the right to take delivery on it for $125 any time in the next three months. And suppose Polaroid, three weeks later, was up to 145 — that is, 20 points over the 125 delivery price. Under the old system (through a private dealer), you had a $2,000 profit (all options are for 100-share blocks) but you had to take delivery of the stock, pay for it, and then turn around and sell it to pin down your profit.

Under the new system on the Chicago Board Options Exchange, you merely tell your broker to sell a Polaroid option calling for delivery at 125. He resells your option and you pocket the profit of $2,000 — minus, of course, the $1,000 the option cost you in the first place. You also have to deduct from your profit the costs of the dealings: commissions to the broker and taxes.

But suppose Polaroid only went up to 135, giving you a potential profit of only $1,000. You could still have sold your option for the $1,000 it cost you. That would have meant no profit. But meanwhile, at no cost to yourself, you had a chance to make money on any rise in Polaroid beyond 135.

Now let's take another case, of a man who bought Polaroid at 110. The price is up to 125, just as in the first case. He has a potential profit of $1,500, but he thinks the price will go even higher. Therefore he doesn't want to sell the stock but he does want to pin down and make sure of his profits.

There are two ways he can use the option system for this purpose. He can buy a put at $125 a share, to guarantee that he can sell his stock for $125 even if it goes down. Or, he can sell a call, promising to sell the stock at, say, 125 any time in the next three months. He would get about $800 for the option. If the price goes up 5 points, to 130, he has to deliver the stock, which is worth $13,000, for a price of only $12,500. But he has received $800 for his option so he is $300 ahead on the deal.

Suppose Polaroid goes down 5 points from 125. The seller of the call keeps his stock—nobody is going to pay 125 for stock he can buy on the open market for 120, so the seller has both his stock and the $800.

There are some special terms in the option market beside the call (an option to buy) and the put (an option to sell). The man who gives the option is called the *writer*. The *expiration day,* of course, is the last day an option can be exercised. Options are usually for three, six, nine, or twelve months. The *exercise price* or *striking price* is the price at which the stock will be exchanged: in the call case above, the striking price was 125; in the put it was also 125. But it could have been any reasonable price ending in 5 or 0. Prices on the Chicago option exchange go up or down in multiples of 5. From private dealers you can buy irregular striking prices like 32 7/8. The *premium* is the amount paid for the option, usually from 8 to 20 percent of the underlying value of the stock.

A put is usually the way to make money when stock prices are going down. Let's go back to Polaroid, selling at 125. You think it is going down, so you buy a put to sell the stock within three months at 120. Again, you pay $800 for the put. The stock actually goes to 110. You buy 100 shares at that price on the open market. They cost you $11,000. Then you deliver them to the man who sold you the put and get $12,000. You paid $800 for the put but you made $1,000 on the delivery, so your profit is $200. You can work out for yourself how juicy the profits can be when Polaroid drops all the way down to $24.

Now is the time for the big warning, which all the information on puts and calls gives you and which your broker will repeat to you. Here is what the Chicago Board Options Exchange has to say: "Even aggressive investors should not ordinarily commit more than a small percentage of their assets to the purchase of options."

You should never risk more than you can afford to lose in options dealings, because you can lose the entire amount you put up if the option expires without showing a profit. In the case of the call you bought on Polaroid for $800, let's say Polaroid goes up from 125 to only 130. That is a profit of $500 on the shares, but you paid $800 for the call, so you have lost $300. But suppose Polaroid goes down. You are not going to pay 125 for a share you can buy on the open market for 120, so you let your option expire without buying anything. You have lost the whole $800.

That's the thing about options: you can make a lot of money, but it's a high-risk business. If you buy a share of stock outright, it will nearly always have some value even if it goes down. But if the price under a call option goes down, you have lost all the premium you paid for it.

However, Donald R. Fischer, a New York broker specializing in options, points out that the high-risk factor is for the buyer of options, not for the option-writer—the man who provides the stock to be optioned. He says, "Options can be the most conservative of investments if you deal right. Where else can you get a steady income even when the market is going down? If it goes down, you get your premium and you keep your stock. If it goes up, you deliver your stock but you still have your premium."

However, there is a warning for the people who write options. Unless they own the stock outright, their possible loss is theoretically unlimited. It is like selling a stock short—the price can go up any amount, but it can only go down as much as the face value of the stock. If you buy Ford at 45, the most you can possibly lose is $45 a share. And you are not likely to lose that on Ford. But if you sell Ford short or sell an option to deliver when you don't have the stock, Ford can go to 450 and you have to deliver it and get only $45 a share.

The SEC says that more than half the options written are never exercised. That means the writer gets to keep the premium and also keeps his stock. It would indicate that the option-writer generally does better than the option buyer. This is particularly true in times of a generally rising or generally falling market. The buyers of calls lost heavily during the big slump in late 1973 when nearly all stocks were going down.

Take the case of Itek. In August, 1973, you could have bought a call on Itek, then selling at 31, for $975 for 100 shares. The striking price was 23 and the option good until December 17. That looked like a good buy in a good market, a chance to get a $31 stock for $23 a share any time in the next four months. Even counting in the premium of $975, that would have made the cost of the stock only $32.75—$23 plus the $9.75 per share you paid for the option. If the stock went up more than $1.75 you could exercise the option and make money.

But Itek didn't go up. Two months later it was selling for $30 a share. No profit, but your loss was only $2.75 per share, $275 in total. You could have taken this loss by selling your option for whatever you could get for it or by exercising it and selling your stock at the market price.

Or you could have held on to the option, hoping the stock would rise again. That wouldn't have helped, though, because the stock continued to go down. By the time the option expired, in December, Itek was down to 13, caught in the big downdraft of that year's energy crisis. So you let the option expire. You lost your $975 completely, and your only consolation was that you had plenty of company in your misery. All the other call buyers were likewise suffering.

The writer of the option, meanwhile, was in clover. True, his Itek stock was down, but he had your $975 to offset his potential loss. And he still had his 100 shares of Itek, so he could wait for it to go up.

On the other hand, the put, which is the mechanism for the bear types who think stocks are going down, would have made you a profit on Itek. The same day the call was offered at $975, you could have bought a put on Itek, expiring in six months and with a striking price of $35. The premium was $675 or $6.75 a share. That option meant the writer had to buy Itek from you at 35 any time in the six-month period. In December, with Itek down to 13, you could have bought the shares for $1,300 and sold them to the writer for $3,500. That would have given you a profit of $2,200 minus the $675 you paid for the option in the first place. It would have worked out to a net gain of $1,525 in four months on an investment of $675.

Both of these calculations, of course, leave out the commissions you would have had to pay. However, even after your commissions, you would have cleaned up *if* you were right about which way the market was going.

Options can now be bought and sold easily, thanks to the Chicago option exchange, which created an open market where none existed before, but *only in certain stocks and only for calls.* Chicago was planning to add a trade in puts later. The exchange deals only in well-known shares — thirty-two different companies, early in 1974. Among them were such blue chips as AT&T and IBM and such swingers as Polaroid and Kodak. Other stocks are added to the list from time to time. In April, 1974, the SEC authorized the American Stock Exchange in New York to set up a stock options market, but it was not yet in operation as this book went to press.

Most option writers are big individual holders of stocks for investment, bank trust departments, insurance companies, or pension funds. By writing options, they can make deliveries from their inventories of stock and pick up a good income from premiums — as much as 30 percent a year on some stocks. If you, too, would like to be an option writer, speak to your broker. You could write a three-month option on a block of 100 shares. If it is not exercised, you still have the stock and you can write or sell another option on it. Theoretically, you could write as many as four options a year on that single block of shares. And, since the usual premium is around 12 percent of the value of the stock, you could in theory make as much as 48 percent a year on the value of the stock. Of course, you would have to take a loss on some options, but if you wrote enough of them and the market was going your way — up in the case of calls and down in the case of puts — you could do considerably better than break even.

Another possibility is to invest in Able Associates Fund, 17 Birch Drive, Manhasset Hills, New York 11040. This is a no-load mutual fund that invests up to 90 percent of its funds in stocks listed on the Chicago Board Options Exchange and then uses its portfolio to write options on that exchange. The minimum investment in this fund is $1,000. The advantage is that with this modest sum you could spread your option writing over a wide range of stocks. As an individual option writer, you would need hundreds of thousands of dollars to achieve this same spread.

The other options we mention in this book — silver bars, coins, or foreign exchange — are traded on the American Board of Trade in New York. This operation was only introduced about the middle of 1973, but it provides machinery

for anybody who wants to invest in any of these. One advantage of the American Board of Trade system is that premiums are fixed in advance—for instance, the premium on
a three-month put or call on a single 1,000-ounce bar of silver
at the time of writing this is $454. For a one-year option (on
which you have four times as long a time for the price to
change) it is $676.

One great advantage of options in these markets is sim-
plicity. If you wanted to buy foreign exchange futures, say
10,000 Swiss francs, you would have to go to the International
Monetary Market in Chicago (through a broker, of course).
And your possibility of loss in futures is greater than in options: the currency you bought for futures delivery might go
down so far you would lose 10 percent or even 25 percent of its
value. But by buying an option you could never lose more than
the amount you paid for the option.

American Board of Trade options are for three, six,
nine, or twelve months. Silver bar contracts are for one, two,
five, or ten bars. Silver coin options are for one, two, five, or
ten bags, a bag being silver coins with a face value of $1,000.
This might be 4,000 quarters or 10,000 dimes or any combination adding up to $1,000.

In the foreign exchange field, the options you can buy
range from 2,500 to 25,000 Canadian dollars; 1,000 to 10,000
pounds sterling; 10,000 to 100,000 Swiss francs; or 10,000 to
100,000 German marks. Commission rates range from $20 for
the small options to $90 for the big ones in foreign exchange,
or $10 to $45 in the silver options.

To sum up, the advantages of buying options are as
follows:

1. The risk is limited to what you pay for the option—you
can't lose more.

2. There are high potential profits—your gains are
theoretically unlimited, since all the profits above the striking
price plus premium are yours.

3. You get some tax benefits—options held for more than six months produce a long-term capital gain, which is taxed at only half your normal income tax. If you lose, your loss is a capital loss and can be offset in general terms against any gains.

4. Less capital is required—if you buy stock on margin, you have to put up 65 percent of the cost. But you can buy an option for 10 to 20 percent of the value of the stock and you get all the advantages of any price rise.

Now for the disadvantages:

1. You can lose everything you put into an option if the market goes against you. If you bought stock outright, you could wait for it to go back up.

2. Unless you are dealing in a stock listed by the Chicago option exchange, you might have trouble selling an option before its expiration date. This could be important if you needed money in a hurry or wanted to cut your losses and sell an option that had gone sour.

So there you have the outline of the put and call market: it has two sides to it, one highly speculative and the other highly conservative.

Buying options is certainly not for widows and orphans—it is extremely risky. Option *writing* may be for them, however, if they are well-heeled enough to offer options on stock they own.

If you have money to risk, option buying is the way to take a high risk in return for big profit possibilities. Consider this example: from July to October 1973 a call on Texas Instruments went from $5.50 to $48 on the Chicago market.

And if you own stock, option writing is the way to squeeze more income out of it. Suppose you own 100 shares of AT&T and you want to make more income out of it than the 5 percent dividend return it provides you. Offer your stock to an option buyer. He will make all the profit if AT&T goes up spectacularly. But meanwhile the premium he pays you for this chancy privilege will perhaps double your income or more from old Ma Bell.

4

Overseas Banking

THERE ARE SOME people who just cannot stomach the wild gyrations of the stock market, no matter what potential profits they can make. If you are one of them, this chapter is for you.

What you basically want is a guaranteed fixed interest rate every year plus the assurance that your $100 investment will always be worth $100 whenever you want it back.

You face two problems here. The first is devaluation of the currency in which you are invested. The second is internal devaluation — inflation of prices of the things you can buy with your currency.

If you had held all your money in United States Government securities before the devaluations of the dollar in 1971 to 1973, for instance, you would have lost as much as 40 percent of the value of your investment in less than two years, even though the securities had the full faith and credit of the United States behind them. The dollar value would have been the same, but you would have been 40 percent ahead if you had held securities denominated in marks, Swiss francs, or yen.

This is not only a dollar problem. The British pound was devalued by 14 percent in 1967 and has dropped even further since then. The German mark has only recently become a stable currency. The Japanese yen and the French franc have also suffered disastrous devaluations within the twentieth century. Even the Swiss franc has been debased against gold.

So, how do you avoid losing money when the dollar is devalued? Or the mark, the yen, or the franc, since any of these currencies might also be marked down by the existing government?

For a start, you avoid the weak currencies and put your money into the strong currencies. We talk a great deal in Chapter 12 about how to predict future monetary trends. That same information will be valuable to you if you are planning to put your money in less risky ventures than the currency futures market, which we discuss in that chapter.

The futures market, as recorded on the Chicago Mercantile Exchange International Monetary Markets tables and other such sources, gives you the consensus of the monetary experts about the trends of various currencies. The strong currencies tend to be quoted at higher exchange prices for delivery six months or one year ahead than they are for immediate delivery. The weak currencies tend to be quoted at lower and lower exchange rates the further the delivery date advances into the future. Investors in the currency futures market have millions of dollars backing the positions they have taken. When a large number of high-powered investors think the German mark is going to go up and back their opinion with hard cash, it is very likely that this prophecy will be fulfilled.

You should check these figures with reasonable frequency since political events can change the monetary situation. For example, say there is another outbreak in the Arab-Israeli war. The United States backs Israel and the Arabs

ban oil exports to the United States and cut back oil production. But the United States gets only 10 percent of its oil
from Arab countries, so, although the Arab action might
cause a gas shortage, it doesn't affect the United States economy nearly as much as it affects the economy of Europe,
which depends on the Arabs for as much as 90 percent of
its oil. The Arab boycott thus weakens the German mark
and strengthens the United States dollar.

We come now to your second problem — internal inflation. As long as your money is invested in *any* paper currency
there is no way around the problem of inflation. It exists and it
will always exist as long as the government can manipulate the
printing press. You just have to find the highest interest rate
you can in order to counter the effects of inflation on your
holdings. In some cases this is not possible. It is not possible,
for example, when United States savings accounts are paying 4
percent interest and the yearly inflation rate is 6 percent. It is
not possible in Argentina, where the local commercial banks
are paying 18 to 24 percent on savings accounts and the
inflation rate is more than 70 percent. In such cases you
have to take refuge in real values such as gold bullion, gold
coins, silver coins, or silver bullion.

The fact is, of course, that the strong currencies in the
foreign exchange market are the ones least affected by inflation. That is one reason for their strength, and at times you
may be better off earning 5 percent yearly in Swiss francs than
8 percent in United States dollars. These were the prevailing
rates in 1972-73, for instance, in the Eurodollar market. At
the end of that period you would have been about 35 percent
ahead on the francs thanks to the upward revaluation of the
Swiss currency.

Buying Foreign Bonds

Now that you've chosen the currency you think is the strongest, how do you go about investing your money at a fixed
interest rate with maximum safety?

First, you could buy World Bank Bonds. The International Bank for Development and Reconstruction, com-

monly known as the World Bank, is a multibillion-dollar international institution. Most of the world's nations are members of this bank, which finances development projects in underdeveloped nations, among other programs. It is based in Washington D.C. The World Bank issues bonds in a number of different currencies, including German marks, Swiss francs, Japanese yen, and United States dollars. The World Bank's dollar-denominated bonds are given an Aaa rating by Moody's, a leading United States bond-rating service. (This is the highest possible rating, also given to United States Treasury bonds and notes and direct obligations backed with the full faith and credit of the United States Government. Bonds with this rating, according to Moody's, are "judged to be of the best quality. They carry the smallest degree of investment risk and are generally referred to as 'gilt edge'.") It seems reasonable to suppose that the World Bank bonds issued in other currencies are of equally high standing.

Two sister organizations that also issue bonds in various currencies are the Inter American Development Bank (also rated Aaa by Moody's) and the Asian Development Bank.

World Bank bonds in foreign currencies are not liable to the United States Interest Equalization Tax. In some countries, such as Switzerland, they are also exempt from local withholding taxes on interest payments. During the 1972-73 period, World Bank bonds yielded around 5 percent in Swiss franc issues, 6 percent or more in German marks, and 8 percent in United States dollar issues.

Perhaps the simplest way to buy World Bank bonds is through a bank or broker in each country:

United States dollar bonds—through any American broker.

Swiss franc bonds—through any Swiss bank, such as the Union Bank of Switzerland, 45 Bahnhofstrasse, Zurich.

German marks bonds—through any German bank, such as the Dresdner Bank, 7-8 Gallusanlage, Frankfurt am Main, West Germany.

Japanese yen bonds—through Japanese stock brokerage firms, such as Nomura Securities, 100 Wall Street, New York 10005; or Nikko Securities, 1 Chase Manhattan Plaza, New York 10005.

British pound bonds—through any British bank, such as Lloyds Bank International Limited, 40-66 Queen Victoria St., London, EC4.

Many of these banks and brokers will be able to give you advice on other foreign bonds you can buy, including British government bonds and Swiss Federal government bonds.

Or, if you want to simplify matters and boil your worldwide bond investments down into one package, you could do so through Bond Invest, a mutual fund with a worldwide portfolio of bonds. It is sold by the Union Bank of Switzerland. Yield in recent years has been around 7 percent.

Opening a Foreign Bank Account

Some of these foreign banks may also be eager for you to open a savings account in their local currency. Provided your timing is right, you can make windfall profits by opening such an account. For example, if you had opened a Swiss franc savings account in Zurich in early 1971, the revaluation of the Swiss franc would have increased the value of your account in dollars by more than 30 percent in two years. You would also have received interest of about 4 percent a year.

Opening a foreign account is very simple. You just write the foreign bank for an application form, fill it out, and return it with your personal check for the initial deposit. Most big foreign banks, such as the ones mentioned above, are able to correspond with you in English. Regulations and interest rates vary in each country.

Some of the strong-currency nations take measures from time to time to keep out an unwanted flood of weak currencies (such as United States dollars in 1972-73). In Switzerland, for example, a typical savings account may earn as much as 4.5

percent for money on deposit for a year. But in 1973 depositors not resident in Switzerland were restricted to a maximum 50,000-franc deposit (about $16,000). From 50,000 to 100,000 francs no interest was paid, and deposits above 100,000 francs were penalized by a 2 percent quarterly *deduction* from the account. This was intended to encourage small foreign depositors and keep the big foreign money out. Early in 1974 the penalties and restrictions were removed and the interest rate was raised to 5 percent for depositors.

By the time you read this book the regulations may well have changed again. In any event, it is easy to circumvent them. You can open a Swiss-franc account with a bank in Austria, where there is no limitation on the amount, no negative interest rate, no prohibition on payment of interest on amounts above 50,000 Swiss francs, and no withholding tax on interest. One such bank is the Bankhaus Deak Limited, Rathaus Strasse 20, Vienna. You can also keep Swiss francs on deposit with a bank in London such as Lloyds Bank International for fixed periods of one, two, three, or six months and receive monthly interest. This might vary from a 2 percent yearly rate for a one-month deposit to 3 percent for a six-month deposit. In times of turmoil on the foreign exchange markets, the interest rate might sink to practically zero as scared investors from all over the world seek refuge in the Swiss franc, which has traditionally been the world's safest currency. These short-term deposits are an ideal solution, in fact, in periods of world monetary uncertainty, when one has funds available but does not know what to do with them until the situation becomes more stable.

Swiss banks, incidentally, will usually not open a secret numbered account unless it is for a very substantial amount. A big Swiss bank will turn you down if you have a mere $20,000 to deposit, although smaller banks may not be so snooty. This kind of account is largely unnecessary in any event. Swiss banks resist any kind of prying by foreign authorities into *any* of their accounts without a Swiss court order. In fact, the banks are so discreet that they have a habit of sending mail to their clients abroad without any return address on the envelope. (There are countries where such a return address would swiftly make the addressee the target of an investigation.) Numbered accounts, generally speaking, are for political victims of totalitarian regimes, Latin American dictators insuring against a future fall from power, international narcotics dealers, and Mafia bosses. And in these last two cases they are none too effective, because the Swiss authorities cooperate vigorously in prosecuting international criminals. For an ordinary citizen a numbered account is superfluous.

Banks in other nations may offer you unusual deals from time to time. Finansbanken A.S. of Copenhagen, for example, has been offering 8 percent interest on funds deposited for a year (in Danish crowns). The rate is raised to 9 percent if the depositor buys one share in the bank. The share costs about $400 at the time of writing and itself yields about 6 percent.

High interest rates available in Mexico have attracted large amounts of American money in recent years. The Mexican peso has shown a rocklike stability against the dollar for the last twenty years, holding unchanged at 8 United States cents to the peso since 1954. This fact, and interest rates of 10 percent or more, have been a magnet to savvy Americans, particularly at times when United States savings accounts were only paying 4 percent or so.

One such Mexican bank is Nacional Financiera, Isabel la Catolica 51, Mexico 1, D.F. This is Mexico's official development bank, owned 51 percent by the Mexican government and 49 percent by private investors. Its assets total about $3 billion, and it finances many of the country's industrial firms. Nacional Financiera offers easily marketable *titulos financieros*, bonds yielding 8.75 percent as well as six-months deposits yielding 9.25 percent and one-year deposits yielding 10.5 percent.

The Sociedad Mexicana de Credito Industrial, Paseo de la Reforma 213, Mexico 5, D.F. a private firm, also offers

mortgage bonds, financial bonds, and promissory notes
yielding about the same interest rates as Nacional Financiera.

Taking Advantage of United States Opportunities

Finally, one should always keep in mind that, in spite of its big
devaluations in 1971-73, the American dollar was not always a
weak currency nor will it always be one. After World War II it
was for many years the strongest currency on earth, with all
the war-torn nations of the world desperate for more and more
dollars to finance their reconstruction. Such a situation is
unlikely to recur, but in early 1974 the greenback
strengthened considerably against other currencies, and you
may want to have all your money in dollars if this strength
continues.

If so, you can usually do better than 5 percent from a
bank savings account if you look around. United States
Treasury Bills, for example, posted yields of about 9 percent
during 1974. The bills are promises to repay your money,
backed by the full faith and credit of the United States Government, within periods of three, six, nine or 12 months. The
three-month and six-month bills are sold every Monday; the
nine-month and twelve-month bills once a month. The
minimum purchase is $10,000. You can go to the auction at
the Federal Reserve Bank (there are a dozen Reserve Banks, in
New York and other cities), and compete in bidding, or, you
can mail in your check before the auction and ask for a bill at
the average bid price. Further details may be obtained from
the Division of Administration Services, Federal Reserve
System, Washington D.C. 20551. The bills are subject to
federal taxation but are exempt from most state and local
taxes.

It may well be that you are not yet rich enough to deal in
$10,000 certificates. If so, you can buy three-month and six-
month Treasury Bills in amounts as small as $5,000 or $1,000
through the American Board of Trade. The Board pools its
clients' money and then bids for the bills and keeps them in

safekeeping. The charge for this service is $5 per $1,000 and is scaled down for bigger purchases. If you need your money back unexpectedly, you can sell out before maturity by paying the Board a $10 special redemption charge. If you keep the bills to maturity there is no redemption fee. Another alternative is a mutual fund such as the Fund for Investing in Government Securities Inc., American Express Investment Management Company, P.O. Box 7650, San Francisco, California 94120.

If you are already in the big money league, you can invest in bankers' acceptances, where the interest return is higher than with treasury bills—it climbed to over 12 percent in 1974. The minimum investment here is $100,000, and it is a pretty safe one, because an acceptance is a bill, issued usually in a foreign trade deal, which has been "accepted" by the bank. The accepting bank guarantees payment at maturity, usually in 90 to 120 days. The best way to deal in bankers' acceptances is through a bank with which you have close—and substantial—business relations. It is a big-ticket and very limited field.

Somewhat further down in the big money league, and also appreciably lower in safety, you can deal in commercial paper. This consists of unsecured promissory notes from business firms, and there is about $45 billion worth of it floating around in the American economy. Commercial paper is issued because big businesses frequently find it cheaper to borrow from the public than from their friendly banks, particularly when the banks demand that the firms keep 20 percent of the loan on deposit at the bank, and even more so when the Federal Reserve starts clamping down on bank credit.

The return on commercial paper thus rises and falls with the prime rate that banks charge the major corporations who are their most creditworthy customers. In 1974, you could get close to a 10 percent return from commercial paper. This was obviously much more profitable than putting your money in a 5 percent bank savings account so that the bank could reloan

your money at 10 percent to the Super Dynamics Corporations. You might as well get the 10 percent yourself from
Super Dynamics.

The problem is that it is not so easy to do. The commercial paper field is dominated by huge corporations, financial organizations, and institutional investors. However, the
American Board of Trade has opened a small wedge for the
little man to get into the game. You can buy commercial paper from the Board with a face value of $250, $500, or $1,000.
It comes in maturities of three months or six months, whichev-
er you prefer, and in 1973 it yielded as much as 9.75 percent.
This is how it works. Suppose you decide to invest $1,000 in
six-month commercial paper. You mail in your application
together with a check for $951.25. Six months later you collect
the full $1,000, which includes your $48.75 half-yearly interest. In 1974 the yield rose to 10.25 percent.

The reason commercial paper is not as safe as Treasury
bills is that it has no unconditional government guarantee
behind it. If the United States should get into a serious
depression, some corporations might not be able to meet their
obligations. Even the biggest corporations cannot print their
own money to pay off their creditors. The federal government
can. Furthermore, commercial paper is not backed up by any
collateral.

You can also buy a diversified mixture of these government and private fixed interest securities through mutual
funds such as Drefus Liquid Assets Incorporated, 600 Madison Avenue, New York 10022. This particular fund charges no
sales or redemption fee. The minimum investment is $5,000
(or $1,000 if you apply through a securities dealer). The fund
holds a portfolio of United States Government Securities,
bankers' acceptances and commercial paper. It declares
dividends daily. In mid-1974 it was yielding a net return of
nearly 10 percent. The advantage of this type of fund is diversification and the fact that you do not have to tie up your
money for five years or more in order to get a higher interest
rate. You can buy or sell your shares at any time.

5

Gold—The Ultimate Security

THROUGHOUT history, gold has represented wealth. It is the universally acceptable commodity. When you have gold you have everything else—the power to buy food, housing, land, to survive financial crashes, to flee your own country with your wealth if political and economic conditions become intolerable, and to set yourself up in a new life elsewhere. Gold is the world's ultimate symbol of value, the standard against which everything else is measured.

For a start, let's measure it against the United States dollar. Up to 1934, the dollar was valued at $20.67 per ounce of gold. In that year President Franklin D. Roosevelt marked the dollar down to $35 an ounce and prohibited gold ownership by Americans. In December, 1971, President Richard Nixon notched the dollar down, and the gold price up, to $38 an ounce. Only fourteen months later, in February, 1973, Nixon devalued the dollar again, to $42.22 an ounce. So we have this sequence: the $20.67 price lasted 100 years, from

1834 to 1934; the $35 price lasted nearly 38 years, from 1934 to 1971; the $38 price lasted one year and two months; and the $42.22 price was a fiction, because by 1973 no one was selling gold to anyone at that price anywhere in the world. The "official" price bore no relationship to the actual free-market price of gold, which in 1974 zoomed as high as $180 an ounce on the world's gold bullion markets.

Now, which would you rather have—dollars or gold? In the free markets of Paris, Zurich, and London a lot of foreign speculators have been making their preference for gold unmistakably clear in recent years, pushing the free-market price up and up. As recently as 1968, it was only $35 an ounce because the United States government still had enough gold at Fort Knox to sell any amount needed to hold the price down at the official level. Now, most of the country's gold stock is gone and the United States is no longer able to keep down prices. Early in 1974 the Treasury's gold stock was worth $11.5 billion, while the United States' national debt was $470 billion.

It is not only the United States dollar that these European and other gold bugs are suspicious of—it is *any* paper currency, including so-called "strong" currencies, which in 1973 were notably the Swiss franc and the German mark. Even in those countries inflation was running at about 8 percent a year in 1973, and the value of their money was being clipped at an even higher rate in 1974.

For the fact remains that, in any country in the world and at any time in history, paper money is only paper. Every government on earth loves to spend money to please the public and hates to raise taxes for fear of angering the voters or taxpayers. The easy way out is simply to print more paper money. The government then has funds to finance its projects and doesn't have to force the citizens to fork up. A beautiful solution—except that the money supply keeps rising and the dollar bills, marks, francs, and yen keep flooding into the market. That is why we have inflation and why your money is worth less every year, whether you live in New Orleans or Yokohama.

Meanwhile, gold is gold is gold, and no government

anywhere has ever figured out a way to run it off the printing press. As long as gold is as scarce and as difficult to dig out of the ground as it is now, there is no great danger of any glut on the market. Someone once calculated that all the gold ever mined in all of human history—about 100,000 tons—would only fill a baseball diamond and make a cube 90 feet high on that area.

So, foreigners dump their depreciating paper money and seek security in gold. If you're an American citizen, though, you probably assume you can't follow their example, since Americans can't own gold. But you *can* buy gold perfectly legally. At the time of this writing you can buy gold coins, provided they are dated 1959 or earlier. You can buy raw, un-processed gold nuggets. You can buy jewelry made of gold. You can buy gold mining shares and, by the time this book gets into print you may be able to own gold in any shape or form without restriction. As this book was going to press, President Ford, on August 14, 1974, signed a bill allowing United States citizens to own gold after December 31, 1974. A United States Treasury spokesman said the administration did not favor setting such deadlines and that it might ask Congress to extend the gold ownership ban for a time until international monetary con-ditions were stable enough to accept the measure without dis-ruption. Apparently all that was in doubt was the exact date on which Americans would be allowed to own gold again.

What the measure would do, of course, would be to add a market of more than 200 million Americans as potential buyers to existing gold markets abroad. What this would do to the price of gold was unknown, but one New York coin dealer predicted that its impact would be "tremendous" and that gold prices would start climbing immediately. United States government spokesmen said Washington would sell some gold from its stockpile so as to hold down any violent upward surge in gold prices.

As this book was going to press, American dealers were preparing plans to offer gold bullion to their fellow citizens and United States commodity markets were setting up gold futures contracts for American speculators. We shall get to these further ahead in this chapter. First, let's examine the ways Americans can legally profit from gold no matter what happens to the anti-gold ban legislation mentioned above.

Gold Coins

It is beyond the scope of this book to talk about the numismatic value of gold coins — that is, their value as rare objects. Instead, we'll talk about investing in coins for the amount of *gold* they contain.

Here is a list of the most common coins, those in which there is a fairly large and active trade:

> American $20 Double Eagle
> American $10 Eagle
> American $10 Indian
> American $5 Half Eagle
> American $2.50 Quarter Eagle
> Mexican 50 Peso
> Mexican 20 Peso
> British Sovereign
> Colombian 5 Peso
> French 20 Franc Napoleon
> Swiss 20-Franc Vreneli
> Belgian 20 Francs
> Italian 20 Lire

Here is a sample of the prices of some of these coins in February, 1973, just before the 10 percent devaluation of the United States dollar, and in March, 1973, just after the devaluation. The table is taken from *The Powell Monetary Analyst,* March 31 (published twice monthly by Reserve Research Limited, 63 Wall Street, New York, New York 10005).

COMMON GOLD COINS — Average Dealer's Asking Price (N.Y.C.)

	2/1/73	3/2/73	3/29/73
U.S. $20 Double Eagle	$125.00	$185.00	$158.00
U.S. $10 Liberty	$ 70.00	$ 90.00	$ 90.00
U.S. $10 Indian	$ 90.00	$125.00	$125.00
U.S. $ 5 Liberty or Indian	$ 55.00	$ 75.00	$ 75.00
Mexican 20 Pesos	$ 50.00	$ 65.00	$ 65.00
Mexican 50 Pesos	$115.00	$165.00	$150.00
British Sovereign	$ 24.75	$ 38.00	$ 35.00
Columbia 5 Pesos	$ 24.00	$ 34.00	$ 32.50
French Napoleon	$ 19.00	$ 32.00	$ 25.00
Swiss 20 Francs	$ 19.00	$ 32.00	$ 31.00

You will note that all the coins rose sharply after the February 12 devaluation and then lost part of their gains. The $20 Double Eagle, for example, rose $60 (about 50 percent) in one month and then fell back to $158. This still left it with a $33 gain on March 29 (about 25 percent over two months).

The first thing you need to know is how much gold each of the coins you buy contains. Then you know exactly how much precious metal you are getting for your money. When you buy an American $20 Double Eagle, you are getting nearly one ounce of pure gold. With the Eagle you are getting almost half an ounce. The Half Eagle gives you a little less than a quarter of an ounce and the Quarter Eagle just under one-eighth of an ounce of pure gold. The Mexican 50 Pesos contains 1.205 ounces; the British Sovereign and the Colombian 5 Pesos each have close to a quarter-ounce of pure gold. The French, Swiss, and Belgian 20 Francs and the Italian 20 Lire are all of the same weight and purity. They represent nearly one-fifth of an ounce of gold for each coin. Here are the exact figures:

GOLD COIN(S)

WEIGHT AND CONTENT

American $20
Double Eagle

Gold content: 0.97 troy ounces*
Fineness: 21.6 karats
        (900/1000 pure gold)
Weight: 1.07 troy ounces

American $10 Eagle
(Liberty or Indian type)

Gold content: 0.48 troy ounces
Fineness: 21.6 karats
Weight: 0.53 troy ounces

American $5 Half Eagle

Gold content: 0.24 oz.
Fineness: 21.6 karats
Weight: 0.26875 troy ounces

American $2.50
  Quarter Eagle

Gold content: 0.12 troy ounces
Fineness: 21.6 karats
Weight: 0.13 troy ounces

Mexican 50 Pesos

Gold content: 1.205 troy ounces

Mexican 20 Pesos

Gold content: 0.48 troy ounces

Colombian 5 Pesos
British Sovereign (Queen
Victoria, George V,
Edward VII)

Gold content: 0.24 troy ounces
Fineness: 22 karats (916.23/1000)
Weight: 0.25 troy ounces

French 20-Franc Napoleon
Swiss 20-Franc Vreneli
Belgian 20-Franc
  Leopold II
Italian 20-Lire
  Vittorio Emanuele II
Italian 20-Lire Umberto I

Gold content: 0.19 troy ounces
Fineness: 21.6 karats
Weight: 0.25 troy ounces

*The troy ounce, used for weighing silver, gold, and other precious metals, is equal to 1.0972 avoirdupois ounces, the ounces we use for everyday measurement.

The second thing you need to know is the price of gold on the particular day on which you are buying or selling gold coins. Turn to the *Wall Street Journal,* the *New York Times,* or any other newspaper that carries a good business news section. In the *New York Times,* look up the list of quotations in a column headed "Money." You will find these lines:

Gold (N.Y.) H&H Base Price $91.20
Gold (N.Y.) Engl. Selling Price $91.35

The *Wall Street Journal* spells these cryptic initials and abbreviations out for you in an item titled "Silver and Gold Prices":

> U.S. gold prices: Handy & Harman's base for pricing gold content of shipments and for making refining settlements was $91.20. Engelhard Minerals and Chemicals Corp.'s buying price for gold was $91.15 and the selling price was $91.35.

These are two firms that refine and deal in gold for use by industrial companies, jewelers, and dental supply concerns authorized to buy gold for use in their business.

The *Times* and the *Journal* also give you the price of gold on the London free market, which on this particular day ranged between $90.90 and $91.25, but other American papers may not. Even so, the two United States firms' quotations are a good reference point because they normally are very close to the prices in London, Zurich, and other free markets for gold abroad.

Let us imagine that, alarmed by the February 12, 1973, dollar devaluation you were buying gold coins on March 2 at the prices shown above in the *Powell Monetary Analyst* table of average dealers' prices. The price of gold bullion that day was about $86 an ounce. If you had bought American Double Eagles at $185, you would have been paying more than twice the dollar price of the coins' one-ounce gold content. British Sovereigns at $38 would have cost $152 per gold ounce. French Napoleons at $32 would have worked out at $160 per ounce of gold.

This was evidently *not* the best time to buy. The damage of the devaluation had already been done. In early February, just before the devaluation, gold bullion was selling at about $65 an ounce. At that time, as you will see from the table, you could have bought French Napoleons at around $19 per coin, which meant you were paying $85 for each ounce of gold content — a premium of only 30 percent.

All these coins sell at a premium over the price of gold bullion simply because they *are* coins. They have the official stamp of the United States, Britain, or some other government guaranteeing their weight and fineness. Of course, they also have a certain scarcity value because they are not being minted any more, and a numismatic value because collectors prize them.

You now know how much gold you are getting for each type of coin. You know how to keep track of the price of gold on world markets. You are also in a position to figure out which coin is giving you the best value in relation to its gold content.

The table of prices shows how prices could rise 50 percent in one month. Can we predict how much you can gain by trading in your paper dollars for gold coins? No. The future is unforeseeable, and nobody can give you an exact blueprint of what is to come.

But you *can* gauge the probabilities of a situation. On August 15, 1971, President Nixon announced that the United States dollar was no longer convertible into gold — not for anybody. Not for foreign central banks, foreign private citizens, and certainly not for American citizens, who had been forbidden to own gold four decades before. On that day, the American dollar became an inconvertible paper currency, no different in essence from the French franc, the Brazilian cruzeiro, or the Argentine peso.

In all those countries, where the local currency has

depreciated in each case to one-hundredth part or less of its value forty years ago, private citizens have learned long since that gold is incomparably a better security than paper money.

A hundred years ago, the Brazilian currency was depreciated to such an extent that the government abandoned it and started printing milreis, the equivalent of one thousand old units. The old units have fallen into such oblivion that not even Brazilian bankers remember what they were called without referring to an encyclopedia. The milrei in turn sank so low that the government issued a new monetary unit, the cruzeiro. If you turned in 1,000 milreis you got one cruzeiro, which was thus equivalent to one million old units. The cruzeiro in turn succumbed to the floods of bills being turned out by the government mint, and its place was taken by the new cruzeiro, which represents 1,000 old cruzeiros. The new cruzeiro is thus the equivalent of one billion old units. After three formal debasements in a century the Brazilian monetary unit had thus shrunk to one-billionth part of its original value. And this is still not the end of the process.

In recent years, the new cruzeiro has been losing its value at a minimum yearly rate of 15 percent.

In this kind of situation, no matter how high the price of gold or gold coins seems at any particular time in relation to the local currency, one can be sure that the price of gold this year will seem absurdly cheap next year, regardless of how exorbitant it seems now in terms of the local paper currency.

Where do you buy or sell your gold coins? Use the most reliable coin dealer you can find, which means you do not do business with the first one you come across. Some of these gentlemen have inflated ideas of how much a middleman should make, and the gap between their selling price and their buying price for the same coin is sometimes unbelievable.

For a test, list the dealers within your reach and check them out by buying one coin from each, as long as you find their selling price is not too far out of line. A few days later, send somebody else back to the same shop with the same coin, offering to sell it. You will be surprised to learn that in some cases a coin that a few days ago was praised as a veritable paragon of excellence is derided a few days later by the same dealer as a worn-out piece of junk.

If you can shame this dealer into treating you fairly by showing him you are not a sucker, you *may* still want to do business with him, as long as you know the value of what you are buying or selling. There are other dealers, however, who are satisfied with a reasonable markup, if you find such a person, you know you can bargain with a fairly reasonable human being.

If there is no coin dealer within easy reach of where you live you can also buy coins by mail from some coin dealers located in big cities. In New York City, for example, Manfra, Tordella, and Brookes, Incorporated, 30 Rockefeller Plaza, New York 10020, periodically advertises gold coins for sale by the piece or in 100-coin lots, which are cheaper. The coins are sent to you by registered, insured mail. A spokesman for this firm says its normal markup is about $2 on a $35 coin. That is, if they are buying at $35 they are usually selling at $37. Another firm with a similar selling and pricing policy is Perera Fifth Avenue Incorporated, 636 Fifth Avenue, New York 10020.

A curious feature of these mail-order firms is that you can usually save money by buying from out of state. In New York City, for example, there is an 8 percent sales tax, which you would not have to pay if you ordered from a New Jersey address. There is also a New Jersey sales tax that is not paid by residents of New York or other states when ordering by mail.

We have been talking about gold coins as an investment in *gold.* You might consider buying gold coins as a sort of insurance policy against the many long years of inflation that might lie ahead. During your earning years, you may want to buy one gold coin, or ten gold coins, every month. This is your "insurance premium." In fifteen or twenty years you will have a couple of hundred or a couple of thousand gold coins stacked up in your bank safety deposit box. When you retire, you withdraw one or ten coins a month and sell them. This is your payout. Compare the results with the payout on your conventional insurance policies — we suspect you will come out far ahead.

Gold Mining Stocks

In recent years the rise in the price of gold has been so explosive that gold mining shares have generally lagged behind. Only when astonishing profit growth was made apparent in quarterly company statements did investors become fully aware of the advantages of investing in gold mines rather than in the metal itself. When a mine can work at a profit selling gold at an artificially held down price of $35 an ounce, as so many did from 1934 to 1968, the profit potential when gold is set free and hits more than $180 an ounce, as it did on free world markets during 1974, is spectacular.

There is a long list of gold mining shares available for you to invest in. The largest gold producer in the United States is Homestake Mining. Campbell Red Lake and Dome Mines Limited are major Canadian producers. A.S.A. Limited is an investment trust with a portfolio of most of the big South African mines. All four companies are quoted on the New York Stock Exchange. International Investors, 40 Wall Street, New York 10005, is a United States mutual fund that concentrates on gold mining shares. For readers outside the United States, mutual funds are also available with a heavy concentration of gold shares, among them S.A.F.I.T. in Switzerland and Jessel Gold & General Unit Trust in Great Britain.

Investors in the United States and other countries can also buy shares in individual mining companies, which are quoted in Johannesburg, London, New York, or all three. These were discussed in Chapter 2.

Gold Futures

You can trade gold in the commodities markets as if it were corn, cotton, or hog-bellies. And you can get all the tremendous speculative leverage these staples of the futures markets have to offer. As this book went to press, the only snag was that you could not participate if you were an American citizen or resident, due to the United States ban on gold ownership.

At the time of writing, the only place in the world to trade in gold for future delivery is on the Winnipeg Grain Exchange, which offers two gold futures contracts. One is for 400 troy ounces and the other is for 100 ounces. Both allow the investor to speculate on the price of gold as far as a year ahead. With gold at around $150 an ounce, each 400-ounce contract is worth about $60,000. The exchange requires a margin of 10 percent, so that the minimum speculation possible would mean an ante of $6,000. The 100-ounce contract is worth $15,000 and requires a margin outlay of about $1,500. It is designed for the little man, and will probably be the model for United States gold futures markets as soon as they are allowed to operate by the repeal of the gold ownership ban.

The New York Commodity Exchange was planning to offer a 100-ounce contract and so was the New York Mercantile Exchange. Similar small contracts were being studied by the Chicago Mercantile Exchange and the Chicago Board of Trade.

In Winnipeg, the brokerage commission on a 400-ounce contract is $75, and on a 100-ounce contract it is $35. Further details on gold futures trading may be obtained from the Winnipeg Grain Exchange, Winnipeg, Manitoba, Canada.

Gold Bullion

American coin and currency dealers were also busy preparing for the day gold bullion sales would become legal as this book went to press. To take one example, Perera Fifth Avenue Inc., 630 Fifth Avenue, New York 10020, was planning to sell ingots of .999 fine gold bullion in sizes of ½, 1, 3, 5, 10, 16, 32 and 100 troy ounces. Larger denominations would also be sold on special order. Perera anticipated that the price of its bullion would fluctuate in close connection with the London and Zurich bullion markets. A spokesman said he expected the spread between bid and asked prices to be less than 5 percent. The latest quotations on gold bullion and coins, as well as silver bullion and coins, may be obtained from Perera's "gold hotline" around the clock, 212-586-2175.

6

Silver—The Hoarder's Metal

Like the price of gold, the price of silver was held at an artificially fixed level by the United States government for years. Then, on May 18, 1967, the United States Treasury withdrew its standing offer to sell silver to all comers at $1.2929 per troy ounce. The effect was much the same as with gold a few years later. The price of silver shot up more than 100 percent. A couple of years later, it lost nearly all that gain and started a series of wild fluctuations that have kept speculators and investors guessing and exchanges busy.

There are two ways to approach this situation—as a speculator and as an investor. Which approach you choose depends on your temperament, your circumstances, and your goals. Are you willing to take high risk of loss for quick, short-term profits? Or are you more inclined to pile up a fortune in silver over the years because you think that in the long run it will be worth more than constantly inflated paper currencies? If you're a speculator, the futures market is for you. If you're an investor, look into the bullion market.

Silver Bullion

For many years Britons and Americans have been forbidden by their governments to own gold. So when they lose faith in their country's currency at times of monetary crises, they tend to turn to silver to preserve their assets. The imagination of the public, fed by newspaper headline writers, is captured by the idea that while the paper money supply is constantly being inflated, nobody can inflate the supply and thus reduce the value of good, solid silver bars.

The very fact that people all around the world tend to hoard silver in times of revolution, war, inflation, and political upheaval can have a tremendous impact on the price of the metal. At times such as the Depression, when paper money gained in value instead of declining, the economic slump reduced industrial demand for silver. Silver prices dropped as low as 24.5 cents an ounce at one point.

Nowadays, consumption constantly outruns production of silver, resulting in an annual worldwide deficit of about 100 million ounces. This by itself should push prices constantly higher. However, there are some jokers in the pack. One is that the global level of hoarding is impossible to predict. Americans and Britons are not the only silver bugs. Indians, for example, are also great silver hoarders. Who can tell how much silver is being smuggled into India? Or out of India, if the price should surge spectacularly elsewhere? Silver prices are also affected by the technical demands of industry. Photography currently accounts for about 30 percent of all silver consumption. If somebody in the Kodak, Polaroid, or AGFA laboratories were to invent a method of making photographs by a process that required no silver, this would reduce demand by 30 percent and drive the price of silver down.

Although the demand for silver is uncertain and fluctuating, the supply is fairly constant and inelastic, for the curious reason that relatively few mines are primarily in business to produce silver. The precious metal is usually only a by-product of such base metals as zinc, copper, or tin. If the price of the mine's main product does not go up and silver represents only a relatively small percentage of total sales, even a steep increase in the price of silver may still not make it worthwhile to increase production.

About 60 percent of the world's silver is produced by four countries: the United States, Mexico, Peru, and Canada. You can keep track of production trends by reading such specialized newspapers as *American Metal Market*, 7 East 12th Street, New York 10003, and by requesting literature from the Office of Mineral Information, Bureau of Mines, Washington, D.C. 20240.

Now, where do you buy silver bullion? There are a number of possible sources, and here are some of them. Probably the cheapest way is to buy a nearby futures contract on the Chicago or New York commodity exchange and take delivery of it. The trouble is that the minimum amount you can buy in this way is 5,000 ounces in Chicago and 10,000 ounces in New York. At $5 an ounce that would be a lot of money. You would also have to pick up your bullion at a designated warehouse and if you do not live in the Chicago or New York area that would be out of your way.

There are also scores of firms across the country that sell and deliver to you silver bullion. In some cases they call themselves exchanges but they are in fact private merchants. To see if the prices they offer you are in line with the prevailing market price, check first with the "Silver and Gold Prices" item in the *Wall Street Journal*. You should also be aware that many of these firms will only buy from you the silver bars with their own stamp on them, so that you might have no alternative but to sell the bullion back to the firm that sold it to you. The firm would then hold you as a captive customer with no place else to go, and you would be at the mercy of its resale policy, which might not offer you a fair market price.

Perhaps the biggest firm in the business is the Pacific Coast Coin Exchange, 3711 Long Beach Boulevard, Long Beach, California 90807. It offers standard silver bars of 1,000 troy ounces. Each bar weighs about 70 pounds and is a foot long by five inches wide by four inches high.

There are other places where you can buy in smaller quantities, but generally speaking the smaller the ingot you buy the higher the price per ounce. I.M.C. Mint Corporation, 315 East Second South, Salt Lake City, Utah 84111, sells ingots as small as 1, 2, 3, 5, 10, 25, 100 or 500 troy ounces as well as the standard 1,000-ounce bar. Similar small lots can be bought by mail from a major precious metals firm, Engelhard Industries, Pine & Durham Streets, Attleboro, Mass. 02703. There are other such firms around the country. The silver all these firms sell you is certified .999 fine (that is, 99.9 percent pure). It is usually delivered by registered, insured mail if there is no regional office near you. Obviously, the smaller your purchase the higher will be the proportionate cost of mailing and other sales expenses.

You can also buy silver from the United States government whenever Washington decides to auction off surplus silver from its stockpile. The minimum amount the government will sell you is usually 5,000 ounces, for which you have to pay hard cash. For further details write to the General Services Administration, Office of Information, 18th & F Streets, Washington, D.C. 20405.

The disadvantages of silver bullion thus are that it is bulky to store, sold in large quantities and hard to buy at a fair price in smaller amounts. It may also be hard to sell when you want to get rid of it.

Silver Coins

You can avoid some of these difficulties by buying silver coins instead of bullion. There is a large and organized trade in United States dollars, half-dollars, quarters, and dimes minted in 1964 or earlier. Up to that year the coins contained 90 percent silver. Since 1965 they have been made of base metals without any precious metal content at all.

You can buy pre-1964 silver coins by the piece from your neighborhood coin dealer or in bags containing $1,000 face value silver coins from such firms as the Pacific Coast Coin Exchange.

The advantages of United States silver coins is that you can buy them in small amounts, the United States government stamp on them is a first-class guarantee of their silver content, and they are easier to sell than silver bars.

When buying or selling you can verify that you are getting a fair price by glancing at the nearest month on the table of quotations from the Chicago or New York silver coin futures markets. We shall discuss these coin futures markets further on. Another way to check is to know the silver content of your coins.

Every U.S. silver coin in circulation and minted through 1964 contained:

Dollar	0.72464 troy ounces
Half Dollar	0.36225 troy ounces
Quarter	0.18113 troy ounces
Dime	0.07245 troy ounces

(The troy ounce is equal to 1.0972 avoirdupois ounces)

The wastage on the older and more worn coins is surprisingly small. In a $1,000 bag the average will work out to about 715 to 720 ounces of silver instead of the 724.64 you should get in a bag of uncirculated coins without any wear and tear.

Once you know the silver content of your coins all you have to do is look at the "Gold and Silver Prices" in the *Wall Street Journal*, or the spot price of silver in your local newspaper if it carries a good commodities section, and you can work out the current value of the coins whenever you want to buy or sell.

You can buy both silver bullion and the $1,000 silver coin bags on margin, but so far we are assuming that you are buying silver with the purpose of holding it as a long-term investment. In this case your primary consideration is safety; therefore you should not be operating on margin. A wise way to invest in silver is to make regular purchases of moderate amounts. In this way you will average out your purchase price, and you won't make the mistake of putting everything into silver bullion at an emotional moment when everyone is talking about silver as an inflation hedge and the price is skyrocketing.

Silver Futures

If your goal is short-term speculation and what you want is a quick killing in the silver market, the picture changes completely, and your strategy should be as different as the blitzkrieg is from the war of attrition. In the silver futures market, price swings are magnified perhaps tenfold by your low margin, and your gains and losses are swift and dramatic.

In the United States, silver futures are traded on the New York Commodity Exchange, the Chicago Board of Trade, and the Pacific Commodities Exchange in San Francisco; in England, they are traded on the London silver market. Your first step in silver speculation is to find a commodities broker. If you are active in the stock market, your own stockbroker may be able to help you, since many brokerage firms are active in the commodities field. Otherwise, there are scores of firms all over the United States and in many foreign countries with whom you can deal. Some of the biggest, with branches in many American cities and abroad, are the following:

Bache & Company, 100 Gold Street, New York 10038
Merrill Lynch, One Liberty Plaza, New York 10006
E.F. Hutton & Company, One Battery Park Plaza, New York 10004
Reynolds Securities Incorporated, 120 Broadway, New York 10005

Having chosen your broker, you then open an account. You will be assigned an account executive, who will handle all your buy and sell orders. If you are a novice in the game, you may want to start out by taking this man's advice on when to buy and when to sell, if you are favorably impressed with his knowledge and competence. You may assume that he knows more about the market than you do initially, and it is obviously in his interest that you should make money.

However, you must also realize that your broker has other interests of his own, which are not your interests. First and foremost, his goal is to make as much money in commissions out of your account as he can. This is where you must watch out for yourself. Your loss is not only the cost of the commissions. As we shall see in a later chapter, to be constantly in and out of the market taking small profits can be a fatal mistake in commodity future trading. These markets are risky and your profits *have* to be big ones to offset that risk.

So keep a tight rein on your broker. Insist that he call you before he makes any trade for you and that he explain briefly why he wants to buy or sell at that particular time. Do not allow him to make any trade without your explicit approval. Some of these gentlemen, even in large and reputable brokerage houses, have itchy pants and can't sit still even after having received such instructions. If your broker starts making trades for you without phoning you first, report him to the office manager, explain the problem, and move your account to another firm.

You will soon find out how your executive is doing for you, and if he gives you his reasons for every trade you will also learn what he is doing right or wrong. Meanwhile, you should be reading every item you can on silver in the newspapers, magazines, and market letters. You can receive these letters from a number of brokers by clipping their coupons when they advertise market reports on silver. You will be surprised to find how interesting this reading matter is to you when your own money is on the line.

Once you have sufficient confidence in your own knowledge and judgment and have proved to your own satisfaction that you have a strong enough stomach to relish the wild swings of the futures market, you may want to cut yourself loose from your broker's advice and decide entirely on your own when to buy and when to sell.

The main thing you will be watching in the newspapers is the table of futures market quotations that appear every business day. The typographical details vary in each newspaper, but generally the information you want looks something like this:

Commodity Futures Trading in Detail

CHICAGO BOARD OF TRADE
SILVER

	Open	High	Low		Close	Prev. Close	Life of Cont-High	Low
Aug.	278.10	278.10	278.10	†278.10-	—	†278.10	282.00	163.80
Oct.	298.00	299.00	289.50	291.50-	291.30	†293.00	299.00	176.50
Dec.	302.00	303.60	294.00	296.30-	295.20	297.60	303.60	178.56
Feb.	305.80	307.50	299.50	299.50-	299.00	†301.30	307.50	191.80
Apr.	309.00	310.50	302.50	303.00-	—	304.30	310.50	205.30
June	312.00	313.10	304.00	306.00-	305.50	†307.40	313.10	219.50
Aug.	314.50	315.50	308.00	†307.50-	308.00	†309.50	315.50	233.00
Oct.	316.00	318.80	309.50	309.50-	—	†311.50	318.80	287.50

COMMODITY EXCHANGE INC.
SILVER

	Open	High	Low	Close		Prev. Close	Life of Contr. High	Low
Sept.	293.50	296.20	288.50	s291.10-	—	s291.20	296.20	164.00
Dec.	300.50	302.50	292.00	297.20	—	s297.20	302.50	176.50
Jan.	302.20	305.00	296.00	s299.20-	—	s299.20	305.00	179.00
Mar.	307.00	307.90	301.00	s302.40-	—	s302.30	307.90	193.80
May	310.00	310.00	303.50	s305.20-	—	s305.00	310.00	208.40
July	313.50	313.80	306.50	s308.30-	—	s307.90	313.80	255.00
Sept.	316.50	316.50	310.00	s311.20-	—	s310.80	316.50	233.50

Total sales, 4,647 lots; Sept., 1,183; Dec., 1,820, Jan., 193; Mar., 474; May, 391; July, 306; Sept., 280.

The table is from the *New York Journal of Commerce* and it details trading operations on Tuesday, July 17, 1973.

Let's start with the very first line of the bottom table, under the heading *Commodity Exchange Inc.* This is the New York silver futures market. The table tells you that on July 17, 1973, silver contracts for delivery in September, 1973, opened at 293.50 cents per troy ounce, were quoted as high as 296.20 and as low as 288.50 cents during the day's trading, and finally closed at 291.10. The previous day's closing price was 291.20. During the previous year (Life of Contract) the quotations had varied between a high of 296.20 and a low of 164.00.

Thus, on this July day, we would be pretty near the high end of the previous year's price range. Nevertheless, let us suppose that you think the trend is still upward, at least for a couple more months. You decide to buy a September, 1973, contract. Your decision is strengthened by the amount of trading activity in this month, which you know from the figures given below the table: Total sales—4,647 lots. This means that 4,647 contracts were traded that day.

You will also note that more than half of them were traded in the two closest months: 1,183 for delivery in September, 1973, and 1,820 for December, 1973. Once you get into the deliveries due farther ahead—in the 1974 months— activity drops off sharply. From this you conclude that, due to the greater activity in the September, 1973, delivery, you will find it easier to find a buyer or a seller in that month— that is, you will have greater liquidity.

You call your broker. The next day, he buys you a September, 1973, contract on the New York Commodity Exchange at 290—that is, at $2.90 per troy ounce of silver. Since the standard contract in New York is for 10,000 ounces, the total value of the contract at this price would be $29,000 (plus a $45 commission and a 50-cent Exchange fee). This looks like an enormous investment; in fact, you would probably be trading on about a 10 percent margin, which means you would put up only $2,900 of your own money.

This gives you powerful leverage. If your contract goes to 291 the next day, its total value rises to $29,100, and in twenty-four hours you have a $100 gain on your $2,900 investment. It is easy to see that a fluctuation of one cent per ounce would mean a gain or loss of $100 on your contract.

Of course, if your contract went down 29 cents an ounce, it would wipe out your entire $2,900 investment. However, do not get alarmed too soon. The maximum daily fluctuation the Exchange allows is usually 10 to 20 cents an ounce. And, in normal markets, you can protect yourself before this 29-cent disaster overwhelms you by putting a stop-loss order in at the same time you buy your contract. Let us say you are willing to take a maximum loss of $300 if the market goes against you. Since you bought at 290, you put in a stop-loss order at 287. This means your broker will automatically sell out your contract if it should ever drop to 287. Your possible loss is thus limited to $300.

Not only does the stop-loss order limit your possible

losses, but it can also protect your gains. Suppose you were right in predicting a rising market and that in a week's time your contract is up to 300 (which means you have a $1,000 gain). You move your stop-loss order up to 297 (this would give you a $700 gain if you sold at that price). Even if the market then turns down, you will be automatically sold out at 297. You thus have an assured gain of $700, whatever happens subsequently.

The stop-loss order is not completely foolproof, however. If there is a sudden, calamitous drop in the market, the broker may not be able to execute your order until the price has fallen through your stop-loss limit. However, this kind of drop is highly exceptional; it is usually caused only by some catastrophic news, for example, a sudden United States government decision to dump all its silver stockpile on the market at once — an extremely unlikely eventuality. In normal times, the stop-loss order should give you effective protection.

Let's move on now. You are watching the silver futures table in the newspaper every day and you notice that your contract month is fluctuating constantly around the 300 mark, sometimes a little higher, sometimes a little lower. It begins to look to you as if the market advance is losing steam and that the price is bumping around its top. Early in August you decide to sell out at 300. The total contract is now worth $30,000 (less the $45.50 commission and fee) instead of the $29,000 it was worth when you bought it. This is a gain of nearly $1,000 and it is all yours. Not bad for an investment in which you put down just $2,900 only about three weeks ago.

You are now out of the market, but you are still on the sidelines watching developments. You note that the market now seems to be in a definite downtrend. By October, 1973, you are convinced that the market will be considerably lower over the next year or so. You tell your broker to sell a September, 1974, contract, which he does at 280. That is to say the contract totals $28,000 and your margin is $2,800.

By selling this contract you have undertaken to provide

10,000 ounces of silver for delivery in September, 1974, for which you are to receive $28,000. Of course you have no intention of making any such delivery. You will simply *buy* a contract later on, and this obligation to accept 10,000 ounces of silver in the future will cancel out your obligation to deliver 10,000 ounces. The vast majority of contracts in all futures markets never come down to actual delivery. They are simply liquidated by a countervailing buy or sell order, either at a profit or a loss — if your judgment is right, at a profit.

Let us assume that you have protected yourself once again by a stop-loss order to *buy* at 283, but that it has not been touched off because the market has continued to fall. By December, 1973, your September, 1974, contract is down to 250 and you decide to cash in your profits. You buy a September, 1974, contract at 250. You now have a contract to purchase 10,000 ounces of silver for $25,000 and another contract to sell 10,000 ounces at $28,000. The difference, less commissions and expenses, is all profit for you. Your contracts cancel out each other, and you are out of the market, nearly $3,000 ahead on a $2,800 investment made three months before.

Please note that the above examples are only hypothetical, with all figures rounded off for greater clarity and with up and down price trends assumed merely for the purpose of illustrating market movements. They have no connection with what actually happened in the market in the 1973-74 period. If you want to turn this example upside down, assume that the market went down when we said it went up and up when we presumed it would go down — in other words, that everything turned out exactly the reverse of what you had anticipated. In this case, provided your stop-loss orders functioned properly, you would have lost $300 closing out your original long position (the first contract you bought), and you would have lost another $300 closing out the short position (the contract you sold). Your total loss would be $600 plus commissions.

These examples illustrate the importance of the stop-loss order in cutting your losses short while you let your profits run.

We have been talking here of margins in the neighborhood of $3,000 (they vary from time to time and from one broker to another). This may be more than you want to risk on the silver futures market. In this case you may prefer to trade on the Chicago market, where the contract is for only 5,000 ounces rather than the 10,000 in New York. The money figures we have given above would thus all be cut in half. At 290, your Chicago contract would be worth $14,500 and the margin payment would be only $1,450 on the same scale. The Pacific Coast contract is the smallest of all—a mere 1,000 ounces. This market was just being inaugurated as this book went to press, but if it generates a sufficient number of contracts to insure liquidity it will be a good place for the little guy to start out. You would require a margin of about $500.

In London, the unit of trading is 10,000 ounces per contract and you can buy or sell spot silver or for delivery three, six, or twelve months ahead. The delivery months in New York are different from those in Chicago. This accounts for price discrepancies between the two markets, the March delivery in New York, for example, not being exactly comparable with the April delivery in Chicago.

Silver Coin Futures

Much of what we have said on *silver* futures is also applicable to *silver coin* futures.

There are two markets for trading American silver coin futures in New York. There are also two markets in Chicago, one for American and the other for Canadian silver coins.

These coin markets arose as a result of the debasement of the currency. As we have noted, up through the year 1964 all United States dollars, half dollars, quarters, and dimes were made of 90 percent silver. Since 1965 they have mostly been made of a mixture of copper and other base metals, with an intrinsic value of about one twenty-fifth of their face value.

In the futures markets the old 90-percent-silver coins minted through 1964 are the United States coins traded. The Canadian coins traded are those minted in 1966 or earlier, with an 80-percent-silver content. You never find these coins in your loose change any more because they have been worth as much as four times their face value due to their silver content. As Gresham's law pointed out long ago, bad money drives good money out of circulation.

On the New York Mercantile Exchange each contract is for a face value of $10,000 in dimes, quarters, and half dollars. The margin requirement varies, but assuming it is 10 percent of face value, you could buy or sell a $10,000 contract for $1,000 plus a $10 commission. Obviously, the leverage is very high here, and a fluctuation of only $100 in the quotation of a $10,000 contract would give you a 10 percent gain on your $1,000 margin outlay.

You may want to play for lower stakes. If so the American Board of Trade offers you contracts with a total face value of as little as $1,000. On this market the contract months cover a 12-month span, October, January, April, July, and October of the following year. On the New York Mercantile Exchange, the delivery months run as far as 15 months ahead.

On the Chicago Mercantile Exchange the United States silver coin futures contract is for a $5,000 face amount of dimes, quarters, or half dollars contained in five canvas money bags, each containing $1,000 face amount of coins minted prior to 1965. The Canadian silver coin futures contract is for $5,000 face amount of Canadian dimes, quarters, or half dollars minted prior to 1967. Because older Canadian coins have a lower silver content than older American coins, the Chicago Exchange calculates that every $1,000 bag of United States silver coins contains 715 ounces of silver, while every $1,000 bag of Canadian coins contains only 585 ounces of silver.

Silver vs. Coin Future Spreads

Because the underlying value of the coins is the value of the silver in them, there is a close relationship between the price of silver bullion and the value of the coins.

This difference in the prices of bullion and coins is not constant. It varies, and the variation has given rise to a curious market in which you try to make a profit out of the relationship between the price of silver bullion and the price of silver coins. Let's take a brief look at this highly specialized field.

To establish a spread, you buy a silver futures contract and at the same time sell a silver coin futures contract. Your profit or loss will then depend on the relationship between these two contracts. In this kind of speculation, it does not matter to you whether the entire market goes up or down. What is important is the spread between the two contracts — whether silver coins rise in relation to silver bullion or vice versa. This kind of deal is offered by the American Board of Trade, which claims it is "a low-risk but profitable trading approach."

Before you get involved in this market, however, you had better make sure you understand both the silver bullion and the silver coin futures markets. Even the Board of Trade admits that this field is "so highly specialized and technical that it can be engaged in profitably only by seasoned professional traders and investors."

If you are still intent on trying, write for further details to the American Board of Trade, 286 Fifth Avenue, New York 10001. The Board says that "initial investment for margin is only $300 per single program unit. For the full year April 1, 1971, through March 31, 1972, returns on two indicated program spread trades would have totalled $453, for an annual gross return of $151 on capital investment as margin." We wish you as much luck in the future.

7

Copper—A Political Commodity

$\mathbf{M}$ORE THAN ANY other commodity handled on futures markets, copper is the plaything of politics. International finagling has more to do with the price moves than the supply and demand situation.

This means that, if you enjoy watching and reading about international politics, you may make money by investing in copper futures. And it won't be an idle investment — toward the end of 1973, copper went up 25 percent in one month. It was then selling at the highest price on record and cost more than silver once did. In 1974 it went even higher.

Copper is traded on the New York Commodity Exchange, the Chicago Mercantile Exchange, and the London Metal Market. You should probably deal on the New York or Chicago exchanges because it is simpler and your orders can be carried out more quickly.

There are times, though, when the London dealings

might be better, since they open earlier than the American markets. Let's say you heard something late one afternoon that made you think copper prices would go up. That would be too late to buy in New York, where the market closes at 2:10 P.M. So you order a purchase in London — you can usually find a broker in the late afternoon who will take your order for execution in London. That way you could use your knowledge before the New York market was open for other people in America to act on the same information.

A copper futures contract in New York is for 25,000 pounds of copper. The price is quoted in cents per pound — although the way prices have been climbing, the quotations are just as likely to be in dollars and cents per pound. A change of one cent in the price quotation amounts to $250 on a contract, so profits can pile up quickly.

Price rises or falls are limited to 2 cents per day, so you can't make a million overnight. Nevertheless, 2 cents amounts to $500 a day on a single contract. If you wanted to plunge and had ten contracts, you could theoretically pick up $5,000 in just one day. Of course, one could lose that amount in one day, too, if the market moved down.

Just how much margin you have to put up on one contract is between you and your broker, but it would probably be around $2,000 to $3,000. In Chicago, where the contract is for only 12,500 pounds, your margin would be lower.

Trading terms are a little different in London. The contract there is for twenty-five long tons, or 56,000 pounds of copper. Prices are quoted in pounds sterling per long ton. A move of one pound sterling is worth £25 — about $58 — per contract. There is no maximum daily limit in price changes. Trading begins at 7 A.M. New York time.

Starting to trade in either market is simple. First, pick a broker. As a general rule, "biggest is best" unless you know someone you trust in a smaller firm. Talk to a customer's man, the person who deals with the public and holds a client's hand when a deal goes sour. Once he knows just what sort of investing you want to do and how much money you can risk, he will give you the figures: so much in your deposit account and so much margin on the copper. Don't be hurt if he refuses to take your account — brokerage houses like to earn commissions, but they get into trouble if they help lose money for people who can't afford to lose it. So they must make sure their clients can stand any potential loss.

While you have been looking for a broker, you must have decided which way you think copper prices are going. So you buy or sell one or two futures contracts based on your judgment of what is going to happen. Then you can sit back and wait to see how good a prophet you are.

Here's where dealing in copper futures begins to get tricky. Because copper is so much affected by governments' actions, a boom won't necessarily push up the price of copper and a depression needn't push it down. Furthermore, there is little connection between the price of copper for today's sale and the price of futures.

For instance, late in 1973 the spot copper price was 60 cents a pound, but the futures price for delivery the following month was $1.02 per pound. However, 60 cents was the price paid by major users, customers who bought thousands of tons of copper under a contract running for a year. Most of these contracts were signed more than six months before, when copper prices were much lower. A better indication of the real price of copper on the spot market is the scrap copper price, which is reported daily in many newspapers. The scrap price and the nearby futures price are usually close together.

At first glance, it would seem like good business to buy a few tons of copper now, at 60 cents, and sell them in a month at $1.02. But remember that *you* can't buy copper at 60 cents — that is the price for large users buying under contract. If you wanted to buy copper, you would either have to pay the scrap price or buy futures and take delivery. That is what the copper mills do when they can't get enough 60-cent copper to fill their orders.

Another complicating factor is that a reduction in business activity — the copper tubing makers getting fewer orders, for example — does not mean lower prices for the metal itself. That is because the big mining companies have a way of evening out their cash income. When the price is high, the companies just mine a lower grade of ore, perhaps rock that is only ½ percent copper. The metal price is high enough to give them a profit on this low-grade ore. But when the price falls, the companies start on their seams of richer ore, which contain perhaps 1½ percent copper. Because they are working ore with more copper to the ton, they can still make money. So a bust in the economy does not mean a bust in the copper business.

Most important, though, is how government actions affect prices. The United States government sometimes controls prices directly. In 1973, the government kept domestic copper prices under contract at 60 cents a pound, even though the price overseas was more than $1. The government just flatly said the copper companies couldn't raise prices.

As a bargaining tool, the United States government usually has a copper stockpile of about a quarter of a million tons, approximately enough to supply United States industry for three or four months. This stockpile is supposed to be held as a reserve for use in case of war. However, when copper prices go up there is always a chance that the government will sell stockpile copper to keep prices from going to high. This in fact happened early in 1974 — the entire government stockpile was sold out. Usually, the threat of this action is enough to halt any sky-high price rise.

Foreign governments also are a force to be watched. The world's largest copper producers are the United States and Canada and, probably, Russia. (Russian production figures are only guesses, though, since Russia uses all or nearly all the copper it mines and its government doesn't give out any figures.) But after those three, the largest producers are developing countries whose governments are generally nationalistic, not always friendly to foreign firms, and given to quick changes in government or government policy. These countries include Zambia (formerly Northern Rhodesia, until the British gave it independence), Chile, Zaire (the former Belgian Congo), and Peru. Among them these four produce 60 percent of the world's copper exports — that is, copper that is sold to the hundred or so countries that do not produce their own.

Since the United States and Canada sell most of their copper under long-term contracts and Russia uses most of its own, these four countries substantially control the floating market, the copper sold on a hand-to-mouth basis or used as the basis for dealing in copper futures. (Of course, some African copper is also sold on contract, but all the rest of it gets into the free market.)

Such a situation gives each country an important leverage in setting prices. If one of these governments does something that slows the flow of copper, the price goes up. If something happens that hurries up copper supplies, the price goes down.

For instance, when Chile nationalized its copper industry early in the 1970s, many foreign technicians left the country. This seemed to threaten the volume of output, so copper prices went up. Later, when the army took control of Chile, the government retained control of the mines, but there were fears the army would not be able to control the miners. Again prices went up. When somebody blew up a bridge on the long railway that carries Zambian copper to the African ports for export, prices again went up.

The result of such developments has been to drive copper prices to the highest levels in history. They stayed there even during the fright that the energy crisis of 1973 might result in an economic depression, proof that politics affect copper prices more than economic conditions do.

Another factor the copper speculator has to consider is whether prices will continue to go up or whether the high price will make users turn to some substitute. Aluminum can be used for electrical wiring in place of copper. Some automobile companies are already using aluminum radiators instead of brass ones (brass is a mixture of copper and zinc).

What may keep copper prices high is the antipollution

drive. In 1972, the President's Council on Environmental Control estimated that the cost of pollution control in the United States would be $287 *billion* over the next ten years. This was about the biggest figure being passed around Washington, being exceeded only by the national debt and the gross national product.

Of course, not all this would have to be spent to clean up copper operations. But the cost of air pollution control alone was figured at $591 million. Copper's pollution is mainly of the air and mainly in the West, where the people affected are few and far between. While there is some water pollution from copper ore scrap piles, the ecologists' main complaint against the industry is that the smelters pollute the air. Antipollution forces have demanded that smelters either be shut down or that expensive air cleaning systems be installed. In some cases the smelters have been shut down because they were so old that it was not worthwhile to put in the air cleaners.

The ecology measures affect the price of copper in two ways. If pollution control equipment is installed, its cost must be added to the cost of smelting and this tends to raise the price of copper. If the smelter is shut down, that reduces the supply of copper. Again the effect is to raise the price.

Adding all these factors together, copper would appear to be in a bullish market for at least the middle years of this decade. But whether prices will continue to rise or just level off on a high plateau is something only the future can tell.

One indication will be when you don't find any copper pennies in your loose change any more. As inflation goes on its merry way the copper Lincoln penny may soon disappear. The critical point is when copper hits $1.20 a pound in the metal markets — at that point it costs the United States Treasury more than a penny to make a copper penny. And when copper costs $1.50 a pound, it becomes profitable to melt your pennies down and sell the copper in them. Early in 1974 the United States Treasury banned the melting or export of pennies and was looking around for some substitute material. You may soon have pennies made of aluminum or some other cheap metal, just as your half-dollars, quarters, and dimes are now made of base metals instead of silver.

8

Diamonds—
A Global Monopoly

$\mathbf{A}$ DIAMOND is the hardest and one of the most valuable substances found on earth. For one carat—1/142 ounce—you might have to pay $1,900 for a high-quality gem. Even the lowest-quality diamonds—those used as grinding material in industry—may be worth three times as much as gold.

For this enormous price you are getting no more and no less than a minute piece of carbon, squeezed into a pellucid crystal by cataclysmic pressures in the bowels of the earth.

So how do you get yourself some diamonds? Well, there is a place in southwest Africa where you can pick these sparkling treasures off the beach and desert sands by hand. The only drawback is that this bleak desert area, known as the Skeleton Coast, is perpetually guarded by dogs, barbed wire, radar, and jeep and helicopter patrols. If you *are* allowed in, you are x-rayed on the way in and out.

One outfit, Marine Diamond, came up with an ingenious

solution—they decided that there might be diamonds in the seabed off the Skeleton Coast that might have been washed out by the African rivers. The company set up a dredge off the coast, sucking sand and gravel from below the surface. It found diamonds, quite a few of them, but a storm hit the coast and did such damage to the dredge that the profits were not enough to cover the repair costs. So the venture was abandoned in 1971.

In the early days prospectors used a simple technique to pick up diamonds in this dusty waste inland. They would walk out into the desert just before sunrise and just before sunset and wait for the rays of the rising or setting sun to pick out the flash of a gem here and there in the sand.

Nowadays things are not so simple, and you would not be permitted such free and easy pickings in the diamond fields. The sparkling gems have to go through a complicated process of mining, cutting, polishing, and marketing before you get your chance to lay your hands on them—and each step will make them more expensive for you to buy.

The entire diamond-bearing area on the Atlantic coast of Southwest Africa is controlled by De Beers Consolidated Mines Limited, a giant concern that also controls most of the diamond mining in the Republic of South Africa. De Beers has a stranglehold on the sales of about 85 percent of all the diamonds sold in the world. This incredible worldwide monopoly sells only to about 220 customers. The company itself chooses its customers, and they are forced to take whatever batches of stones De Beers cares to offer them. They are not even allowed to inspect their diamonds beforehand. The Central Selling Organization in London, controlled by De Beers, is so powerful that even the Soviet Union, a major diamond producer itself, swallows its Communist principles and cooperates with this capitalist octopus. The United States government, however, will not allow De Beers to operate directly on American territory.

In any event, the 220 buyers are merely told by De Beers what the price is, and they have no alternative but to pay. De

Beers does very well on this system — and this is only the first step of the process that makes the price of a diamond what it is by the time it gets to you. From the Central Selling Organization in London, the rough diamonds are fanned out to Amsterdam, Antwerp, Bombay, New York, Tel Aviv, and other markets, where they are bought by cutters. The cutting process halves the weight of each diamond and doubles its price. The diamond cutter then sells to a dealer at a 10 percent markup, and the dealer in turn sells to a jewel manufacturer, also at a 10 percent markup. The manufacturer sells to a wholesale jeweler at a 25 percent markup, and the wholesale jeweler sells to a retail jeweler at another 25 percent markup. Finally, the jeweler sells it to you, and *his* markup is usually 50 to 100 percent. So, by the time a man buys the girl of his dreams that diamond ring, he has made a lot of people rich and happy along the way.

De Beers justifies this system by claiming it protects everybody by maintaining a stable pattern of steadily rising prices and pointing to the wild fluctuations in other commodities as horrible alternatives. In fact, the tightly controlled price of diamonds has risen at a steady rate year by year, and the average price of a one-carat diamond gem has more than tripled from 1964 to 1974. As long as De Beers controls the world market it seems reasonable to anticipate a similar rate of appreciation in the foreseeable future.

The problem is that it is going to take you at least five years to catch up with the 100 percent markup of the jeweler you bought from, to say nothing of the other markups before the diamond got to him. So let's see if we can short-circuit the system and eliminate some of the middlemen.

One way of doing this is offered by Empire Diamond Corporation, Empire State Building, New York 10001. This firm is one of the world's biggest diamond cutters and is a wholesale supplier to wholesale and retail jewelers. But it will also sell diamond jewelry directly to the customer at a price it claims will "save at least 25 percent of the cost of a comparable diamond bought elsewhere." You simply ask for Empire's illustrated catalogue of rings, earrings, and other items, make your selection, and order by mail. After you get your order, you have ten days to decide whether you want to keep it. During this time you can have the item appraised, and Empire says that "unless it is valued at 25 to 50 percent above our price we will refund the cost of the appraisal plus the postage to return the diamond."

Such an appraisal by an independent expert is a necessity wherever and however you buy a diamond, because no layman is able to make an accurate assessment merely on the basis of a visual inspection. You need an expert with the professional equipment for the job. Many reputable jewelers will give you an appraisal for a reasonable fee, or you can look up Appraisers in the Yellow Pages of your telephone book. Or, you can contact a diamond and jewelry appraiser through the Appraisers Association of America Incorporated, 541 Lexington Avenue, New York 10022, a professional society with members in 211 cities and towns in 38 American states, Washington, D.C., Puerto Rico, Canada, England, and Holland, who specialize in valuing more than 200 different kinds of articles and goods.

Another shortcut is offered by Investment Diamonds Incorporated, Suite 520, Johnson Building, Muncie, Indiana 47305, which claims to deal with cutters who deal directly with De Beers. This firm sells you cut, but unset, diamonds, and buys them back from you at "bid and ask prices based on the firm's intimate current knowledge of the diamond market and upon scientific measurement."

Each diamond "is microphotographed to prove its clarity (the presence or absence of blemish). Special technical instruments are used to exactly determine each diamond's color, fineness of cut, and weight. Each buyer receives along with the diamond a certificate which describes and identifies the diamond and includes a microphotograph of the diamond. No two diamonds are ever exactly alike."

When you buy you pay the "ask price" plus 4 percent commission. Investment Diamonds says it will "buy back any diamond bought through the firm at its bid price and no commission." When you buy from Investment Diamonds, you mail your check (the minimum purchase is $600) and receive your diamond by registered insured mail. If you prefer not to send any money the package will be mailed to your bank. In either case you have ten days to inspect the diamonds, have them appraised, and send them back without paying for them if they are not satisfactory. When you want to sell you ask for the current bid price and if you find it acceptable you mail your diamond and its microphotographed documentation back to Investment Diamonds.

Some sources in the diamond trade claim that this firm's prices tend to be high in the retail range, except for the minimum-size one-carat stones. Here again, note the absolute indispensability of a thoroughly disinterested professional appraisal.

Here is a recent example of Investment Diamond Incorporated prices. The ask price of a one-carat diamond, rated Quality 10 (in the top 10 percent of all gem diamonds mined, used in fine jewelry and not available in every jewelry store) is $945. With the 4 percent commission, you would pay $982.80. The bid price at which you can sell the stone back to the firm is $900.

As a hedge against inflation, you may want to buy diamonds in London and arrange to have them stored there. If the dollar should be devalued another 10 percent your diamonds would be worth 10 percent more when sold. One of the London dealers is Diamond Selection Limited, 46 Hatton Garden, London. This firm says that if it sold you a stone of the best quality in 1973 for $5,483 (an increase of 204 percent over the 1969 price), it would have bought that diamond from you in 1973 at $5,072.

Rather than seeking shortcuts in the diamond market, you can also go to where the trail ends in your search for bargain prices. The end of the trail is the pawnbroker. Actor Richard Burton paid $1 million for the 69-carat diamond he bought for Elizabeth Taylor. Lesser-known men are always buying lesser-priced diamonds, and a certain percentage of them will always get into financial difficulties even if they are less extravagant and in a less chancy field than show business. In such cases the diamond will often be pawned — at far below its wholesale value — to meet pressing debts. And in a certain percentage of these cases the owner will not be able to redeem his diamond. The pawnbroker will then try to sell the diamond. There are pawnbrokers all over the United States, and some of them operate on a national scale through the mails. One of these is Fidelity Loan Bank, 42 South Clark Street, Chicago, Illinois 60603, which has been in the business since 1892. You can write this firm for a list of what is available — it constantly has new items coming out of pawn — and any item that interests you will be mailed to your bank. If you can provide satisfactory references, the diamond will be mailed directly to you. You can hire an appraiser to check on the quality of the jewel and advise you whether it is worth the price you are asked to pay. If not, you mail the package back at Fidelity Loan's expense. As a general rule the price range of the diamond jewelry offered by Fidelity Loan seems to run from $1,200 to $20,000 and up, although you may sometimes get some items for less than $1,000.

While it is quite true that such jewelry is usually pawned for far less than its full value, a pawnbroker would be a poor businessman indeed if he did not try to get the full retail value out of them from you. You should not therefore assume that you are automatically getting a bargain on this kind of deal. Your appraiser should be able to give you an accurate price assessment as well as a reliable quality appraisal.

So far we have been talking about gem-quality diamonds, but only about 20 percent of all diamonds mined are good enough for use in jewelry. The other 80 percent are still a valuable industrial material because they are nearly one hundred times harder than any other substance in nature. Industrial diamonds are widely used for grinding, polishing, and cutting.

You can buy industrial diamonds from the United States

government, but it is a highly specialized field and you have to know the business well in order to resell the diamonds to an industrial firm at a profit. If you think you can swing it, write to the Minerals and Ores Branch, Stockpile Disposal Division, General Services Administration, 18th & F Streets, Washington, D.C. 20405, and ask for a bid invitation on the next industrial diamond sale.

It may have occurred to you by this time that if you cannot dig up the diamonds on the Skeleton Coast yourself, the next best thing would be to own a piece of De Beers. You *can* buy a piece of De Beers, and you only need a few hundred dollars to do it. De Beers is a publicly owned company and you can purchase its shares in Johannesburg, London, or New York. The company was earning about 9.5 percent in the early 1970's, although it doesn't pay all its earnings out in dividends. Diamond prices have gone up regularly at the De Beers sales. After almost annual increases from 1967 to 1972, De Beers raised its prices a total of 28 percent in three steps during 1973. Since it controls the world market it can do this practically at will, and as a shareholder in the global monopoly, you would obviously be sitting pretty every time it did.

9

Worldwide Real Estate

Wild Mustang Ranch, Colorado, less than $61 an acre.

Pueblo, Colorado, working cattle ranch. Excellent hunting, $55 an acre.

Maccan, Nova Scotia, 500 acres all evergreen woodland on paved highway, $12,500.

Moose River, Nova Scotia, 20-acre farm, 6-room house and barn wired and water, $7,000.

Jamaica, Montego Bay, hillside villa, 3 bedrooms, tropical garden, 1 acre, close to beach. Proved income property, $45,000.

These real estate advertisements were taken at random from a recent issue of the *Wall Street Journal.* They all appeal to the urge to get away from one's humdrum, everyday existence as a commuter in the crummy suburbs of a decaying

106

city and to start life over again in a faraway place, where the dream is still untarnished by reality. Who hasn't dreamed at one time or another of getting away from it all and living a lazy, carefree life on a tropical island?

It's not as difficult as you might think—in fact, you don't even have to leave the United States. Head for the United States Virgin Islands, an exotic paradise only three-and-one-half hours from New York by plane. The islands have miles of shimmering beaches washed by the clear blue Caribbean, and a beautiful tropical climate, with an average temperature of 78 degrees—you get your money back for every day it drops below 70. There are quaint restaurants and activities such as snorkeling to keep you busy. All of this is true, just like the advertisement says.

But before you buy your dream house and tie a twenty-five year mortgage around your neck, you should know that some other things are equally true. The cost of living is 10 to 20 percent higher than on the continental United States because everything has to be brought in by sea or air. Land costs at least $20,000 an acre. The natives are poor and often resentful of the cost of living, the cost of land, and the fact that everything of value seems to end up in the hands of rich strangers from elsewhere.

Much of this understandable resentment prevails throughout the Caribbean, from Trinidad to Grenada to Jamaica, creating potentially explosive situations. The atmosphere of tension is only heightened by the certain number of tourists who are loud-mouthed and arrogant, and who talk of being cheated by "shifty natives." So if you are looking for an unspoiled paradise in the tropics, do not look for it in the big tourist centers. You are not likely to find it.

It is a pity, because you can get some beautiful deals at times. How about this one? A three-bedroom villa in Jamaica with its own swimming pool, only a few minutes drive from the beach, with twelve acres of banana trees (500 trees to an acre) plus 250 coconut trees on the property. The whole estate costs about $250 a month to keep up, including the salaries of a handyman, a maid, a washerwoman, and a cook. With the help of a good Jamaican lawyer, you pay taxes of only $25 a year. You rent the house to American tourists for $300 a week in season (December to April) and $150 a week out of season. You get tourists to stay there by advertising for them yourself or you register with the Jamaica Association of Villas and Apartments, which has an office in New York and might provide as much as a third of your customers. If you have the place run by a management company in Jamaica, this firm will also find you guests.

In a word, you get yourself a permanent vacation home in the tropics that pays for itself, plus a working banana plantation for extra income. The asking price is $40,000. If you can't swing the price the previous owner will transfer his 10 percent mortgage from a local Jamaican bank.

Before you decide to buy, you can rent the place for a week or two and investigate every angle, while you are living on the property.

One of the authors of this book was actually offered this deal a few years back. He did not take it and does not regret the decision.

There are just too many snags in such bargains. You know the problems that come up in maintaining your own home. Imagine what they would be like if you had to solve them while living two thousand miles away. Every time a major plumbing job or other difficulty came up in Jamaica you would have to make the plane trip from New York, Detroit, or wherever you live. Your only alternative would be to hand the house over to a local Jamaican management agency, pay a fee that would eat into your tourist income, and still face the possibility of padded maintenance and repair bills.

Meanwhile, your banana plantation is being run by a contractor who never seems to show any profit for you, and from two thousand miles away it is impossible to find out why. The household staff are reasonably honest and hardworking, but to supplement their Jamaican salaries of $20 a week, they feel they have a right to take home large amounts of food for their large families when the day's work is done. So your grocery bill is enormous. Then a certain percentage of your American tourist guests will be the type of people who break things and set the mosquito netting on fire by smoking in bed. The owner who was selling this particular property, a Canadian, was already facing all these problems, and a little inquiry revealed precisely why he wanted out of his tropical paradise.

There were other more formidable problems on the horizon. How long can one expect a poor island nation like Jamaica to tolerate a situation where rich, foreign, absentee landlords pay $25 taxes a year on such large, income-producing properties? Sooner or later, there will be a political demand for higher taxes, and perhaps even a ban on foreign ownership. Even as this is written, lawmakers in Canada itself are considering a ban on foreign ownership of land in Ontario after hitting foreigners with a 20 percent purchase tax. Oklahoma bars alien owners altogether. Legislators in American states like Vermont have actually clamped down on their fellow Americans, laying punitive taxes on out-of-state buyers of Vermont land. There is even more reason for a country like Jamaica to enact such laws.

For this and other nationalistic reasons, price trends are not always upward in foreign real estate. The Bahamas, another tropical paradise, are a good example. As the islands approached independence from Britain in 1973, the new government made it harder for non-Bahamians to get work in the islands, and many foreigners decided to leave rather than face an uncertain future. Their departure and the general uncertainty among investors about coming policies of the new government brought the prices of luxury homes down to bargain levels, in some cases halving the price of a $100,000 villa in a three-year period.

Still, the lure of a faraway tropical island is strong for the winter-bound Northerner, and even now there are places to be found beyond the tourist centers. But you have to go far out into the Pacific, and even there your only guarantee of getting away from it all is the sheer number of atolls and islands sprinkled across the ocean. Once you have pinned down the particular islands that interest you most—the 2,000 islets of Micronesia, for instance—write for information to the administrative center, in this case the Department of Commerce, Government of Guam, Agana, Guam, USA 96910.

In some vacation paradises, the tourist boom has been so great that the tourists now outnumber the native population. One such country is Spain.

Every year about 30 million tourists travel to Spain. The result has been a building boom that has pushed up real estate prices 15 to 20 percent a year. The range of properties available is wide. You can buy anything from a small apartment for $8,000 to a luxury villa for $250,000. The building boom has run all along the coasts of Spain and Portugal, and a number of firms have started offering condominium and vacation homes to Americans. The main idea is that you spend your vacation there and rent the property out the rest of the year through the developer, who takes care of all the details. You thus get a low-cost vacation, plus an income-producing property, without any of the headaches of running things yourself.

This could be fine if you plan to spend every single vacation at the same place, but not if you like some variety from year to year. There are other difficulties too. Suppose you were to buy a condominium apartment in Spain. How much do you know about Spanish real estate? The laws, the regulations, and the customs are different in many respects from those in the United States. All the legally binding documents are in Spanish, and the English translation you receive is usually inaccurate. Is your Spanish good enough to comprehend the fine legal distinctions?

You are protected here to some extent if you buy only from firms that register with the SEC, which compels each firm to make full disclosure in their prospectus of possible drawbacks as well as the advantages. The SEC has ruled that when condominiums are sold to Americans primarily as investments in income-producing property and not mainly as residences, they must be registered by the developer, just as foreign bonds and securities must be registered by the issuers.

New York and various other states also require such real estate firms to register their sales offerings, and, if you insist on seeing proof that the seller has complied with both the SEC and the state authorities, you have additional protection.

Here is one example. A firm called Sofico will sell you an apartment on the Spanish Mediterranean coast, which you lease back to Sofico for twenty years at a guaranteed rate of 12 percent a year on your money. Sofico takes charge of renting the apartment and maintaining it. All you do is tell them when you want to spend your vacation there and collect your money the rest of the year.

Free vacations, no administrative worries, plus a 12 percent guaranteed return on your investment. It sounds like a great deal. However, the guarantee of a Spanish real estate firm is apparently not really as good as it might seem. It is only a promise to pay unless *fuerza mayor* makes payment impossible. In Spanish law *fuerza mayor* is any event beyond the guarantor's control, which covers a lot of territory—sales territory, for instance. Knowledgeable sources in Spain say that firms of this type are highly dependent on keeping up sales of new apartments to keep themselves solvent, and that if they should run into sales difficulties they could face financial collapse.

The only chance the apartment owners would then have to protect themselves would be to take over and form a committee to run the project themselves. With the investors scattered hundreds or thousands of miles apart, from Germany to the United States, most of them ignorant of the Spanish language, this could be a difficult proposition. Individual owners would then find it hard to rent out the properties, even in association with each other, without the sales organizations of the real estate firms, which rent out apartments wholesale to package group tour operators in New York and elsewhere.

The investors would also find it hard to get out of their investment. Selling an apartment might be difficult in competition with the firms that are selling brand new apartments with big promotions and easy financial terms.

Still, Sofico continues to operate successfully, as do other outfits in the same field. Among these are Real International, Inmobiliaria Bilbao (an affiliate of a major Spanish bank), and Eurovosa.

Real International (159 East 64th Street, New York 10021), is a company based in Lausanne, Switzerland, that has been authorized to sell in New York State and Washington, D.C.

As part of its promotion, Real offers to fly you to Spain at a group rate of only about $240 to inspect its apartments in Marbella on the Costa del Sol. It will sell you condominiums or townhouses for a minimum $8,000 down payment. If you buy, your plane fare is deducted from the price.

A Real spokesman says that most buyers are Europeans and that the typical American buyer is an elderly person a few years from retirement. A buyer can live in the apartment or can rent it out through Real for eleven months a year and spend a yearly month's vacation there. The average sale, according to the spokesman, is an apartment, with a $12,000 down payment, plus another $12,000 spread over two years.

Real will also sell you homesites for $8,900 or more, but if you are planning to build in Spain you should be aware that it is almost impossible for a nonresident to get a mortgage there. It will take you a year or more to achieve resident status.

Another investment you can make abroad is a membership in a local country club. Suppose you buy a home in the Alicante area of Spain. For a $2,200 investment plus the payment of annual dues, you and your family can have membership in the Almaina Park Golf and Country Club, which contains a 250-acre golf course on a 625-acre property. There are areas on the property set aside for homebuilding, a hotel, condominiums, swimming pools, stables, trap shooting, a health spa, tennis courts, and game rooms. The membership entitles you to part ownership and participation in any income from the club's facilities. According to Almaina, other clubs in southern Spain have seen their shares grow in value from an average of $1,000 to more than $6,000 in less than two years.

You are offered similar deals in Mexico. At Puerto Vallarta, the Los Tules Club offers you a villa or apartment on a 26-acre property with a private beach on the Pacific, a swimming pool, restaurant, discotheque, tennis courts, horses, and other amenities. Your membership costs $10,000 and lasts ten years. Your vacation home in this club is reserved for you and your family or guests for at least forty days in the prime season (December to March) and for as much as eighty days out of season. You pay no management or maintenance charges, so that on the $10,000 payment your forty-day vacation for ten years would work out at $25 a day.

Now, the fact is that in such cases you may not be buying property at all. You are merely committing yourself to spending your vacations at this particular place for the next ten years. If you have been there before, liked it, and think you would enjoyably spend your next ten vacations there, you will probably get a bargain. But your investment will be entirely in the fun you get out of it and not in any prospect of other profits.

There are all kinds of other real estate and vacation property deals you can make abroad. If the idea of a castle in Europe, a second home in the Caribbean, or even a ranch in the Rockies or a ski lodge in Vermont appeals to you, one place to start looking is a 288-page sales guide published by Previews Incorporated, Realtors, 49 East 53rd Street, New York 10022. The guide costs $5.

Another source of information is the magazine *Condominiums USA and Homes Overseas,* 50 Union Avenue, Irvington, New Jersey 07111.

The farther away the place is, the more enchanting and alluring it appears. But distance is precisely the main problem involved in buying, maintaining, and running foreign real estate. Of course, if you plan to *live* abroad, many of these objections disappear. Once you are around all the time to watch over your property yourself you are no longer at the mercy of administrators, agents, developers, and other middlemen. You are there to watch out for your own interests.

In these circumstances there are a number of friendly countries that will be only too glad to have you. One of these is Costa Rica, a small, stable, democratic republic in Central America that has eternal spring weather. The thermometer hovers around 72 degrees all year long. Kernan Turner, a newsman who spent a year in Costa Rica on a research grant, reports that Americans who have retired to Costa Rica find they can live as well in San José on $500 a month as they did in Miami on $1,000 a month. A homeowner can also enjoy the luxury of employing a full-time maid and a handyman to mow the lawn in front of an eight-room house that might cost $10,000 or $20,000. If your income is $1,000 a month, this obviously leaves you with an additional $500 to invest each month. According to Turner, some American residents have taken up mining, prospecting, farming, and dealing in semiprecious stones to keep themselves busy. Costa Rican law allows you to own land outright, operate a business, work for the government, or teach at the National University. You are allowed to buy $7,000 worth of household furniture, plus a motor vehicle every five years, free of all import duties. To qualify for the benefits you only have to prove you have a permanent income of $300 a month. It does not matter what age you are.

How do you do it? Decide, first of all, that you will learn at least enough Spanish to communicate in a friendly way with the Costa Ricans. Then write to the Costa Rican Tourist Bureau (Instituto Costarricense de Turismo, Apartado Postal 777, San José, Costa Rica). They will give you the details of a law specifically designed to attract retirees and other foreign residents to Costa Rica. The English-speaking community is small, but large enough to support a local English-language newspaper, the *Tico Times*.

Costa Rica is off the main tourist path. Mexico, a nation nearer home, is very much on it, receiving about $1 billion yearly from the American tourist trade. But it offers the same advantages of relatively cheap living, plus the luxury of domestic help that disappeared many decades ago in the United States. This is another nation where the welcome mat is out for foreigners with a steady, assured income, like United States Social Security. Many Americans live in Guadalajara and other areas. However, there are some restrictions about working and about owning real estate in frontier areas. A good place to inquire about living in Mexico is the Mexican Consulate, 8 East 41st Street, New York, or the Consejo Nacional de Turismo, Direccion de Pensionados, Mariano Escobedo 726, Mexico 5, D.F.

There are other nations in the world where you can take up residence without too much trouble, buy yourself a place, live more cheaply, and have more money available to invest in other things. There are even Americans living well on United States Social Security in such Communist nations as Poland and Yugoslavia (but inquire first — there *are* some Communist countries on the United States blacklist). You can live in Switzerland if you can prove to the Swiss authorities that you have sufficient means to live without having to take up remunerative work.

In most countries you can reside for three months at a time without any requirement except a valid passport, and it is no trick at all to divide up your year between four or five European countries, if you have the means to rent a place and pay for your meals.

The point of all this is that if you are a non-travelling homebody, then your split-level ranch house in Trenton, New Jersey, or wherever, is obviously the best place for you. But if you are the wandering, footloose type and you have enough income from Social Security or from your investments, why should that house become a millstone around your neck? Sell it. Invest the proceeds in a wide spread of real estate and use the additional income to finance part of your living expenses wherever you want to live around the world.

Here is just a sample of the real estate investments you can make in various countries and keep completely free of every problem of administration, maintenance, finance, repairs, and general headaches except your personal taxes on the dividends you collect every three months.

In the United States, you can achieve a wide spread of property investment through a real estate investment trust, of which there are dozens quoted on the stock exchanges. Real estate trusts are exempt from corporate income taxes provided they pay out 90 percent of their income in dividends. You can take your pick here of several varieties of trusts. One type, such as Real Estate Investment Trust of America (ticker symbol REI on the American Stock Exchange) specializes in buildings *per se*. This particular trust has office buildings, shopping centers, and other properties from California to Massachusetts. It has been paying dividends since 1889.

Another type of trust buys long-term mortgages rather than properties themselves. An example of this is BankAmerica Realty Investors (ticker symbol BRLTS on the over-the-counter market). A third type of trust specializes in short-term mortgages. One of these is Chase Manhattan Mortgage Realty (symbol CMR on the New York Stock Exchange).

If you are unable to decide which type is for you, you can solve the problem by investing in REIT Income Fund (ticker symbol RET on the American Stock Exchange), which invests in a portfolio of other real estate investment trusts and thus achieves an enormous spread of investments.

Perhaps arm-chair ranching appeals to you. If so, there are a number of investments you can make in which your effort and trouble are limited to phoning your broker to buy you some shares and then reading the annual report. One of these is Tejon Ranch Company. As a shareholder, you would be part owner of one of the largest landholdings in California —

270,000 acres of land used for cattle raising, farming, oil and mineral exploration, and real estate development. It is quoted on the American Stock Exchange, and a yearly report may be obtained from Tejon Ranch Company, Suite 550, 10850 Wilshire Boulevard, Los Angeles, California 90024.

All the American trusts we have mentioned are quoted on United States stock exchanges. They are supervised by United States authorities and there is a ready market for their shares. There are also similar trusts available abroad. In foreign countries, however, one should immediately be on one's guard because these safeguards do not necessarily exist.

One possible investment is a 25,000-peseta (about $440) share in the Expo Hotel being built in Barcelona, Spain. The advertising material says "guaranteed minimum dividends of 12% are budgeted into the pro-forma projections. The projections, however, based on Spain's present low rate for hotel rooms, show a return of 20% the first year and 23% annually after that."

That sounds like a great investment. Let us note, however, that "no stock sales are made in the U.S., but many Americans have written directly to Empresas Asociadas. . .for information concerning the investment opportunities. The address is Avenida Generalisimo 87, Madrid 19."

We learn further that Expo Barcelona is scheduled to open in 1974, followed by similar hotels in Madrid, Bilbao, Zaragoza, and Seville. The same firm also sells shares in the drugstores of a chain it built in Madrid and other Spanish cities.

All of the firm's statements may very well be true. This is a Spanish company, and Spaniards generally put a considerable amount of trust in their own real estate concerns. They become distrustful when an American promoter is involved in the deal. The point to note is that no stock sales are made in the United States. This indicates that the offering may not have been registered with the SEC. It is possible, therefore, that full disclosure of all the material facts in the offering may not have been made, as required by the SEC. If the reader writes to the firm in Spain and makes an investment transacted in that country, he may thus be unable to count on any protection from United States authorities if things do not work out as he expected. It would also be a prudent and reasonable precaution to find out how and where one could sell this share should one decide to cash in on the investment.

This resale problem is avoided by some British property trusts, which buy your shares back from you in the same way as United States mutual funds do. For example, the Property Growth Agricultural Bond (sold by the Property Growth Assurance Company Limited, Edward House, 73 Brook Street, London W1) offers you an interest in several dozen farms located in Norfolk, Lincolnshire, and several other countries in the north and west of England. You get one investment package without any of the chores of farming, plus a life insurance policy thrown in, equalling or exceeding your investment. This company operates under the supervision of the British Department of Trade and Industry. The minimum investment is £250 (about $600), and for a minimum investment of £1,000 (about $2,500) you can make automatic yearly withdrawals of up to 7 percent. Otherwise, you do not receive any income because all earnings and capital gains are plowed back in.

This is how it works. The fund invests in farm lands, which are disappearing in England at the rate of 1,000 acres a week due to the encroachment of housing, industry, roads, and other aspects of urban life. As a result, the average sale price of farm land in England has increased by 6.5 percent a year for the last twenty years, according to an official British government estimate.

The fund does not operate farms itself. It rents them out to tenant farmers. In some cases it buys lands and leases them back to the farmer. When you buy a bond, you are in fact paying a one-shot insurance policy premium. Ninety five percent of your payment is invested in land, and the other 5 percent goes toward insurance costs. Supposing you invest £500. If you are up to 35 years old, you are insured for at least £800, which your beneficiaries will receive if you die before cashing in your bond. If you are 56 to 76 years old, your insurance is only £500—or the full value of the bond if its value has risen above your £500 investment.

The fund is divided into units. When you buy a bond you are told how many units the bond represents. The price of the units fluctuates and is quoted daily in the *Financial Times* of London. The value of the units is calculated periodically by independent appraisers, who estimate the value of each farm in the portfolio at least once a year. When a farm is sold at a profit, the gain benefits the unitholders. For running the fund, Property Growth Assurance charges a monthly service fee of 1/32 percent.

There are dozens of British property bonds that operate in the same way as these agricultural bonds, except that they invest in real estate rather than in farm lands. Perhaps the largest of these is the Abbey Property Bond Fund, Abbey Life Insurance Company, 1-3 St. Paul's Churchyard, London EC4. The fund was started in 1967, and by 1973 had risen in value by 81 percent.

When you buy one of these bonds, you are purchasing a share in a portfolio of about 200 office buildings, shops, factories, and warehouses with a total valuation of around £200 million (about $500 million). The minimum investment is only £100, about $250, and the bonds are revalued once a month by an independent appraiser. The life insurance coverage ranges from £2,814 to £1,000 for every £1,000 invested, depending on one's age. There is a 5 percent initial charge when you buy: you also pay a management fee of ½ percent a year. You may cash in your bond with the fund at any time, at the current valuation price.

Merchant Investor's Property Bond, Old Broad Street Securities Assurance Limited, 125 High Street, Croydon, England, is another such bond. The minimum investment is

£250, and the insurance coverage from £2,600 to £1,000 per £1,000 invested. As in the case of most other property bonds, the current price may be checked in the *Times* of London, the *Financial Times,* and other major British newspapers. The value of this bond appreciated by 40 percent between the initial launching in June, 1970, and July, 1973.

Another property bond, Fortune Property, Hill Samuel Life Assurance, NLA Tower, Croydon, England, offers as an additional feature loans of up to 75 percent of the value of your bond.

From what we have said above you will gather that these agricultural and property bonds are misnamed. They are not really bonds at all. You do not invest $1,000 in a piece of paper that pays a fixed rate of interest and for which you will be repaid exactly your $1,000 twenty years later in drastically inflated paper money. They are more in the nature of an investment in land and real estate plus a life insurance policy. Both the investment and the policy make you the beneficiary of any increase in value of the property over the years. They protect you against inflation, whereas conventional bonds are mere inflation traps.

A variation on this is a type of British fund that invests in real estate companies rather than buying property itself. This resembles a United States mutual fund, with a specialized portfolio of shares in the real estate field. One of these is Ebor Property & Building Fund, Ebor Securities Limited, 4 Great St. Helens, London EC3. Another is Jessel Property & General Fund, Jessel Britannia Group, 155 Fenchurch Street, London EC3. The sales charge on British mutual funds, or unit trusts as they are called in Britain, is usually 5 percent.

Finally, you can spread your real estate investments around the globe by putting your money in mutual funds and investment trusts with holdings in real estate.

In Switzerland, the Swiss Bank Corporation (6 Paradeplatz, Zurich) runs a real estate fund named Swissimmobil, which is entirely invested in Switzerland and holds more than 100 properties, including apartments, offices, shops, and garages. SIMA is a similar Swiss real estate mutual fund run by the Union Bank of Switzerland, Bahnhofstrasse 45, Zurich.

You can buy a wide cross-section of Israeli real estate through Africa Israel, a company quoted on the Tel Aviv Stock Exchange. Despite its name (it was founded by South African settlers) it concentrates on Israeli real estate. In the United States you can buy it through Leumi Securities Corporation, 18 East 48th Street, New York 10017. Other possibilities in Israel are the Israeli Land Development Company and the Property & Building Company, both quoted on the Tel Aviv Exchange.

In the Far East, the Hong Kong Land & Investment Agency Company Limited is one of the biggest companies in Hong Kong real estate. It is quoted on the Hong Kong exchange and also in London. During the wild Hong Kong stock market boom its share price rose from 80 to 300 times earnings in three months.

In Australia the Universal Property Income Trust, Universal Units Limited, 375 George Street, Sydney, invests in modern rental apartments in the Sydney metropolitan area and in other Australian real estate. The minimum initial investment is 500 Australian dollars (about $700) and subsequent investments of at least 100 Australian dollars.

If you investigate further, you will undoubtedly discover for yourself other funds and trusts that invest in real estate in other nations such as Canada. The terminology used abroad is sometimes confusing for Americans. Mutual funds, for example, are in fact real-estate-based investments in New Zealand. One of the largest of these is the Fund of New Zealand, 42 Customs Street, Auckland, New Zealand.

10

Tax Shelters

TAX SHELTER enterprises used to be a sort of private game preserve for the rich upper crust, but not any longer. Inflation has boosted people's incomes and pushed hundreds of thousands of taxpayers into the 50 percent income tax bracket or higher, which is the level where this kind of deal becomes potentially profitable.

The tax shelters arise from various tax breaks that Congress has created for the benefit of certain industries, such as real estate, oil and gas drilling, cattle feeding and breeding, equipment leasing, citrus crops, movies, and plays. Although they are sometimes called "loopholes" or "tax gimmicks" there is nothing illegal about them.

A tax shelter in any of these fields enables you to convert your tax bill into profits or earning assets. You can do this by postponing tax payments to a more convenient time, taking advantage of special deductions or lower tax rates, and turning current deductions into possible future assets.

   The United States Treasury estimates it loses about $1 billion a year in revenue as a result of tax shelter programs, and it is out to plug the leak. The department wants to limit artificial accounting losses obtainable through these programs and force people to speculate with their own money, not with the tax dollars they owe to Uncle Sam.

   In April, 1973, the Nixon administration sent to Congress a bill that would significantly reduce the benefits of tax-sheltered investments. Congress was occupied with other matters in 1973, but was expected to attend to the problem some time in 1974 or 1975.

   This whole investment area revolves around the tax laws, which may be very different when you read this book than when it was written. Therefore, before doing anything at all with regard to the kind of deals mentioned in this chapter, you should check with a good tax lawyer or accountant and find out what the current tax situation is.

   The major tax shelter programs are in oil and gas drilling, livestock, and real estate, but there are many others, such as Broadway plays, pistachio nuts, and chinchilla farms.

   E.F. Hutton & Company Inc., One Battery Park Plaza, New York 10004, is one large brokerage house that has paid a good deal of attention to tax-sheltered investments. It points out that tax shelters are most productive for investors in the 50 per cent income tax bracket and above—which means those with a minimum annual gross income of $40,000 to $50,000. Hutton adds:

> As a prospective tax shelter investor you should have a high income, a large tax bill and a clear understanding of your own investment goals. If you're properly qualified, if you're prepared to live with the risks; if you're able to wait two years or longer in some cases before getting your money out, it may be possible for you to benefit tremendously from a well-thought-out tax shelter investment program. A hasty, ill-conceived tax shelter decision, on the other hand, can ruin an entire year's tax planning, play havoc with your checkbook and seriously impair your overall investment picture.

   Albert Barrette, a tax shelter specialist with Hutton, says

that in four years' experience in the field he has found that cor-porate executives who are accustomed to think in terms of thousands of dollars in their business, tend to have a quicker and more successful grasp of tax shelter plans. Professionals such as doctors and dentists tend to think in terms of smaller dollar amounts and find it more difficult to come to a business decision.

Like other brokers, Hutton offers help in planning your tax shelter investments but stresses that it cannot ensure the tax consequences of any transaction and that you must rely on your own accountant or lawyer for advice on these matters.

Hutton points out that there are two aspects of such in-vestments—tax benefits and the possible profits on the deal—and stresses that the tax benefits may supply motivation but that an investor should always look to making a profit as the final justification for going into a tax shelter investment.

A lot of people are apparently not doing this. In 1965, partnerships in the major tax-shelter industries reported $1.4 billion in net profits against only $900 million in net losses. Six years later, the balance had swung around to $4.2 billion in net losses and only $2.4 billion in net profits.

It is only common sense that a loss is a loss. The only tax shelter plan that is of any use to you is one that makes a profit. You then get the tax savings on your gains. So the first question to ask must be: is this project going to make a profit? What the tax benefits are is only the second question.

How do you do it? The usual form a tax-sheltered in-vestment takes—in whatever field—is a publicly registered limited partnership. In this kind of deal there is one general partner who has a number of limited partners. The general partner runs the business and usually has unlimited liability for any losses. Due to this nasty fact, he tries to write as many advantages for himself into the contract as he can for self-protection. You and the other limited partners can lose only the money you actually put in. You are not liable for anything more, provided you are not assessable, a factor that we shall get to further ahead.

Here is an example of a tax-sheltered program. XYZ Petroleum Corporation (the general partner) offers limited partnerships to investors for a total of $8 million. Your minimum allowed investment is $5,000. The partnership is called the XYZ 1974 Exploration Program Limited, and it plans to drill for oil and gas in Louisiana, New Mexico, various other U.S. states and Canada. XYZ Corp. contributes 20 to 35 percent of the total exploration costs. You and the other limited partners chip in the rest. If the exploratory drilling is successful, the revenues are shared in direct proportion to the expenditures made by each. Once the total original investment is recovered, XYZ Corporation takes 50 percent and you and the other limited partners get the remaining 50 percent. The program then goes into a development phase, in which XYZ Corporation pays for all the additional development drilling and collects all the revenue until it recovers its expenditures. After that the limited partners share 50-50 in the net income from the development wells. If no oil or gas is discovered, XYZ Corporation's money and everybody else's goes down the drain.

Now here are the tax advantages. In the early stages of the program, you can write off the drilling expenses against your current income. This reduces your out-of-pocket investment. In the following years—if the program strikes oil or gas—22 percent of the gross production revenue from a successful well is tax free (up to a maximum 50 percent of the net revenues from a producing property).

Such, at least, were the tax rules when this tax-sheltered program was issued. When considering a similar plan on whatever date you read this book, the first thing to do is to check with a good tax lawyer or accountant and find out what the ground rules are at that time. The situation may have changed considerably.

Each program has its own varying provisions, and some are of bewildering complexity. You have to read and reread the prospectus to make sure of what you stand to get out of the deal. As a general rule, you should not invest in any programs

that have not been registered with the Securities and Exchange Commission. But even if they have registered, you
should be aware that the SEC does not approve or disapprove
of any of these programs. All it does is insist on full disclosure
in the prospectus of all material facts. If the prospectus says
that the Super Duper Dry Hole Corporation has always drilled
100 percent dry holes, and that as a matter of policy it intends
to continue drilling 100 percent dry holes, it has complied
with the SEC regulations. If you fail to read that warning in
the prospectus and put your money into the company despite
that explicit statement, then you are on your own with your
folly and have only yourself to blame for losing your money. So
rule number one is always: Read the prospectus, using a
magnifying glass on the fine print if you need to. Hutton
warns that all

> tax sheltered investments have certain aspects in common. They're
> almost all complex; they involve various risk factors, and they're
> illiquid. . .hard to sell in a hurry and in some cases hard to sell at
> all. Be prepared for a variety of risks, the risk that your oil wells
> won't produce and so forth. This risk is offset to a degree by tax
> savings, that is, your investment is partially financed with dollars
> which would otherwise pay income taxes. You simply can't call your
> stock broker when the mood strikes you and ask him to sell your share
> of a limited partnership. You may find yourself locked in for two
> years, or even longer. Even those partnerships that promise liquidity
> by agreeing to buy you out on demand have at least an initial waiting
> period.

The tax advantages in these deals are of various kinds.
You can claim business expenses as deductions against your
taxable expenses. Depreciation allows you to write off some
business costs against current income. The government
recognizes that oil and gas and other minerals are wasting
assets. Every barrel of oil produced means there is one barrel
less left underground—so you get a depletion allowance. Hutton points out that "if the property lasts for many years, you
may recover several times your investment in depletion alone."
You can also save money on capital gains and by other means.

How rich do you have to be before you can profit by these

tax shelters? As a rule of thumb, as we have noted, you should be in the 50 percent tax bracket or above. Hutton says that "in most instances a tax shelter investor should have as a minimum, net worth totalling $200,000, or $50,000 exclusive of his home, and income some portion of which is taxed at a 50 percent rate."

Furthermore, "if you can't afford the minimum investment (generally $10,000), can't assume the risk, or must have liquidity, the concept of tax shelters probably isn't for you. Never invest money you can't afford to lose in a tax shelter program."

Here are some potential problems you should look for in the fine print. Unlimited assessability is one of them, particularly in oil and gas drilling programs. Assessability means the sponsor or general partner has the right to ask you for additional funds to complete partnership work. Unlimited assessability is like a time-bomb ticking under your original investment. You may be called on to throw unlimited amounts of good money after what you may already have decided was a bad investment. Other programs are assessable to a specified amount. Or, they are non-assessable, in which case you know where you stand — your original investment is your maximum possible loss.

Real Estate

Now let's consider the most popular type of tax-sheltered investment: real estate. Hutton points out that, in real estate, the general partners or sponsors "usually invest very little cash in their programs. They contribute the expertise to invest in properties." They make their money from some combination of markup on sale of properties, brokerage commissions, property management fees, and a share of income or profit from partnership properties. In other words, the interests of general partners are not necessarily the same as yours, and there may be numerous conflicts of interest in which the sponsor or general partner is tempted to benefit himself and not you. Once again, your only protection in the end is to read all the fine print and retain a good lawyer.

Hutton adds, "Many investors believe that real estate is almost riskless." However, "definite risk is involved. Profitability depends on leverage, interest rates, percentage occupancy, operating costs, competition, and a host of other factors. The key variable, however, is management: the sponsor must have the ability to conduct successful operations before your partnership can succeed."

In real estate the limited partnerships are also known as *syndications.* You and the other limited partners hand over your money to a general partner, usually some kind of real estate firm, to buy and manage an office building, factory, or apartment house. If you know the property involved you can have some idea of the prospects for the deal; however, there are some partnerships in which you do not know this. These are known as *blind pools.* In a blind pool, the general partner collects the cash first. Then, with the money already in hand, he decides what he is going to invest in. This kind of deal obviously requires you to be especially watchful and wary.

Here is a fairly typical example of a partnership in which you do know what you are getting. Capital Resources Real Estate Partnership II, organized in Illinois, offers $5 million limited partnership interests in four apartment complexes under construction in Oklahoma City, Vancouver, Tulsa, and Houston. The announced objective is to provide tax shelter, tax-free cash flow, capital appreciation potential, and equity build-up from mortgage payments. The minimum investment is $5,000. To invest, you must have a taxable income of at least $20,000 a year and a net worth of at least $20,000 excluding your home.

In a net lease property deal, you buy a factory, building, or other real estate and then lease it to a business or industrial firm that manages the property and makes use of it. The lease yields you about 6 percent a year, the property appreciates in value thanks to inflation, and you get tax benefits from depreciation writeoffs.

You have to be rich to make this kind of deal. If you are not so well-heeled you can achieve similar results by buying the shares of real estate investment trusts that go in for this kind of operation. One such trust is Property Capital Trust on the American Stock Exchange.

In fact, any kind of real estate investment trust, of which there are scores publicly quoted on stock exchanges, offers you some kind of tax shelter. The law requires them to pay out 90 percent of their income to shareholders.

Now, about government regulation of tax-sheltered investments: the SEC requirements and the further regulations enforced by some states such as New York are intended to save the small investor from himself. The very nature of the tax shelter deal means that you just have to be a fat cat. If you have a partnership in which the minimum participation is $5,000, the possible loss to a 50 percent tax bracket investor is only $2,500. The possible loss for the little guy in the 20 percent tax bracket, however, is $4,000. The possible gains also favor the rich man in the same way. So if you haven't got it made yet, you'd better stay out of these deals until you strike it rich. But don't give up in the meanwhile — there may be a way for you to make money out of the fat cats who make money out of the tax shelter, as we shall see further on in this chapter.

Oil and Gas Drilling Programs

According to Mortimer Kaplan, former commissioner of the Internal Revenue Service, oil and gas is the kingpin of all tax shelters. Favorable tax treatment and the growing energy shortage have contributed to this.

It is a high-risk field. Only one out of nine wildcat exploration wells strikes oil or gas. Only one out of fifty is a signficant commercial success. However, once a gas or oil field is discovered, about 80 percent of the development wells drilled nearby are successful.

Hutton points out that the typical $5,000 to $10,000 minimum investment in such a drilling program "has brought oil and gas within reach of approximately one million investors in the 50 percent tax bracket or higher."

In most oil and gas limited partnerships, the general

partner is an operating company that explores for and produces oil and gas. It seldom makes a big direct investment in partnership wells. In the partnership programs, the operating company makes money out of management fees and a share of the income if a commercial find is made. You should consider the possibility that the general partner may be tempted to reserve the more promising exploration areas to the wells it is drilling for its own account, leaving the chancier prospects for the partnership programs.

Hutton makes a distinction between three kinds of drilling programs. You have a choice of high-risk, potentially high-return wildcat programs, which only drill wells exploring for new fields; lower-risk, lower-return development programs, which only drill next to existing producing wells; and balanced programs, which drill a mixture of wildcat and development wells. As for the tax shelter, Hutton explains that

> most oil and gas programs offer intangible drilling and other write-offs of 70 percent to 100 percent the first year. Assuming drilling success, your income is partially tax sheltered by the depletion allowance. At least 50 cents of every dollar you receive will be tax free, as long as your partnership's properties produce. Depending on drilling success, the type of wells and other factors, you may begin collecting depletion-protected income within a year. In other cases you may have to wait — up to five years if pipeline construction is necessary. You can collect until the wells deplete — up to 20 years or longer in some cases.

Cattle-Feeding Programs

Another favorite stomping ground of rich investors seeking tax-sheltered investments is cattle. The big trick here is to shift tax liability from one year in which you have extraordinarily high income to another year in which the tax bite is not so big.

Usually you invest in a cattle-feeding partnership. This means that you buy cattle, fatten them up for a few months, and then sell them. The feed costs are deductible the year you invest, and so are prepaid interest and management fees. Hutton says "you can expect a first year write-off ranging up to 200 percent."

When your cattle are sold the following year, your share of the proceeds after various expenses is taxed to you not at capital gains rates but as ordinary income in the year the cattle are sold. "The entire transaction," Hutton explains, "shifts ordinary income from one year to the next—giving you flexibility to pay tax or to invest again, deferring the tax still further."

In case you still have any outdated ideas about the cattle business, raising the critters has become more like an assembly-line industry than old-style ranching. The cows used to roam on the range, nowadays they are kept in feedlot pens containing 100 to 200 animals, fed a scientifically balanced diet designed to maximize weight gain, fattened for four to six months until they reach their optimum weight, and sold to the slaughterhouse. Some of these feedlots might contain as many as 100,000 head—their rich, dungy odor can be smelled miles away.

The general partner in a cattle-feeding program is usually an outfit involved in ranching or meat-packing. The general partner contributes the expertise and management, while you put up the money.

In fact, however, the limited partners don't put up all the money. Most cattle feeding programs are leveraged. The money you send in is only partial payment for the cattle. The partnership borrows more money to finance the rest of the price and the feed to fatten them.

What are the dangers? "Price changes are probably the most significant cattle feeding risk," Hutton says, but "natural disasters (principally abnormal weather) can also influence profitability. Cattle feeding is a high-risk, self-liquidating investment offering very high first year write-offs, no income shelter, and no capital gains. It's exceedingly useful for deferring tax liability, and if cattle and feed prices work out right, for providing exceptional profit possibilities."

It is a self-liquidating investment because feeder cattle

must be sold within 120 to 180 days. Once they have reached their optimum weight, it is uneconomical to keep them any longer.

You can also buy a partnership in cattle-breeding programs. In this case the business is multiplying cows instead of fattening them. The tax shelter comes from deductions for feed and other costs, depreciation, and capital gains.

More Tax Shelters

Cows are not the only possibility. There are also tax shelter programs for breeding chinchillas, mink, hogs, chickens, catfish, and race horses.

One can range even farther afield in the tax shelter preserves. According to Hutton, "citrus and other tree crops encompass a broad tax shelter area: oranges and other citrus, as well as wine grapes, walnuts, pecans, peaches, pistachio nuts, almonds, and avocadoes—to name several." Although the products differ, the tax treatment is basically similar. These crop programs are sometimes considered raw land investments in which farming offers a potentially profitable land use while awaiting capital gains opportunities. Early year losses in tree crop programs are deductible. Leverage and prepaid expenses can boost first-year writeoffs.

"Equipment leasing is a form of tax sheltered investment," says Hutton, which involves "purchase of capital assets—airplanes, railroad rolling stock, computers, ships, pollution control equipment and industrial machinery—leasing these assets and ultimately selling them."

There are other tax-sheltered fields, too. "Movies and plays for Broadway," Hutton says, "are exceedingly high risk ventures which may offer write-offs (by using leverage) of up to 100 to 200 percent the first year, plus the prospect of very high investment return in the form of ordinary income. Most movies and plays are economic failures. However, the few successful ones can offer excellent profit possibilities because properties can be distributed in multiple markets (television, foreign, etc.), thus enhancing potential."

Hutton sums up with this advice:

> Remember: certain tax investments accomplish certain ob-
> jectives. Matching investments with *your* objectives requires in-
> dividual analysis. Because all tax shelters are risky, you should plan
> to invest consistently over a series of years. One-shot investments have
> a way of encountering bad times. Don't subject your life's work to the
> risks of a tax shelter, unless you keep back enough to live on if the in-
> vestment doesn't work out. Investing in any tax shelter means com-
> mitting a substantial amount to an illiquid, risky, complex in-
> vestment. Once you write the check, you're committed for six months
> to two years or longer. Take a little time before you invest to insure
> peace of mind afterwards.

One more word of caution. This is a complicated, tricky
field and we have barely scratched the surface of it. The tax
laws may be changed at any time. You should get additional,
up-to-date information before you make a decision.

A good place to start is Hutton's booklet *Understanding
Tax Shelters.* For constantly updated information you have
the *Tax Shelter Monitor,* published monthly by Berne Clark,
165 East 72nd Street, New York 10021.

And here are three books on the three principal areas of
tax-sheltered investments: *Oil Program Investments,* by
Truman E. Anderson, Petroleum Publishing Co., Tulsa,
Oklahoma; *Cowboy Arithmetic, Cattle as an Investment,* by
Harold L. Oppenheimer, Interstate Printers and Publishers
Inc., Danville, Illinois; *Real Estate Investment Strategy,* by
Maury Selden and Richard Swesnik, John Wiley & Sons Inc.,
New York.

How to Make Money Out of the Fat Cats Who Make Money Out of the Tax Shelters

Everything we said in the preceding pages is fine if you are
making $50,000 a year or more. But what do you do if all
these juicy deals are out of your reach because you don't make
it into the 50% tax bracket yet? Do you just forget about real
estate syndications, oil and gas drilling programs, cattle-

feeding partnerships and say that is for the fat cats but not for you? Certainly not.

In real estate you can put your money into all kinds of investment trusts that specialize in short-term mortgages, long-term mortgages, and other angles. You buy these trust shares through your stockbroker like any other stock.

In oil, gas, and cattle you can become a general partner yourself. You do this by buying the shares of the companies that sell the tax shelter programs to all those fat cats. One such company is Apexco Incorporated, which drilled about eighty wells in 1973 and is quoted over-the-counter (ticker symbol APXO). Others are Basin Petroleum Corporation and Adobe Corporation.

Mesa Petroleum Company (MSA on the New York Stock Exchange) gives you a double-barrelled shot at the fat cats—it sells cattle feeding partnerships as well as oil and gas drilling programs.

Foreign Tax Havens

As we have noted, all these tax shelters may perhaps be on the verge of being torn down through changes in the tax laws. If Congress cracks down on all the tax shelters within the United States, one major result can be anticipated with reasonable certainty. There will be a boom in foreign tax havens. There are plenty of them already, among them the Bahamas, Panama, the Dutch Antilles, the British Channel Islands, Liechtenstein, Luxembourg, Switzerland, Bermuda, and the Cayman Islands.

All these are ready and waiting. The Cayman Islands, for example, is a British colony consisting of three midget-sized islands south of Cuba. These islets are inhabited by about 12,000 people, 4,000 corporations and 90 major banks.

In the Cayman Islands, there are no taxes on personal income, no corporate profits or capital gains, no gift taxes, no estate duty or death taxes. In fact there are no income or profit taxes at all. Nor are there likely to be any in the future for as long as the islanders want to keep such a good thing going and attract so much business from overseas. All this is under the firm royal protection of Her Britannic Majesty Queen Elizabeth II, with none of the restless stirring for independence that caused a queasy withdrawal of foreign funds from Nassau when the Bahamas became independent in 1973. The Cayman Islanders were given the choice of joining Jamaica when that island became an independent nation, but they chose to remain British. So in spite of all temptations to belong to other nations, these descendants of marooned pirates, shipwrecked sailors, and runaway slaves remain true Englishmen.

Full banking secrecy is enforced by the Cayman Islands government. There is no treaty obligation such as exists between Switzerland and the United States in the case of suspicious Swiss bank accounts — to disclose any financial information to foreign governments.

The islands may be lazy tropical hothouses, but the local businessmen are apparently ready and poised to go. Just let the United States Congress crack down on its tax-sheltered citizens. Here is the International Monetary Bank (1000 Grand Cayman, British West Indies), which says it "can form a corporation on behalf of a client within 48 hours of receiving instructions. The cost of formation is $750 including government stamp duties."

The same bank offers to manage the corporation, provide a registered office and mailing address, nominate directors and shareholders, hold statutory meetings, file returns, keep books of record and forward mail. The cost of these management services is $750 a year.

The same bank can "arrange for the registration of a trust within five days and will act as trustee." The cost of registering the trust is $1,000 and the cost of administering it is $750 a year.

The tax advantage of all this is that if you transfer your assets to a Cayman corporation or trust the income is received free of tax.

According to the bank, "income which would otherwise

be channelled through a U.S. citizen or corporation and be suject to U.S. tax is channelled through the Cayman corporation. In this way income arising in the U.S. is only subject to U.S. withholding and capital gains, and income arising outside the U.S. is received completely tax free."

You can get informative booklets on all these details from the International Monetary Bank. Additionally, the Northwester Company Limited, P.O. Box 243, Grand Cayman, will also send you a comprehensive 288-page guide, *The Caymen Islands Handbook and Business Guide.* It costs $7.50, including handling and postage.

All of the above suggests intriguing possibilities. But get yourself a good tax lawyer. The United States Internal Revenue Service is going to be watching you very carefully. And beware of untrustworthy promoters, both at home and abroad. One American oil-well-drilling operation was reported to have taken $100 million from 2,000 of the biggest names in show business, politics, and even Wall Street. According to the *Wall Street Journal,* it did this through a Ponzi scheme — a classic swindle in which money collected from late coming investors is used to pay off earlier investors, who are delighted with their gains and encourage all their friends to invest.

11

Defaulted Bonds and Old Shares

Fortunes have been made since World War II in what seemed like hopeless issues. For example, Americans who bought Japanese bonds immediately after VJ Day for a fraction of their face value hit the jackpot when the postwar government of Japan in 1952 not only resumed debt service of the bonds but also paid off all accrued interest.

—Barron's Magazine

Yes, the defaulted bonds of overturned and defeated foreign governments can sometimes turn out to be unexpected gold mines. The buyers of German bonds hit the jackpot at about the same time as the Japanese bondholders, when the West German government decided to clear up all back debts and wipe the slate completely clean of the Nazi past.

But you cannot count on such big payoffs. They are not likely to happen very often in a world in which most governments have a decided preference for sweeping the sins and debts of their discredited predecessors under the carpet and forgetting about them. But — and this is the big point we want to make here — there are still profits to be made out of defaulted bonds, even if the chances are small that they will be honored.

To prove our point, let's look at the example of Russia. The czarist regime collapsed in Russia in 1917. It was replaced by a provisional government, which in turn was overthrown by the Bolsheviks. The last czar, Nicholas II, and all his family were killed in 1918. Vladimir I. Lenin and his new communist regime then set out systematically to wipe out every trace of the czarist past. Among other things, the Soviets explicitly repudiated a series of bonds the imperial government had issued abroad to finance the war effort against Germany in World War I.

All this happened more than half a century ago. And yet these ancient, repudiated, defaulted czarist bonds are still traded in New York. Why? What possible value can they have? And what profit can you make out of it?

Is there any chance of an imperial restoration in Russia and a czarist resumption of a fifty-year-old debt? None at all. Is there any possibility that the Soviet government will reconsider its fifty-year-old repudiation and pay off the bondholders? Very little indeed. For one thing, some of these bonds have accumulated a ruinous 300 percent or more in back interest, which would obligate the Soviets to pay the original czarist debt four times over.

So where is the profit to be made? These bonds are valueless, right? Well no, not for the sophisticated speculator who knows how to profit by the seesawing ups and downs of hope and fear in the public mind.

When you buy these bonds as a speculation you are not necessarily betting or even anticipating that they will ever be honored. You are simply calculating that their price will fluctuate and that if you buy when they are low you will at some future time be able to sell higher. In order for you to make a profit it is not necessary that the bonds should ever be honored. It is only necessary that their price should vary from time to time, that you find a buyer or a seller when you need one, and that you pocket the difference in price.

The same principle we are discussing here is constantly at work in the stock market. Suppose you have bought stock when prices were depressed. Investors later anticipate a boom in the United States economy and they push up stock prices strongly. If you take advantage of this to sell your stock when prices are high, it does not matter to you whether the expected boom ever arrives or not. As far as you are concerned the boom has already "happened"—in the minds of other investors who pushed up prices—and you have profited by it. If the boom never comes about in reality but turns into a depression instead, it is no longer of any concern to you as long as you have already cashed in your winnings.

In exactly the same way, at the frigid depths of the Cold War, with Americans and Russians glaring at each other over gun-barrels in Berlin, the hope in the public mind of the Soviets ever paying off any lend-lease debts of their own, let alone the czar's, sank to about zero. You could then have bought $1,000 czarist bonds for less than $10 each. In the early 1970s, with the Russians buying half the American wheat crop and seeking other trade deals, and with Soviet leader Leonid Brezhnev visiting the White House and embracing President Nixon, the price went over $100. A tidy profit. There were other ups and downs in Soviet relations through the 1950s and 1960s that could have given you similar gains.

Let's get this perfectly straight—you approach this as an out and out speculation, and you have no expectation that the bonds will ever be honored by the governments in question. You do not buy czarist bonds when Soviet Premier Khrushchev is preaching peaceful coexistence and visiting the United States. You buy them when he is installing rockets in Cuba (as in October, 1962) or when the two superpowers are eyeball to eyeball in a nuclear confrontation. You sell them when his successor Alexei Kosygin is having friendly chats with President Johnson at Glassboro, New Jersey, some years later.

How would this have worked out in terms of actual prices? Lenin repudiates the czarist bonds in 1918: $7.50 per $1,000 bond. Franklin Roosevelt grants diplomatic recognition to the Soviet Union in the 1930s: $85. World War II breaks out: $2.50. The Soviet Union, the United States and Great Britain discuss the post-war world as victorious allies at the Yalta Conference: $210. The Cuban missile crisis of 1962: $10. Russia imports huge amounts of grain from the United States in 1972 and seeks further trade deals: $100.

We are talking here of two bond issues made in July and December, 1916, for a total of $75 million. One is the Imperial Russian Government Three Year Credit, which paid 6½ percent until it was annulled by Lenin in 1918 and which has accumulated about 360 percent in unpaid interest since then. The other is a 5½ percent issue that has piled up about 300 percent interest over the years.

These are not the only bonds on the junkheap of history — to use a communist phrase. You can also buy Chinese imperial and nationalist bonds. These issues include the Hukuang Railways 5 percent Gold Loan of 1911, the China Pacific Development bonds, and a 5 percent bond issued in 1925 by Chiang Kai Shek to pay for damage caused in the Boxer Rebellion at the turn of the century. More than a dozen different Chinese issues are quite actively traded in the United States and London. These have probably been the cheapest of the defaulted foreign bonds in recent years. Early in 1974, they were selling for as little as $10 per $1,000 bond.

Other bonds that have been traded include the Republic of Cuba 4½ percent External Bonds, due in 1977, which were defaulted by Fidel Castro in 1960 and which have ranged in price from $10 to $76 per $1,000 bond since then; the Czechoslovakian government 1960 6 percent external bonds, which were defaulted by the Communists in 1952, whose price range has been $7 to $50; and Polish issues that were wiped out by World War II, such as the 1940 6 percent external bonds defaulted in 1938 (price range $7 to $16) or the 1950 4½ percent Republic of Poland bonds defaulted in 1940 because of the Nazi conquest ($4.50 to $24.50). There are other issues defaulted in the communization of half a dozen East European countries, the most problematic of which is probably the Republic of Estonia 1967 7 percent External Bond issue. This is a country that does not even exist anymore. It was swallowed alive by the Soviet Union, and its bonds have been in default since 1941.

How many buyers and sellers are there in this defaulted bond market? It is hard to get precise figures, but holders of czarist bonds probably number 3,000 or more in the United States. There are somewhere between 10,000 and 30,000 American owners of Polish bonds. There are about two dozen Polish issues that typically were bought in the first place by Polish American citizens, associations, and fraternal organizations.

The market is made by brokerage houses that have made the bonds their specialty. One of these is R.M. Smythe & Company, 170 Broadway, New York, New York. A big dealer in czarist bonds is a New York firm with the curiously ironic name of Carl Marks & Company Incorporated, 77 Water Street, New York 10005. Actually, it is rather pointless to give you the address. Marks is a wholesaler, and you would not deal with this firm directly. You buy and sell through your usual stockbroker. He may well find Marks his best bet to deal with in Russian bonds, since Marks itself may own as much as 10 or 20 percent of the $75 million czarist bond issues.

When you are looking for prices there is not much to orient you except *Standard & Poor's Bond Guide* (345 Hudson Street, New York 10014), and you will probably have to call your broker to get you a quote. But you will find some foreign bond quotations in this small section of the *Wall Street Journal*:

FOREIGN BONDS

Volume: $40,000

Bonds		Cur Yld	Vol	High	Low	Close	Net Chg.
Chile	3s93f	3.4	3	87	87	87	
Cundin	3s78	3.7	3	80	80	80	
El Salv	3s76	3.4	1	88⅛	88⅛	88⅛	+7½
vjKreu	5s59f		5	3⅞	3⅞	3⅞	-1⅛
Nipn TT	6s76	6.1	1	97	97	97	-½
Queb Pr	8s78	8.5	10	94	94	94	-2
Silesa	4½58f		8	30	30	30	
Wars	4½58f		4	30	30	30	

Up to this point we have been assuming that none of these bonds will *ever* be paid off, that a deadbeat is a deadbeat and will always continue to be so, particularly when communists take over a government. This assumption might prove to be excessively gloomy in some cases.

Those people who bought Japanese and German bonds in 1945 seemed crazy at the time. Would anybody in his right mind expect to make anything out of the obligations of hated, defeated, and destroyed Japanese and Nazi militarist regimes whose countries had been pulverized by carpet bombing and the atom bomb?

Yet, only seven years later, the full payoff on the Japanese bonds came when the post-war government in Tokyo was desperately eager to reestablish its good name in the international financial community. By 1960, every penny had been paid off, including back interest. One World War II veteran bought these bonds at one cent on the dollar, and when he came home from the Pacific theater of war he used them as wallpaper. Later on, it was well worth his while to scrape them off the walls. He made a 10,000 percent profit.

West Germany settled with its foreign bondholders for the same reason at about the same time, and investors in pre-Hitler German bonds reaped a rich reward.

If the communist governments pay up on their bonds — which, as we have noted, is not really necessary for you to make a profit — it will be basically for the same motive as the Germans and the Japanese. They will want to reestablish their credit in the world community.

To a large extent this is already happening. In July, 1974, the United States and Czechoslovakia reached a preliminary agreement on a settlement of financial claims against each other dating to the end of World War II. At the same time, the United States and Hungary were in an advanced stage of negotiations on Hungary's default on pre-World War II bonds.

The incentive here was that Czechoslovakia and Hungary, like other communist states, wanted access to credits from the International Monetary Fund and other Western sources. But you cannot very well apply for new loans at the bank when you are still refusing to pay off your old debts.

Other communist nations had already learned this lesson. Yugoslavia settled with its foreign bondholders some years ago. Poland settled in 1972, at least on a preliminary basis. The Polish government agreed to resume interest payments for two years pending a final agreement on the repayment of principal and back interest to be negotiated before July 1, 1975. About two dozen Polish issues were involved, including the Republic of Poland twenty-year 6 percent dollar-Gold Bond Loan of 1920 and the 7 percent City of Warsaw Gold Bond Loan of 1928. These settlements usually do not pay off the whole debt, of course. The preliminary agreement with Poland only provided for partial interest payments of 1.5 percent to 2 percent a year, and it stipulated that clauses promising payment in gold would not be honored. The way the gold price has gone up it would be just too ruinous for the Polish communists to meet their gold obligations in full.

In spite of all this, if you had bought Polish bonds at $60 to $70 per $1,000 certificate at the beginning of 1972, you could have sold them for as much as $300 by the end of the year. When the communist Polish government agreed in principle to pay off its back debts, you would have gotten back $4 to $5 for every $1 you originally invested.

Both the Poles and the Yugoslavs negotiated these settlements with the Foreign Bondholders Protective Council Incorporated, 1775 Broadway, New York, New York. The council was set up in 1933, and since then it has worked out more than forty debt settlement plans with twenty-four foreign nations. This is the first place to turn to for reliable information on the status of any U.S. dollar foreign bonds.

At the time the Polish settlement was reached, the council was also in preliminary negotiations with the communist governments of Rumania and Hungary. It was also endeavoring to get negotiations started with Bulgaria, the Soviet Union, China, and Cuba.

The Soviet government has been the only communist regime to announce its repudiation of the state bonds of a preceding regime. Not even the Chinese communists have come right out and done that. In fact, there have only been two outright repudiations in modern times. The Soviet Union was one and the United States was the other, when it disowned the Confederate bonds after the Civil War.

The unwillingness, refusal, or sheer inability to meet financial obligations is by no means limited to proletarian communist states. This kind of thing also happens even in the highest social circles. Like Rolls Royce, for example.

It is nice to know that sometimes even suckers who get taken for a ride end up making quite a lot of money. It does not happen often, but there are still cases. And in this case the suckers got taken for a ride in a Rolls Royce. The famous British luxury carmaker got into trouble in 1970 when an aero engine it was making on contract for Lockheed Aircraft Corporation far overran cost estimates and plunged Rolls Royce millions of dollars into the red. The British government refused to help out and the automaker went bankrupt. Rolls Royce shares dropped to a few pennies a share.

However, in the United States there were thousands of little investors who knew practically nothing of the financial shenanigans in London, but who did know that Rolls Royce was the finest of the finest, the car maker supreme for kings, sultans, and presidents. Savvy British investors began to unload their practically worthless stock on these people. It reached the point where reputable American brokers refused to accept any orders for Rolls Royce stock from their more ill-informed customers. Even so, according to one estimate, the British shareholders succeeded in dumping nearly 25 million shares on the American suckers, out of a total 64 million shares outstanding.

A couple of years later, in December, 1973, it suddenly turned out that the suckers who were still stuck with their shares might have the last laugh after all. The liquidators of the bankrupt firm estimated that common shareholders might get one dollar a share, perhaps five times more than they paid for them two years before. By that time they had already paid out 60 cents a share in partial settlement.

Despite such exceptions, though, you are far more likely to receive unexpected payoffs from defaulted bonds than from bankrupt common stock. The reason is that bonds are senior securities—they get first preference when debts are being paid off. Common shareholders are not paid until everybody else has been taken care of, and if there are no salvageable scraps left over when the other creditors have had their claims satisfied then they get nothing at all.

For example, the Hudson & Manhattan Railroad Company went into bankruptcy in 1954. Some of the railroad's $1,000 bonds could have been bought five years later at $70 to $80 each. The company owned real estate in Manhattan and other assets but it took a decade of litigation to clean up the mess. When the liquidation was finally completed in 1973 these bondholders were awarded $1,850 per bond (including unpaid back interest). Not bad on an $80 investment. The common shareholders got nothing.

Old Stock Certificates

Old and apparently valueless stock of companies that no longer exist becomes valuable through a series of takeovers rather than through bankruptcy. When an industry is young—the auto industry in the early 1900s or the oceanography industry in the 1970s—there are hundreds of companies in the field and the public is snapping up the shares of all of them. In a few decades there are only a handful left, say General Motors, Ford, American Motors. The Stutz, the Durant, and scores of other makes have all disappeared. What happened to them? Many of these firms were bought up and absorbed by their bigger and more successful competitors. So if your granddad left you some shares in the Phoenix Steam Car Corporation or the Alpha Adding Machine Company, it is not entirely impossible that they ended up converted into shares of General Motors or IBM.

If you have some of these shares lying around, check them out before you throw them away. You can do this through Stock Market Information Services, 235 Dorchester E., Montreal, Quebec, Canada. This firm will trace any securities issued anywhere in the world since 1850. The fee is $20.

Suppose you hit the jackpot with some old company that was bought up by another that was merged into a third and that finally ended up convertible into shares of something really valuable like Xerox or Polaroid. Where could you find some more of these apparently valueless old certificates and cash in on them?

There are a few firms that specialize in these kinds of shares. They are, so to speak, the morticians of the securities industry, at least as far as the Internal Revenue Service is concerned. These firms hold auctions that enable the seller to establish *some* kind of a price, even if it is only one cent a share. He then has the sales slip as proof for the tax authorities in claiming a tax loss.

One such firm is Adrian H. Muller & Son, 103 Park Avenue, New York, which has been in the business for more than a century. Muller holds dozens of auctions every year of practically worthless shares. You might be able to buy thousands of shares of some defunct Ethiopian mining stock for a hundred dollars. They might have belonged to a Rockefeller or some other financial luminary. (Yes, even the big boys get taken for a ride sometimes.)

The chances are, of course, that if you have any dusty and forgotten old stock up in the attic it probably is worthless as a security. But you still might be able to write it off as a loss against your income tax if you establish a price for it at auction.

If you sell through Muller, the quantity of stock and the potential tax benefit should be fairly substantial to make the sale worthwhile. The minimum sales fee is $50, and you also have to pay for the advertising.

Finally, let us suppose you are holding old stocks and bonds in which there is no trading activity, that have no value at all as securities, and that offer no tax benefits. They still might have value as collector's items.

Railroad buffs go for old railroad shares. Autograph hunters have a yearning for old stock signed by tycoons like John D. Rockefeller or Cornelius Vanderbilt. With the United States Second Centennial coming up you should also be on the lookout for anything connected with the American Revolution. There are still some Revolutionary War Bonds in existence engraved by Paul Revere.

12

Foreign Currencies

I<small>F YOU ARE</small> an American, you are accustomed to thinking in terms of dollars. You buy things with dollars and never stop to think about what they would cost in marks, yen or francs. That kind of financial isolationism can be costly — in 1972 and 1973, in fact, you may have lost up to 30 percent of your net worth.

In December, 1971, the American dollar was devalued 7.89 percent. In February, 1973, it was devalued another 10 percent. In March, 1973, it was allowed to "float" in free trading and promptly sank another 10 percent or so against such currencies as the German mark and the Japanese yen. As a result, like 99.99 percent of all Americans, you let your net worth decrease by 30 percent compared to what it would have been had you owned only marks, yen, or Swiss francs during the same period.

It is too late to do anything now about the highly unpleasant situation in 1972-73. But the next time something similar happens, there are ways you can handle the situation. One way, of course, would be to just stand there and get clobbered. This is what more than 999 people out of 1,000 did— they just hung on to their depreciating dollars and hoped for the best.

Or, you could protect yourself against devaluation by changing your dollars into foreign currencies when you see trouble on the way—and its coming is usually plain enough, as you will see in this chapter. You can do this by buying Swiss francs, German marks, Japanese yen, or some other strong currency from a foreign exchange dealer or by opening an account with a bank in one of the countries. Had you followed this plan in the 1972-73 period, you would have come out around 30 percent ahead, in dollars. In the foreign currency, you would merely have broken even, ending with the same number of francs or marks with which you started. In other words, you would not have lost any money and you would be 30 percent ahead of the vast majority of Americans who just sat on their hands and did nothing. We deal with this choice in Chapters 2 and 4 on foreign stocks, bonds, and savings accounts.

But you have a third choice as well. In this case, you do more than merely take defensive measures to preserve your assets. Instead, you go out aggressively to *make* money out of the situation. This is exactly what a handful of multinational corporations and big banks are suspected of doing in 1972-73—and it's very likely that they made hundreds of millions of dollars on their deals.

The basic technique is so simple that there is no reason why you cannot do it as well. The only problem is that of scale, the fact that you are dealing in hundreds or perhaps thousands of dollars while the big financial institutions are throwing around millions. We shall get to that problem later on, but first let's look at how currency speculation works.

Suppose we are back in October, 1971, and you see from the papers that the dollar is in trouble in foreign exchange markets. You suspect that a financial crisis is brewing and that the dollar may be devalued. If you are a big financial operator, you borrow a million dollars, say at 6 percent yearly interest, and you change this money into German marks. By December—barely three months later—the mark's worth has increased 7.89 percent against the dollar. You are already ahead, but you decide to wait for bigger profits. In February, 1973, you are another 10 percent ahead, and by the following month another 10 percent or so. But you still decide to wait until October, 1973, when it finally seems reasonably certain that the dollar is not going to sink much further. Exactly two years have gone by, and at 6 percent you owe $120,000 interest on your borrowed million dollars. The marks you bought are now worth $1.3 million when you change them back into devalued dollars to repay your loan. You are therefore $180,000 ahead. If you had kept the marks in a German saving account at 4 percent yearly interest, you would have received another $80,000 in two years. Total profit—$260,000.

Now, you might calculate that $260,000 profit on $1 million is a 26 percent gain. It is not. *It is all pure gravy.* Those million dollars were not yours, they were borrowed from somebody else and were just working for you. You started out with nothing (except the necessary credit-worthiness to borrow the million), and now after repaying the loan you have $260,000, all of which is pure profit, earned by making use of other people's money.

You do not have to be a big international company or bank to make this kind of deal. You can do it quite simply by opening a savings account in a bank in Switzerland, Germany, or another nation with a strong currency. You borrow dollars in the United States wherever you can find the cheapest interest rate and then send your check for that amount to the foreign bank, which will convert it into the local currency, credit your savings account, and pay your interest in the same currency.

The only trouble is that if you operate on a small scale you incur much higher costs than a billion-dollar multinational company would. You must pay higher interest rates on borrowing, and foreign exchange dealers' commissions are much higher on small quantities.

Foreign Currency Futures

Instead of using this do-it-yourself approach, you may find it more convenient to seek essentially the same results by dealing in the foreign currency futures markets.

Foreign exchange trading in the United States probably amounts to about $500 billion a year. Most of these transactions are handled through international banks, and unless you have a million dollars available the field is closed to you. One of the kingpins in the world banking system of foreign exchange dealings, for instance, is the Morgan Guaranty Trust Company in New York, which was founded by J.P. Morgan, the great financial wizard at the turn of the century. Foreign currency trading through banks mainly represents trade deals. More than 90 percent of such futures deals are settled by actual delivery of the currency contracted for. Deals are rarely for less than $1 million.

Before you become this decade's J.P. Morgan by advancing into the World Series of the monetary game, however, let's see how you can start at the beginning by dealing on two smaller markets, one in New York and one in Chicago.

On New York's American Board of Trade, all you have to ante up is about $300. Each contract is worth about $2,500, and the $300 represents your margin. This is obviously the smallest-risk market, the place to get your feet wet, learn the ropes, and generally find your sea legs in the foreign exchange market.

On the Chicago International Monetary Market, hedging and speculating activities (as opposed to trade deals) account for most of the action. Less than 1 percent of the contracts come down to actual delivery. The size of each contract is much smaller than in the big-money markets, ranging from $40,000 to $100,000 in the different currencies. Your margin is only about $2,000 or $3,000.

On the American Board of Trade, you can trade in Canadian dollars, British pounds, West German marks, French francs, Swiss francs, Japanese yen, and Italian lira for future delivery. In Canadian currency the contract, or basic trading unit, is for 2,500 Canadian dollars, which is approximately equivalent to the same amount in United States dollars. All the other currencies are traded in about the same amounts. The standard unit for British pounds is £1,000; in German currency, it is 10,000 marks.

However, you are not putting up the entire $2,500 out of your own money. Your margin is only $300, and you are thus getting a leverage of about eight to one on your investment. The brokerage commission is $20 per basic unit.

This is a short-term market. You can buy or sell these currencies for delivery thirty, sixty or ninety days ahead. You are therefore concerned with how the United States dollar or the Japanese yen is going to stand not more than three months from the time of purchase. The shortness of the trading period does not exclude the possibility of startling short-term profits. If you had bought thirty-day Swiss francs, for instance, on May 4, 1971, at 23.36 United States cents per franc, your 10,000-franc unit would have cost $2,336, of which you would have put up only $300 of your own money. On June 3, when your contract expired, you could have cashed in your francs at the then prevailing price of 24.46 United States cents, for a total of $2,446, and a gain of $110 on the $300 you put down thirty days before. In the following months, even greater gains would have been possible—by 1973 the Swiss franc was worth more than $0.35—but we are talking here of the possible profits in a maximum time span of ninety days.

You do not have to be an out-and-out speculator to trade in foreign currency futures. You can reduce your risk considerably by trading on a spread basis. In this case, you might buy pounds sterling for delivery in thirty days and simultaneously sell the same amount of the British currency on ninety-day delivery. You anticipate that you may lose money on one contract but make enough profit on the other one to wipe out the loss and end up with a net profit.

Through the use of arbitrage, you can make a thoroughly conservative investment that avoids the usual high risks of dealing in the commodity futures markets. You do this by buying a spot (immediate delivery) contract. On the American Board of Trade, spot contracts are in the same amounts as futures contracts, and they have the same margin require- ments. At the same time you sell a contract of the same cur- rency for delivery in sixty or ninety days. You are now fully protected from losses or gains caused by exchange fluctua- tions. You are also in a position to profit by the difference between the spot rate and the forward rate of exchange. According to the American Board of Trade, "This approach offers an assured return that is equalled by few investment avenues today." A return is only possible, however, when the difference between the spot and the forward rates is enough to cover costs and leave you with a margin of profit.

The American Board of Trade offers you another possibility for trading in foreign currencies—an options con- tract. This is different from the futures market, where you put up margin and assume a contractual *obligation* to buy or sell 10,000 marks or whatever currency you are dealing in, within a specified period. With an option contract you assume no obligation. You purchase only an *option* (known as a put or a call) to buy or sell 10,000 marks within a period of three or six months or one year. If, at the end of this period, you find that it has proved to be unprofitable to exercise your option, you just drop it and forget about it. You are under no obligation to buy anything or sell anything to anybody. The most you can lose is your option premium, which might be $200 or $300 on a 10,000 mark contract.

With this kind of premium you must figure on a 10 per- cent fluctuation in the exchange rate, which does not happen too often, before you can make a profit. However, in ex- ceptional circumstances your profits might be substantial. If the mark goes from around $0.25 to $0.40 in United States money, as it did in the 1972-73 period, your twelve-month call for 10,000 marks would have risen in value from $2,500 to $4,000, giving you a $1,500 gross profit. Your only investment (and maximum possible loss) would have been the $338 option premium and the Exchange's $20 commission. However, such wide fluctuations are not at all frequent.

The American Board of Trade also offers options in Canadian dollars, British pounds, Swiss francs, and other items, such as silver bullion. We go into the details of these in Chapter 3, on options, which are a major form of investment in their own right.

After you've learned the ropes in New York, you may want to try for bigger stakes on the International Monetary Market in Chicago, which was set up in 1972. Before that time, there was little room for such a futures market to operate because every currency had a fixed par value and each nation's government guarateed to keep its currency within 1 percent of that fixed value. In 1971 this world monetary system broke down—this is where the United States dollar came to grief, as you will recall—and the world's currencies were left more and more to find their own value at whatever level they were driven by supply and demand. The hedging and speculating of private dealers then moved in to stabilize a worldwide market that national governments had previously tried unsuccessfully to hold within rigid and artificially decreed exchange rates.

The nations of the world are negotiating with each other in the International Monetary Fund to create a new world monetary system that would once more put governments in control. This is a prickly subject, and the negotiations look as if they are going to take several years. If they succeed in reestablishing fixed exchange rates, this will obviously take most of the incentive out of speculating in currency futures. In the meantime, however, the currency futures market continues to grow although it is still rather thin. By mid-1973 about a quarter of a million contracts, valued at a total of about $35 billion, had been traded on the Chicago market.

On the Chicago market you can speculate in British pounds, Canadian dollars, German marks, Dutch guilder, Italian lira, Japanese yen, Mexican pesos, and Swiss francs. The size of each contract varies according to the currency, as follows:

Contract	Approximate value (in U.S. dollars)
25,000 British Pounds	$ 60,000
100,000 Canadian Dollars	$100,000
250,000 German Marks	$100,000
125,000 Dutch Guilders	$ 50,000
25,000,000 Italian Liras	$ 40,000
12,500,000 Japanese Yen	$ 50,000
1,000,000 Mexican Pesos	$ 80,000
250,000 Swiss Francs	$ 80,000

These may seem like big amounts to be dealing in, but in fact you may only put up a margin of about $2,000 or $3,000. You thus have powerful leverage on your investment.

A typical day's trading on the Chicago market is recorded like this in the *New York Journal of Commerce* (99 Wall Street, New York 10005). In the *Wall Street Journal* and perhaps in your local newspaper the information is printed in a more abbreviated form.

Chicago Mercantile Exchange
International Monetary Markets

	Open	October 23 High	Low	Close	Prev. Close
MEXICAN PESOS					
Dec.				*.07985	*.07985
Mar. '74	.			*.07955	*.07955
June				*.07929	*.07929
Sept.	.07898	.07900	.07898	.07900	.07910
Dec.				†.07873	*.07869
Mar. '75				†.07843	*.07839
DUTCH GUILDER					
Dec.				*.40348	*.40348
Mar. '74				*.40800	*.40800
June				*.41072	.41072
Sept.				*.41080	.41082
SWISS FRANC					
Dec.				†.33500	.33380
Mar. '74	.33670	.33700	.33640	†.33660	§ .33550
June	.33960	.33960	.33930	.33930	§ .33795
Sept.				*.34220	*.34220
BRITISH POUND					
Nov.					
Dec.				†2.4315	*2.4280
Mar. '74				*2.4100	2.4100
June				*2.3900	*2.3900
Sept.				2.3760	*2.3760
Dec.				*2.3560	§2.3560
CANADIAN DOLLAR					
Dec.				†1.00200	*1.00050
Mar. '74	1.00060	†1.00060	1.00060	†1.00060	*1.00160
June					
Sept.					
DEUTSCHE MARK					
Dec.	.41900	†.41925	.41900	†.41905	.41780
Mar. '74	.42170	.42220	.42170	†.42200	.42000
June				†.42260	*.42200
Sept.				†.42450	*.42400
Dec.				†.42750	*.42700
ITALIAN LIRA					
(Comm.) Dec.				*.0017540	*.0017540
(Fin.) Dec.				*.0016800	*.0016800
JAPANESE YEN					
Dec.				*.0037550	.0037550
Mar. '74				*.0037750	*.0037750
June				§.0038250	§.0038280
Sept.		†.0038350	§.0038300	§.0038320	.0038350
Dec.				*.0038700	§.0038700

†—Bid.   § —Asked. *—Nominal.

You will note from this table that in some currencies you can trade nearly a year and a half into the future. You will also note that there is not really very much activity on the market. In fact, in some currencies, such as the Dutch guilder and Italian lira, there was no trading at all on this particular day. If you check the table below, you will see that the only currencies in which more than 10 contracts were traded were the British pound, Japanese yen, Swiss franc, and Mexican peso:

Sales
OCTOBER 23
Chicago

Currencies

	British Pound	Canada Dollar	D-Mark	Italian Lira Comm.	Fin.
Oct.	—	—	—	—	—
Nov.	—	—	—	—	—
Dec.	—	—	1	—	—
Mar.	—	3	5	—	—
June	—	—	—	—	—
Sept.	60	—	—	—	—
Dec.	—	—	—	—	—
Total	60	3	6	—	—

	Japan Yen	Swiss Franc	Mexican Pesos	D Guilder
Oct.	—	—	—	—
Dec.	—	—	—	—
Mar.	—	5	10	—
June	—	9	—	—
Sept.	10	—	2	—
Dec.	—	—	—	—
Total	10	14	12	—

And if you look further down, at the next table, you will find that on this particular day some of the potential markets are extremely small. There are only forty-six Dutch guilder contracts in existence, for example, and in the two-tier Italian lira market there are only thirteen. If you want to buy or sell at an acceptable price you may have to wait a long time to find a buyer or seller. You will find the broadest markets — and thus the greatest liquidity — in British pounds, German marks, Japanese yen, Swiss francs, and above all in Mexican pesos. By the time this book reaches you, of course, the situation may have changed and you should check which are the active currencies at that time.

Open Interest
OCTOBER 23

Chicago

	British Pound	Canada Dollar	D-Mark	Italian Lira Comm.	Fin.
			Currencies		
Oct.	—	—	—	—	—
Dec.	60	10	105	9	4
Mar.	17	10	64	—	—
June	2	—	4	—	—
Sept.	180	—	404	—	—
Dec.	180	—	408	—	—
Total	439	20	985	9	4

	Japan Yen	Swiss Franc	Mexican Pesos	D;Guilder
Dec.	28	68	62	3
Mar.	40	166	778	21
June	114	22	1.080	22
Sept.	252	1	1.683	—
Dec.	127	—	1.523	—
Mar.	—	—	1.267	—
Total	561	257	6.393	46

Predicting Future Trends

If the idea of making money out of money attracts you, re-member this warning from the publishers of the *Foreign Exchange Letter:* "Foreign exchange currencies should be used as investment, speculative or hedging media only by people who know what they are doing—who have the information they need to make sound investment decisions."

What makes one currency go up and another go down? How can you get the information you need? There are many publications to help you. From the Chicago International Monetary Market, you can obtain useful material such as the booklet *Understanding Futures in Foreign Exchange* and the *Foreign Exchange Futures Study Course.* Write to the International Money Market, 444 West Jackson Boulevard, Chicago, Illinois 60606. The I.M.M. can also put your name on a mailing list to receive free brokerage house market letters, which keep you up-to-date on the latest developments. Brokers who are members of the I.M.M. include Merrill Lynch, Bache, and other firms with offices all over the United States and abroad.

Through the American Board of Trade you can subscribe to the *Foreign Exchange Letter* ($24 a year), a biweekly review of foreign exchange trends, with charts, graphs, and commentary. Write to the *Foreign Exchange Letter,* 286 Fifth Avenue, New York 10001. From the same source, you can order the book *A Textbook on Foreign Exchange,* by Paul Einzig, which explains the workings of the international currency market.

Other sources of information and advice are *Green's Commodity Market Comments,* published biweekly at 565 Fifth Avenue, New York 10001, and *The Powell Monetary Analyst,* also published biweekly at 63 Wall Street, New York 10005.

Pick's Currency Yearbook (published in the fall by Franz Pick, 21 West Street, New York 10006) gives you an annual look at the misdeeds of the world's monetary authorities from Albania to Zaire during the preceding year. The yearbook is a good source of alarming data about the depreciation of all paper currencies.

For a start, let's examine what made the United States dollar plunge so dramatically in 1971-73. The answer is simple. There were just too many dollars floating around in the world. All through the 1960s, the United States piled up yearly deficits in its balance of payments with foreign nations, to such an extent that by 1973 the number of dollars in foreign hands amounted to a staggering $100 billion — about $70 billion of them in foreign central banks.

As soon as the dollar was declared inconvertible into gold on August 15, 1971, foreigners lost confidence in what were essentially unbacked scraps of paper. They began to dump their dollars, and it was not reasonable to expect the dollar to strengthen to any great extent until that enormous pile of dollars abroad had been reduced. Any increase in the demand for dollars would be met promptly by a horde of foreigners eager to dump the dollars they already owned.

The balance of payments is thus a big factor in making the value of the dollar rise or fall against the mark, the yen, or the pound. While for years the United States was spending more abroad than it earned, Japan was accumulating huge sums of dollars and other foreign currencies by constant foreign trade surpluses in the 1960s. The result was a 40 percent upward revaluation of the yen in 1971-73.

How do you keep track of such changes? The figures are published monthly—you just have to know where to find them. On the second week of each month the United States, Canada, Great Britain, and Italy publish their latest balance of payments figures. These figures are reported in such papers as the *Wall Street Journal* and the *Financial Times* of London. A big deficit for Britain is bad news for the pound; a big surplus for Canada will tend to strengthen the Canadian dollar on the futures markets. Other countries publish their figures at different times; Germany, for instance, releases the information in the first week of the month.

The balance of payments includes all kinds of transfers of money from one country to another—investments, dividends and interest payments, military expenses, and other items—as well as the mere trade in cars, grain, and other shipments of goods. All these data take some time to put together and add up. The actual trade figures are quicker and easier for governments to calculate. Consequently, the foreign trade figures usually appear sooner. They give you an indication of how things are going for each nation, but they are only a partial indicator of the entire picture. And, in some countries, they are none too reliable an indicator, either—governments are not above juggling the figures for their own purposes.

The United States usually publishes its foreign trade balance in the fourth week of each month. This is the sort of news item you should be watching for:

WASHINGTON, March 25, 1973—The U.S. Department of Commerce announced that the U.S. foreign trade deficit for 1972 reached a record $6.4 billion. The trade deficit in December was $563 million, the largest monthly deficit since June. The 1972 deficit is more than three times the size of the 1971 deficit.

It will not surprise you to learn that the dollar was in big trouble in foreign exchange markets at the time of this report.

What else makes the value of the dollar fluctuate daily against other currencies? One big factor is interest rates. If interest rates are 3 percent higher in the United States than in Germany, then the price of German marks for delivery a year ahead will tend to be 3 percent higher in terms of dollars. The price thus compensates the interest rate differential — assuming that all other factors are equal, which they seldom are for very long. If there are no government restrictions on the movement of capital, German money will tend to move into the United States to take advantage of the higher interest rates, and this inflow will strengthen the value of the dollar against the mark until the interest rates are equalized in both countries. But in fact there usually are restrictions of one kind or another, preventing perfect equality.

To keep track of interest rates in major countries is a fairly simple matter. You will find daily information on United States rates in your newspaper. The key rates are the discount rate, which is the interest the United States Federal Reserve (the United States government's central banking system) charges major American banks for the use of money, and the prime rate, which is the interest big commercial banks charge the corporations who are their biggest and most credit-worthy customers.

You can compare these with rates abroad by checking the British bank rate, which is published weekly and will be found in major financial dailies such as the *Wall Street Journal.* Other foreign figures and reports, such as the Canadian Treasury Bill rate and German government credit policy, are published monthly.

Another big influence on the foreign currency market is the price level in each country. In the early 1970s in the United States prices rose to such a high level that some American products were priced right out of world markets. At the same time Japanese prices were held down to a level at which they swamped the American market. Japanese competition almost wiped out some sections of the United States electronics industry in its own home market. A critical factor was wages.

If American wages rise, it costs more to turn out American products — they will be too expensive to compete with Japanese goods.

When wages and prices are rising, inflation is the result. It is, therefore, important to watch the rate of inflation in each country. If French wages, prices, and inflation rise faster than in other countries you can be sure the French franc will soon be in trouble.

Most of these figures are published monthly. Washington publishes the United States wholesale price index in the first week of each month. The wholesale price index gives a pretty good advance warning of what the cost of living is going to be in a few months, when these prices work their way down to the retail stores. In the fourth week of each month, Washington publishes the consumer price index, which shows how inflation is pushing the cost of living up. In the middle of the month you can get official government figures on personal income in the United States and on the average wages of American workers. Most other major governments also publish comparable figures monthly and you will find them in major business dailies.

These are all predominantly economic influences that may drive the price of the dollar or the pound up or down. There are also political factors that weigh heavily on the foreign exchange market. A country with a weak and unstable government is pretty sure to have a weak and unstable currency. Such was the case in France in the 1950s, when there was a new prime minister in Paris every few weeks. Once General deGaulle had established a firmly based government, he scrapped the constantly debased old franc and created the new franc, a completely new currency worth 100 times as much as the old. From there on, the new franc reflected the stability of the Gaullist regime.

In the United States the Watergate political scandal constantly weakened the dollar in 1973 because foreign currency operators suspected it had undermined the Nixon administration's ability to govern effectively. In Germany, the

Christian Democrat Party is generally considered to be more committed to an antiinflationary, hard-money policy than its rival, the Social Democrat Party. So a Social Democrat victory at the polls might presage a weakening of the mark.

All these political events will be reported in your newspaper, and they are usually front-page news when they happen. As a foreign currency speculator, you should learn to interpret their implications for the value of the dollar, the yen, or the mark.

All these factors—balance of payments, interest rates, differing inflation rates, elections, and changes of government and other political events—create a climate of expectation among foreign currency operators. These expectations themselves can become such a strong psychological factor in the market that they create self-fulfilling prophecies. In 1971 and 1973, for example, so many financial people anticipated a revaluation of the German mark that billions of dollars flowed into Germany to take advantage of the upward move when it occurred. This massive influx itself forced the German government to abandon the fixed mark exchange rate it was committed to maintaining. The government simply could no longer afford to go on buying up billions of inrushing dollars just to hold down the price of the mark. The German central bank then stepped aside from the market and let the mark find its own level through supply and demand. And, as the speculators had anticipated, the massive demand then drove the price up.

Specific Foreign Currencies

Now let's make a brief thumbnail sketch of the various currencies in which you can trade and review some of the factors affecting their stability.

British pounds

Great Britain has to import enormous amounts of raw materials from abroad and is dependent on foreign trade for its very survival. Any slump in world commerce will be a bad blow for the British economy. Any devaluation of the pound will make the imported materials dearer and thus aggravate the problem. Inflation has been high in recent years, running from 6 to 12 percent a year, and the growth rate of the British economy has lagged behind that of other nations. This has tended to keep the pound under downward pressure since World War II. However, one bright spot on the horizon for the pound sterling is the discovery of big oil and gas fields in the British sector of the North Sea, which may make the British self-sufficient by the late 1970s or early 1980s and thus plug a $2 billion yearly foreign currency drain for imported oil.

Canadian dollars

About two-thirds of all Canadian exports go to the United States market, and Canada takes about one-quarter of all American exports. The two economies are so closely linked that the American and Canadian dollars seldom fluctuate very far apart in value. This could be a relatively low-risk currency in which to start speculating for this very reason. Another factor that makes speculation easier is that Canadian economic and political news is widely reported in the United States.

German marks

In the 1920s, Germany experienced a horrendous inflation, in which money literally was not worth the paper it was printed on. Its currency completely collapsed once again after World War II. These bitter experiences have burned deep into the German mind. Consequently, this nation above all others has a horror of inflation. This psychological reason alone tends to make the mark a strong currency, because no German government dares go too far down the inflationary path. The West German economy is vigorously capitalistic. The country's exporters have flourished, despite successive revaluations of the mark that have made their products more and more expensive in world markets.

Dutch guilders

Holland is a small country, and, perhaps more than any other nation, is dependent on the state of world commerce. No less than 40 percent of its gross national product goes for export.

Italian lira

Italy, too, is dependent on world trade for survival. It has to import most of its raw materials. Nearly half its exports go to other Western European nations. This ties its currency closely to theirs, as does its membership in the European Common Market.

Japanese yen

Japan is another nation with inadequate natural resources and a top-heavy dependence on world trade. The United States supplies about a quarter of its imports and takes about one-third of Japanese exports. The Japanese economy has grown at an astonishing rate. By the end of this century the Japanese gross national product might surpass that of the United States. Since World War II, the perennial Japanese surplus of exports over imports made the yen one of the strongest currencies.

Swiss francs

Although Switzerland is a small country, it is a haven for huge amounts of foreign money. It is a neutral nation that is less likely than any other to be involved in a major war. It is also renowned for its fiscal and monetary conservatism. All these factors make the Swiss franc one of the strongest currencies in the world. In trade it is closely linked with the West European nations, which provide nearly two-thirds of Swiss imports, in particular Germany, which provides nearly one-third.

United States dollars

Despite the dollar's weakness in recent years, it represents the world's biggest, most powerful, and most productive national economy. The United States accounts, in fact, for about one-third of the entire world economy. The United States is also the richest nation in natural resources among the major capitalist powers, and it is the least dependent on foreign trade — only 4 percent or so of its gross national product comes from that source. All these factors will surely make themselves felt when the United States cuts its military and other commitments abroad, which have progressively undermined its currency since World War II.

Mexican pesos

Mexico is a country whose currency is linked overwhelmingly to the United States economy. It sends about two-thirds of its exports to the United States market and receives about two-thirds of its imports from the United States. Its currency has maintained a rocklike stability of 12.5 pesos to the dollar since 1954. This close connection with the dollar makes the peso a relatively low-risk currency to start out as a speculator.

Another way to make money with Mexican pesos is apparently being tried by many people, if the large number of contracts in this currency on the Chicago futures market is any indication. Here is how the method works. Usually you can get 2 percent more on your money in Mexico than you can in the United States because Mexico is a poorer country, capital is more scarce, and therefore interest rates are higher. It follows that if you have a good, cheap source of credit in the United States, you can borrow money in dollars, convert them into pesos, lend the pesos in Mexico at a higher rate, and make a nice profit on the interest differential. You could do this through Nacional Financiera, the Mexican development bank mentioned in Chapter 4.

Your only major risk is the possibility that the peso will drop in value against the dollar and wipe out your interest rate profit margin. You can protect yourself against this possibility by selling a peso futures contract for delivery in six months, or whatever the term of your peso loan is in Mexico.

You have now wrapped up a practically foolproof situation that yields perhaps 1 percent. This may seem low, but remember that most of the deal is on margin—you might put down only $2,000 or so on an $80,000 peso-futures contract in Chicago. When working such a deal you are hedging, the exact opposite of speculating.

In most other cases in the foreign currency market, however, you are likely to be speculating in what is a very high-risk field. As a foreign currency speculator, you are assuming all the risks that American importers, German exporters, and other businessmen in world trade want off their shoulders. The makers of Volkswagens don't want to be priced out of the United States market by a rise in the value of the mark. Japanese manufacturers of hi-fi equipment want to avoid losing customers abroad through an overvaluation of the yen. American importers of Swiss watches don't want to lose business by a revaluation of the Swiss franc. American exporters of soybeans are afraid of losing money if they get paid in depreciated British pounds.

The main business of these people is to turn out cars, make hi-fi equipment, sell Swiss watches and American soybeans. Their main business is *not* the foreign exchange market, and many of them do not want to be in this market at all. They seek protection in the foreign currency markets by buying or selling foreign money to offset the liabilities they have assumed in marks, yen, pounds, or whatever in world trade.

But they will not be able to get such protection unless there are speculators like you in the market willing to assume that risk. By speculating in foreign currency, you are therefore greasing the wheels of world trade. You do not need to put up large amounts of money, but what you do put up is ventured at great risk. In return, the market can give you huge returns—if you are shrewd and lucky.

13

How to Speculate and Win

THREE OUT of every four speculators in the commodities markets lose money, according to a government study. How can you be sure you are the fourth, that makes a fortune? The same government study suggests some techniques that will help you win. We'll get to those techniques later in this chapter, but first let's take a look at the losers and see what makes them losers.

You might have the idea that the loser is invariably the little guy, the outsider with only a contract or two, who gets clobbered by the big full-time operators who have more money, more time, and better inside information. This is by no means always the case. In fact, it is often the big-time professionals who take the biggest losses. This appears to be particularly true in the cocoa futures market.

There is something about cocoa futures that seems to drive cocoa experts mad. Speculating in cocoa can turn a studious, serious, honest technician into a rigid dogmatist who is so convinced of his own infallibility that he becomes a loser on a colossal, heroic, epic, legendary scale. In 1970, a cocoa specialist in Basel, Switzerland, took the local branch of the United California Bank of Los Angeles on a cocoa-buying spree that ended up with a $40 million loss for the bank. He became so convinced that a cocoa tree disease and the Biafra-Nigeria civil war would disrupt the world cocoa market that he managed to buy more than 14,000 contracts, which represented half the cocoa in the world. What in fact happened was that cocoa production just chugged along in West Africa, civil war or no civil war, and the price rise he anticipated never happened.

In 1973, William Baird & Company, a British firm, revealed a loss of nearly $4 million as a result of unauthorized operations by its cocoa dealer. This feat was eclipsed, however, by Rowntree Mackintosh Limited, a British chocolate and food company, which admitted a loss of $48 million at about the same time. Rowntree also blamed its cocoa expert, but this expert was selling cocoa futures, not buying them. The market is quite impartial—buyers and sellers get treated with equal severity if they make mistakes and persist in their errors.

The *Wall Street Journal* had this comment: "A characteristic of the cocoa business seems to be that a dealer gets carried away," Sir Donald Barron, Rowntree chairman, said in an interview. "A man can develop 'an absolute conviction that his view of future price trends is correct, even though the market as a whole is moving the other way. In the process a dealer 'plunges deeper and deeper into his position' he said. The Rowntree dealer involved 'still believes' that he was doing the right thing for the company, the chairman said, reaffirming the formal announcement that there isn't any evidence of fraud or personal gain."

These, in fact, are textbook examples of why so many speculators lose in the futures markets. The futures market is no place for pig-headed people who insist that they always know better than anybody else and that they are always right.

Cocoa is not the only example. Professional, big-time operators have taken terrific beatings in other futures markets as well. In 1973 the Union Bank of Switzerland, one of the big three Swiss banks, reportedly lost $50 million in foreign exchange speculation, and a big German bank, the Landesbank Girozentrale, dropped about $110 million. In mid-1974 the Franklin National Bank of New York took a loss of nearly $46 million in foreign currency deals. The bank was so badly hurt that trading in Franklin shares was suspended. In June, 1974, the Herstatt Bank of West Germany broke all previous records with an estimated $200 million loss, and was ordered into liquidation by the West German authorities. European bankers are secretive people and bankers who lose $200 million tend to be especially tight-lipped, but apparently Herstatt's foreign exchange expert was betting that the German mark would go down. It went up instead, and broke the bank.

On the other side of the coin, we have the winners. They tend to be shy people — perhaps they don't want any unnecessary problems with the Internal Revenue Service. But there are plenty of them. Several hundred speculators are reputed to have made more than $1 million each in soybean futures in the 1972-73 period. Studies show, in fact, that a successful speculator can be wrong more than half the time and still come out ahead if he uses the right techniques.

The question for you is how to end up in the winner's corner. For the brutal fact is that most speculators lose money most of the time in the commodity futures markets. According to one estimate, the novice speculator might last eighteen months in the futures markets before he is wiped out. There are even some ex-brokers who admit they never had a single customer who ended up with a profit as a commodity speculator. According to others, professional insiders have simply too much of an edge over the outsider — they are actually in the copper business or the grain trade and they have access to information that the outside speculator simply does not get, or in any event receives too late.

Some critics also complain that United States commodity

markets as they are now constituted allow manipulation by a few powerful individuals. "Floor traders," according to one critic, "can sell sufficiently large quantities of a given commodity to induce a panic sell-off. By trading for their own accounts during such breaks, traders reap windfall profits. These profits come, of course, from the average American investor, who is ignorant of such surreptitious machinations and who is unknowingly the victim of a capricious market. Contributing to such artificial price movements are tax spreads, or the initiation of a completely hedged position between two floor trades for tax purposes only. To the analyst, professional as well as amateur, the distortions in volume and open interest figures that result can be disastrous. Yet such action, if arrived at by open outcry on an exchange floor, is perfectly legal."

What protection do you have against such manipulations? In 1974, as this is written, nothing is really 100 percent foolproof. Some exchanges are regulated by the Commodity Exchange Authority, which operates under the Department of Agriculture. Regulated commodity markets include boneless beef, cattle, orange juice, corn, cotton, fresh shell eggs, feeder cattle, live hogs, milo, oats, pork bellies, potatoes, soybeans, soybean meal and oil, wheat, and wool. The remainder are unregulated markets that are not directly supervised by the Commodity Exchange Authority, and in these the policing depends entirely on the integrity and efficiency of the exchange itself. In fact, only the Chicago Board of Trade and the Chicago Mercantile Exchange have full-time auditing employees. However, in 1974 Congress was at work on a bill to create a new Commodity Futures Trading Commission which would have much tougher enforcement powers and authority to regulate *all* American commodity markets.

Perhaps your best protection is the size of the market. The bigger the market, the harder it is to rig. So check the open interest figures before you plunge into any market. If you can count the contracts in thousands you are safer than if

there are only a few hundred. Where there are tens of thousands of contracts in existence, the manipulators are going
to have a hard time making a dent in the price trend. If
there are only a few dozen contracts on the market, this is no
place for you to be. It is not merely a question of possible
manipulation, it is a question of liquidity, of finding a buyer
or a seller at all. We shall get to some of these problem
markets further on in this chapter.

"Of all the ways of speculating," says Merrill Lynch,
among the biggest brokers in the business, "one of the most
risky is speculating in commodity futures. But commodity
speculation also holds out the lure of big, quick profits."

"A person of small means, cautious temperament, and
inexperience should avoid the risks of the commodity futures,"
Merrill Lynch adds. "But a knowledgeable and well-financed
trader can find opportunities for high profits on the commodity exchanges — if he knows what he is doing."

So what does it take exactly to be a successful commodity
speculator? We can tell you this with some statistical precision,
using the results of a nine-year study made by the United
States Department of Agriculture. The department's Commodity Exchange Authority examined 417,906 futures trans-
actions made over nine years by 8,922 traders in wheat, corn,
oats, and rye futures. Of these, 142 were hedgers and do not
concern us here, since they were the very opposite of
speculators, they were trying to dump all their risks on to the
speculators. The other 8,782 were speculators like you, and
only 25 percent of them ended up with a net profit.

Here is what the winners did right, according to the
government study. If any one trading technique of the winners
could be called the most important one, this was it: *Limit
losses; let profits run.* This rule is absolutely essential for your
success as a trader.

The government study says that the losers "showed a clear
tendency to cut their profits and let their losses run." Why?
Because that is human nature. As the Association of Commodity Exchange Firms points out in a booklet, "it comes easy

to take a profit (that is a happy occasion). It is more difficult to take a loss (this is an unhappy occasion—one has to admit one is wrong). It is typical to feel that, when the market prices move against one's position, the market is wrong and will eventually correct itself to one's own estimate of the situation. So one holds on against a current trend: he lets his losses run."

On the other hand, the average speculator is seduced by a fatal siren song—the saying that one never goes broke taking a profit. So as soon as he has a small gain, he cashes in quickly, impelled, perhaps, by a broker who is eager for frequent commissions and prepared to nibble his clients to death with small profits. The combination of these two tendencies is absolutely disastrous.

To imitate the winners in the government study, you should do exactly the opposite. Every time you buy or sell a contract, put a stop-loss order under it. This ensures that if the market turns against you by even a small amount, you will be sold out automatically. Your losses are always cut short. The smart trader also never meets a margin call. When he is asked to put up more margin, he accepts this as incontestable proof that he was wrong to begin with and simply abandons his entire position in the market.

On the other side of the coin, the winner, according to the government study, is never in a hurry to cash in his profits when the market is going his way. If you do like him you just let your profits run. You know that when a particular commodity is rising or falling it is likely to continue doing so for some time. You wait until the first serious sign that this trend is coming to an end, moving up your stop-loss orders behind you, before getting out of the market with your loot.

If you follow the above system, you will ensure that your losses will always be cut short by stop-loss orders or by the refusal to meet margin calls. You also make sure that your profits pile up for as long as possible until the first setback touches off the stop-loss order you have trailing behind you.

If you find yourself on a long winning streak, you may even add to your position in pyramid fashion. Suppose you buy three corn futures contracts to begin with. The price rises. You buy two more. The price goes up again. You buy one more. You are now in a very strong position, for if the market begins to go down, your single top-price contract will be the first to show a loss, and you can still sell out the other five lower-priced ones at a profit. This is the typical winner's technique.

The typical loser does just the opposite. He buys one contract. The price goes up. He becomes more enthusiastic and buys another two. The price goes up again and he buys three more. He is now in a very vulnerable position, because as soon as the market turns he is liable to take a loss on his three top-price contracts. These will wipe out any profit he still can make on his three lower-price purchases.

Now let's analyze the winner's technique mathematically. It allows you to end up with an overall profit *even if you are wrong six or seven times out of ten*. The mathematics is obvious when you stop to think about it: seven losses of $5 each equals $35. Three profits of $50 each equals $150. Your net profit balance on ten trades: $115.

What it all boils down to is that the leverage of the futures markets *forces you to think big* if you want to be successful. "The dangers are too great for a man who expects to be content with a small profit," Merrill Lynch warns. "You should not initiate a trade unless your profit objective is substantial...it is foolish to initiate a position in wheat with a profit objective of less than 6 cents a bushel, or in soybeans with a profit objective of less than 8 to 10 cents."

Merrill Lynch cites case histories of five speculators who made small profits on no less than 79 percent of their trades and still wound up losing money in the end. It then cites another case in which the speculator made twenty-seven trades at a loss against only seventeen at a profit, but they were big gains and left him with a net profit of $3,593.

The government study spotlights other characteristics and techniques of the successful speculator. The study concluded that the big speculators were not any more successful than the smaller ones. Even more remarkable, it found that "special knowledge of the commodity traded seemed to have little effect on the outcome of speculative trading." Perhaps the operators without "special knowledge" were those avoiding hot tips.

Most studies stress that reliable information (not necessarily inside knowledge) is essential to you as a speculator. Throughout this book we have shown you where to get information on individual commodity markets. There are more general sources available, covering every field that might be of interest to you.

For a general view of how the United States economy is doing, write to the Superintendent of Documents, Government Printing Office, Washington, D.C. 20402 for *Survey of Current Business.* This monthly publication of the United States Department of Commerce (annual subscription $20, single copy $2.25) gives you a battery of statistics on everything from commodity prices to construction figures; lumber sales; wool, cotton, and copper production, imports, exports, and consumption; monetary statistics; foreign trade figures; grain and livestock production figures; cocoa, coffee, and sugar imports; as well as many other items.

A similar publication is the Commerce Department's monthly *Business Conditions Digest,* which runs charts and graphs on the gross national product, employment, and the money supply, as well as a number of indexes and indicators of the future intentions of businessmen and consumers. These figures are used by business analysts and forecasters. Yearly subscription is $15, single issue $1.50.

You can also get broad information from private sources. One of these is the Commodity Research Bureau, 1 Liberty Plaza, 47th floor, New York, New York 10036. The bureau provides regular periodical information on commodities, in addition to its *Commodity Year Book,* which comes out each July ($19.95 per copy). The bureau's other publications include a weekly bulletin on the various commodity futures markets, a weekly service of 150 price charts, and a daily computer trend analyzer showing trends in dozens of different commodity markets.

All big brokerage houses also distribute market letters on most major commodities. Among those who do are Merrill Lynch, Bache & Company, the Siegel Trading Company, and Reynolds Securities Incorporated.

Commodities (1000 Century Plaza, Columbia, Maryland 21004) is a monthly magazine devoted entirely to articles and information on the commodity futures markets.

Consensus (P.O. Box 19086, Kansas City, Missouri 64141) is a weekly publication that offers you the United States Department of Agriculture crop, livestock, and price reports and other important data, together with charts on commodity trading and transcripts of different market letters.

The *Yearbook* of the Chicago Mercantile Exchange ($4.50 postpaid from the Exchange, 444 West Jackson Blvd., Chicago, Illinois 60606) contains the daily price ranges for the previous year of all the commodities traded on that exchange. It gives the contract specifications of each commodity, as well as statistical information on live cattle, pork bellies, hogs, eggs, lumber, milo, potatoes, beef, turkeys, hams, and other products.

Advisory Services

If you had an infallible, surefire, foolproof way of making money in the commodities markets, the stock market, or in any other market, would you shout it out to everybody from the rooftops? Or would you keep it a secret and quietly go about your business making money for yourself? Would you advertise in the papers offering your Midas secret to the public at large?

That is what a number of investment advisory services do. In the stock market alone, where such services have to register with the Securities and Exchange Commission, there are about 4,000 of them, with nearly half a million customers. They plug everything from the Garfield Drew odd-lot theory, which assumes the little investor is always wrong, to the Investors Intelligence Sentiment Index, which theorizes that the majority of investment advisers are always wrong. You pay your money and you take your choice.

Now what do these services have to offer you in the way of making a profit for yourself? The common sense answer is that if they were 100 percent sure of their own judgement they would not be peddling the service to you or to anyone else, but would be using it for their own benefit.

You should be on your guard for other reasons besides this basic flaw. For example, if a service has a large following in a small market, perhaps it can manipulate that market to its own advantage. It could do this by running a favorable recommendation on a penny stock or a thinly traded commodity that it happens to own and then unloading the merchandise on its unwary subscribers at inflated prices.

Merrill Lynch has this recommendation: "If you are an inexperienced trader in commodities, trade only in broad markets."

Until you really know what you are doing, here are some of the markets you should probably stay away from.

Propane Gas

Propane gas is used mainly on farms and outlying homes beyond the urban gas distribution network. Since 1960, its normal price range had been from 2 to 8 cents a liquefied gallon; but in early 1974 an unusual combination of causes pushed the price up as high as 50 cents. Washington then began planning to impose a strict mandatory allocation of propane so as to ensure an adequate supply to big farm states, where it is of critical importance in drying crops.

Propane gas is traded on the New York Cotton Exchange in contracts of 100,000 gallons. At 20 cents a gallon this would amount to $20,000 and the minimum margin would be around $1,000.

This is leverage with a very high profit potential, but at the time of writing there are less than 600 contracts in existence. Until the market gets bigger let's stay away from this one.

Take a look also at this tabulation of one day's trading:

N.Y. COTTON EXCHANGE

	Open	High	Low	Close		Prev. Close	Life of Contr. High	Low
PROPANE [M.B.]								
Sept.	†22.40	22.90	22.85	†22.90-	—	†22.40	25.40	6.05
Dec.	†23.10	23.60	23.60	†23.60-	#	†23.10	26.00	7.90
Jan.	†23.20	—	—	†23.70-	—	†23.20	26.00	8.00
Mar.	†23.50	—	—	†23.70-	—	†23.50	25.50	8.95
May	†23.90	—	—	§24.10-	—	§23.90	24.60	8.70
July	†24.30	—	—	§24.30-	—	§24.30	26.00	17.35
Sept.	†24.50	—	—	§24.50-	—	§24.50	26.00	23.70

Now that looks like a mighty impressive table. But read the footnotes:

†—Bid   —Asked   *—Nominal   s— Settling Price

Nearly all those quotes were bid prices or asked prices in which no seller or no buyer was found. In fact there was practically no trading at all, as you will confirm by checking this tabulation of actual sales figures:

Sales

LIQUEFIED PROPANE Gas (M.B.)
—Sept., 6; Dec., 2. Total, 8

Buyers and sellers were so scarce and so far apart in their demands that only six September and two December contracts were sold. In all other months nobody was able to buy or to sell at what he considered a reasonable price. This is no market to be in if you want to get out in a hurry.

This maybe is a good place to lay one fear to rest. Perhaps you have had a nagging worry that in trading commodity futures you will suddenly find yourself facing a mountain of 30,000 pounds of boneless beef dumped on your doorstep because your futures contract expired, or that forty steers from that live cattle contract will soon be bellowing in your front yard, or that 112,000 pounds of sugar will be stacked up against your front door. In the case of propane, you have even more to worry about—this gas is stored under pressure and may explode. But have no fear, it will *never* be delivered to you. The worst that could happen is that you would be required to take delivery of your 100,000 gallons at a designated storage point near Houston, Texas. You would then get a certificate of ownership and a $120 bill for each month's storage while you figured out what to do next.

Fuel Oil, Heating Oil, Gasoline, Crude Petroleum And Charter Tanker Rates

The energy crisis brought on by the Arab oil embargo against the United States in October, 1973, set off a race between American commodity markets to meet the situation by creating futures contracts in oil industry products and services.

First off the mark was the New York Mercantile Exchange, which in April, 1974, announced it was planning to initiate trading in fuel oil and heating oil contracts as well as futures contracts in oil tanker freights. If trading in these contracts proved successful, the exchange said it would also consider futures contracts in gasoline and crude oil.

As this book was going to press these markets were not yet functioning. When they do start up you might see how much activity they generate in daily trading before you plunge into an uncharted oil futures market.

The Mercantile Exchange announced these plans:

Fuel oil (the variety used by heavy industry) would be traded in contracts of 750 barrels each, for delivery up to eighteen months ahead.

Heating oil contracts would have the same specifications and delivery dates.

Tanker freight contracts would be traded in units of 500 tons each, with deliveries scheduled as far as three years ahead — an unusually long time span in commodity markets. One freight contract would allow speculation in the cost of chartering a tanker to carry oil from the Persian Gulf to Rotterdam, Holland. Another contract would cover the route from the Persian Gulf to Aruba, a Dutch island in the Caribbean. These two contracts would allow you to speculate in the highly volatile cost of carrying Arab oil to Europe and America.

At the time of writing, the Mercantile Exchange had not announced any specifications of gasoline or crude oil futures contracts. The New York Cotton Exchange, which was planning a crude oil futures contract with a Rotterdam delivery, said it would offer contracts of 5,000 barrels each.

Potatoes

The United States produces about 300 million hundredweight of potatoes a year. Of these, 125 million are served on the dining table, 38 million are used for frozen French fries, 34 million are made into potato chips, 30 million are consumed on the farm where they are grown, 23 million are dehydrated, 17 million are required for seed, 7 million are used for starch and flour, 9 million are fed to livestock, and 4 million are canned. The United States, incidentally, is a relative lightweight in the potato league—the Soviet Union produces six times and, Poland more than three times as many potatoes. Nevertheless, the futures market is an all-American one since there are almost no imports and exports.

According to USDA reports, people eat just about the same number of potatoes whether the price is high or low. The major influence on price, therefore, is the variation in the supply. Changes in the supply can result in dramatic price changes. In June, 1972, for example, Hurricane Agnes pounded the northeastern states for about a week. The damage to the potato crop pushed prices up from $2.25 per 100 pounds to as high as $9.50 in the following months.

In spite of the highly leveraged positions possible in potato futures, however, this is a good market to avoid. Potato futures are traded on the New York Mercantile Exchange (contract of 50,000 pounds of Maine potatoes for delivery in New York), and on the Chicago Mercantile Exchange (contract for delivery of 50,000 pounds of Idaho potatoes). The Chicago market, at least, is small enough to make unethical manipulation quite feasible. In September, 1972, seventeen companies and individuals were accused by the Commodity Exchange Authority of participating in opposing power plays to rig the Chicago market for their own benefit. It seems prudent to stay out of this market and let the sharpsters slug it out with each other. At the time of writing, only a few hundred contracts were in existence.

The New York market, with an open interest of 13,000 contracts or so at the time of writing, is somewhat larger. The minimum margin on Maine potatoes is $400 to $800, depending on the prevailing price per bushel. The commission per contract is $28.

This market has also been the target of recent criticism. In fact a bill was actually presented by a Maine Congressman proposing a ban on all trading in potato futures. It was backed by a number of trade and growers associations who consider the futures market detrimental to consumers, the trade itself, and traders in the futures market.

The United States Department of Agriculture Crop Reporting Board issues periodical estimates of potato crop production as of August 1, September 1, October 1, November 1, December 1, and the end of the fiscal year as well as storage stocks as of January 1, February 1, and March 1.

Eggs
This is a fairly active market, with trading reaching about $35 million a day in Chicago. The contract is for 750 cases of 30 dozen eggs each, commonly known as one carload. In other words each contract you buy represents 22,500 dozen eggs. Eggs are also traded on the Pacific Commodity Exchange. In July, 1974, the Chicago Mercantile Exchange started a second egg market—this one for nest-run eggs, which are ungraded eggs as opposed to the older, graded shell-egg contract.

The United States Department of Agriculture's Crop Reporting Board gives monthly production figures as well as monthly statistics on hens and pullets of laying age on United States farms, egg-type chicks hatched by commercial hatcheries, and the egg-feed ratio (the number of pounds of laying feed equivalent in value to one dozen eggs). The USDA also reports on cold storage holdings of eggs, the monthly average price received by farmers, and the average wholesale price of eggs at Chicago.

However a number of people are unhappy with the egg market for various reasons. Like the potato futures market, the egg market is in danger of being legislated out of existence. This does happen occasionally—the onion futures market, for example, has already been banned by an act of Congress. One egg producers association has indicated it will support legislation to ban trading in egg futures.

Platinum

Ounce for ounce, platinum is one of the most valuable materials on earth. It is nearly twice as dense as lead and at times it has been as much as eight times more valuable than gold.

Platinum futures contracts are traded on the New York Mercantile Exchange in units of 50 ounces each. The minimum margin is $1,000 and the minimum commission $40. Delivery months are January, April, July, and October.

There are two problems with the platinum futures market. The first is that among the 26 most actively traded commodities, platinum ranks about twentieth. Unless public interest in the futures market builds up, you may have to sit on your contract for some time in such a thin market. The second problem is that the Soviet Union produces more than half the world's platinum (about 2 out of 3.5 million ounces), and Soviet policy, as Winston Churchill once remarked in another connection, is "a riddle wrapped in a mystery inside an enigma." The platinum futures market, in a word, is a sort of Russian roulette. The Russians publish no figures—you do not know how much they are producing, how much they are selling, where they're selling, or at what price. There is no reliable way of discovering these things.

To compound the problem even further, the United States produces a minuscule 30,000 ounces a year and consumes about 40 percent more platinum than is produced in the entire free world. It has to import about one million ounces a year and is dangerously dependent on the Russians for this strategic material. Washington protects itself by maintaining a stockpile, which in recent years has been around 500,000 ounces. This stockpile creates further uncertainty, since some of it might be dumped on the market if relations improve significantly with Moscow.

Platinum is indeed a highly interesting investment, but not through the futures market. In countries where it is illegal to own gold, the white metal is a glittering attraction to people who want to protect themselves against paper currency inflation. It comes in small sheets or bars that weigh 50 ounces each. You can fit many of these tiny ingots into a bank safety deposit box. At $200 an ounce, each ingot is worth $10,000. If you are not yet rich enough to deal in such amounts, you can buy smaller quantities.

One possible source for buying platinum is Newport Metals Company, Newport, Rhode Island 02840, which sells ingots of 50 grams, equivalent to 1.6075 troy ounces. The price is based on the New York Mercantile Exchange quotations. Another seller is the Metropolitan Rare Coin Exchange Incorporated, 1398 Avenue of the Americas, New York 10019, which sells platinum bars of one and ten ounces.

However platinum is not sought only or even primarily by hoarders of precious metals. It is a working metal, and about 70 percent of platinum production is used by the electrical and chemical industries. The oil, dental and medical equipment, jewelry, and glassmaking industries each use about 5 percent. Perhaps more significant is the possible use of the metal in a gadget to clean up automobile exhaust fumes. If the demand for this anti-pollution device increases, it could cause a prolonged worldwide platinum boom, and if you own shares in the producing companies you may do very well indeed. South African platinum mines, notably Impala and Rustenburg, supply about half the free world's consumption of the metal. South African mining sources estimate that by 1975 the auto manufacturers will need an additional one million ounces, and they believe they control the only source of supply where production can be increased swiftly to meet the demand.

In 1973 Rustenburg was building up its capacity to a potential 1.3 million ounces a year. Impala has a ten-year contract with General Motors to supply 300,000 ounces of platinum and 120,000 ounces of palladium a year. Impala shares are not available in the United States, but you can buy shares in Union Corporation Limited, which owns 46 percent of Impala. You cannot buy directly into Rustenburg either, but you can buy shares of Potgietersrust Platinums Limited, Waterval (Rustenburg) Platinum Mining Company Limited, and Union Platinum, each of which owns about one-third of Rustenburg.

Palladium

Everything we said about platinum futures applies in spades to the palladium futures market, which is a much smaller affair. Palladium is traded on the New York Mercantile Exchange in 100-ounce lots. The open contracts usually amount to only a few hundred. You thus have a very thin market. The Russians control about two-thirds of the world's supply of palladium, but the United States accounts for more than half the world's consumption. Washington keeps a strategic stockpile of *one billion* ounces of palladium that also hangs over the market like a potential avalanche.

Palladium and platinum belong to a related group of metals that also includes rhodium, iridium, osmium, and ruthenium. You might call palladium the poor man's platinum. For years before 1963 the price of palladium varied between $15 and $24 an ounce. In the 1960s it pushed up to the $40 level, and by 1973, with the possible auto emission boom pushing it higher together with platinum, palladium rose to the $80 level. Platinum hit a high of $300 an ounce in July, 1968, and in 1973 was trading somewhat below $200 an ounce — despite the prospect of its imminent widespread use as a catalyst in pollution devices.

Mercury

This is a dying industry and a dying futures market. Mercury futures are traded on the New York Commodity Exchange, but the open contracts usually number less than two dozen.

Behind this there is a situation of dwindling United States production. In previous years production had ranged from 15,000 to 30,000 flasks a year, but in 1972 it dropped to 6,300 and in 1973 to about half that amount. (Each flask contains 76 pounds of mercury.) By 1973, only a dozen small mines were working in the United States. Mercury hit a high of $725 a flask in July, 1965, and dropped to a low of $145 in April, 1972. If you are connected with the mercury business you might make some good profits with well-timed buying and selling, but the futures market has little to offer the outsider.

This is a real insider's market, since a mere eighty firms account for most of the United States consumption of about 50,000 flasks a year. World production is somewhere around 280,000 flasks. Mercury is produced mainly in Spain, Italy, Mexico, and Yugoslavia. The United States depends on these countries for about half its supplies. As in other similar commodities, Washington maintains a strategic stockpile of about 200,000 flasks, which can, and on occasion has, upset the market considerably by government disposal programs.

Cattle Hides

The United States is the world's biggest cattle hide producer. However, this is only a small futures market on the New York Commodity Exchange. If you don't have inside knowledge of the business, stay away from it.

Price changes depend on factors that are hard for the layman to ferret out, but that may be highly profitable for the insider. For instance, in 1973 a spokesman for the British Footwear Manufacturers Federation stated that many Latin American countries had a plentiful supply of leather, which they were retaining to expand their own footwear industries, while the world price of leather was rising due to leather shortages. The only public information available is through esoteric trade publications, such as the British trade journal *Leather* or the newsletter on the American hides and leather trade published by the Tanners' Council of America, 411 Fifth Avenue, New York 10016.

The trade itself is big business. The United States produces about 35 million hides a year. According to the Tanners' Council, the United States exported 18 million pieces in 1972, a large part of which came back to the American market. The council's report said, "We bought more than $1 billion in shoes and leather goods abroad made from the raw material we furnished."

Price changes in hides can be dramatic. In 1972, prices of top-quality United States cowhide rose 150 percent to as much as 50 cents a pound. One big reason was that Argentina, source of about one-tenth of the world supply, banned all hide exports because it was trying to rebuild its cattle herds. Australia and Brazil, which account for another 10 percent of the world supply, took similar measures. It was a golden opportunity if you were in the know, but there seems to be no really practical way of getting into the futures market at a profit unless the market expands considerably and you are able to get better information than is readily available now.

Wool

This is a curious market. Wool prices, both spot and future, showed spectacular increases in 1973, rising from the lowest level in the last twenty years to about three times that level in a few months. Despite all the profit leverage offered by the futures market, however, there was practically no increase in trading activity. "This strange combination of soaring prices and practically no volume," *Barron's* magazine commented, "led to rumors that someone was trying to corner the market."

The futures market is an adjunct of the New York Cotton Exchange, and the contract is for 6,000 pounds of grease wool. The open interest amounts to a few hundred contracts.

Futures prices in New York tend to follow the prices in Australia and New Zealand, where wool is sold at big auctions. Australia accounts for about one-third of the world's wool production of five to six billion pounds a year; New Zealand and the Soviet Union each account for about 10 to 15 percent. Argentina, South Africa, and Uruguay together produce around 20 percent of the world total. The United States has been producing less and less wool every year. Production dropped from about 270 million pounds in 1940 to approximately 115 million pounds in 1973, despite a government subsidy on homegrown wool. It thus imports more than half its wool from abroad.

The decline is due mainly to the fact that wool faces growing competition from man-made fibers for clothing. The vagaries of fashion can have a drastic effect on the market, as wool comes into or falls out of favor. The United States sheep herd has been shrinking for years, and a sudden upsurge in demand cannot be met too readily. Sheep cannot be grown overnight.

Because of these and other factors, this is in fact a moribund futures market, in which the exchange has been buying up broker's seats for about $200 each. However, if you think the wool futures market might stage a revival sometime soon, you might consider asking the exchange to sell you one of these seats as a speculation. Markets do revive sometimes, and wool might follow the example of the coffee futures market, which suddenly revived after years of inactivity.

Flaxseed

Flaxseed futures are traded on the Minneapolis Grain Exchange in the United States and on the Winnipeg Grain Exchange in Canada. The United States and Canada account for about half the total world production of flaxseed, producing around 10 million bushels each. Flaxseed is used in the paint industry and for livestock feed. Flax itself, of course, is a raw material for the textile industry, being the source of linen.

The flaxseed futures market serves as an example of the dangers of a small market. In August, 1973, trading in flaxseed was suspended for several days after days of trading in which the contract price rose constantly the maximum limit of 20 cents a day. These limit rises paralyze the market, since all trading stops as soon as the allowable increase is reached and no business is done until the following day. The shorts—that is, people who have sold contracts—are then locked in and can only watch helplessly as the market rises day after day without giving them a chance to get out before their losses pile up into disastrous proportions.

The problem became a crisis in this case when it became known that the United States flax crop would be only three-quarters of the level previously predicted. This created a situation in which everyone was a buyer and there were no sellers. It was even suggested by knowledgeable sources that somebody had cornered the market and was refusing to sell until the price went through the roof. The shorts, meanwhile, were getting squeezed to death.

How to Avoid Getting Squeezed

Obviously, you don't want to get yourself boxed into such a corner in any market, big or small. As a general rule, therefore, you should avoid contracts that are too close to their delivery date, because you may find yourself trapped as a result of the "technical position" of the market.

The trap is inherent in any futures market. It works like this. When you buy a futures contract you are actually *creating* a brand new contract by assuming an obligation to buy a commodity at a stated time in the future. When you want out, you sell a contract. This cancels out the one you bought, and then no one has to receive or deliver the commodity contracted for. All that happens is that some hard cash changes hands to settle the difference in price between the contract bought and the contract sold—hopefully, at a profit for you.

The number of contracts in existence at any one time (the

"open interest") may be greater or lesser than the commodity stocks actually held and approved for delivery in warehouses approved by the exchange.

This discrepancy usually does not matter until the time for delivery of a contract finally arrives. When it does come there may not be sufficient stocks of the commodity to satisfy all the open contracts. This is unfortunate for a lot of people who must deliver a commodity which they cannot possibly deliver because of the shortage of certified stocks. The "longs" then squeeze the "shorts" who find they have to pay much higher prices than they anticipated in order to fulfill their obligation to deliver.

Commodity Futures

When you trade in commodity futures you will find you have some advantages over dealing in the stock market. When you buy shares you pay a commission. When you sell you pay another commission. If you buy shares on margin, you must pay interest on the money lent you by the broker.

In commodity trading you don't pay any commissions until your transaction is closed. This means that if you buy a contract you don't pay any commission until you have liquidated it by selling a second contract. If you sell a contract, your commission isn't due until your position is closed by buying a contract.

Your margin is much greater in commodity futures than in the stock market, and you pay no interest on it at all. The reason for this is that, strictly speaking, nobody has lent you any money until the delivery date of your contract arrives. And you are never going to take or make delivery. Instead, you are going to cancel your position with a buy or a sell order before the delivery date arrives. You are thus putting up only 10 percent or so and getting about 90 percent of your speculative funds interest-free.

However, do not assume that there are no carrying charges in commodity futures. There are, but they are built into the price of the futures contract. Thus, you pay them indirectly. All other things being equal, the price of wheat for future delivery will be the current or spot price plus the carrying charges from today until the date of delivery. The carrying charges are the storage costs—which in the case of wheat might be 1.75 cents a bushel per month—plus the cost of fire insurance and the interest that might have been earned by the money invested in the wheat. Altogether, these charges might come to 2.5 cents a bushel per month. You should therefore add 2.5 cents a month to the current price of wheat in order to find out what the cost of wheat *should be* worth six months or a year ahead.

What *should be* of course, may not be what actually is. The futures price of wheat may be higher in anticipation of a poor crop next harvest or lower in expectation of a big one. If the futures contract is selling for more than this differential above the current price, it is said to be at a "premium."

To be a speculator you must have one essential qualification that should be obvious. You must have funds that are genuine "risk capital," the loss of which will not put you into a disastrous financial position.

How much should you have? As a minimum, your risk capital should be at least three times the original margin required to buy or sell one futures contract of the commodity in which you are interested. There is a psychological reason for this, too. If one has every trading dollar committed on one contract, a slight turn in the market may cause one to panic or force one to take an unnecessary loss through liquidation.

What else do you need to be a winner—to be the one speculator out of four who makes money from the three losers? Merrill Lynch sums it up this way: "Before you buy or sell a futures contract, plan your profit objective and the maximum loss you are willing to take. Study the market in which you plan to trade, or secure the services of a knowledgeable advisor or broker. Never act on "hot tips." Make your profit objective at least three times greater than the potential risk of loss you assume. Don't fight the market. If the price is going against your opinion, wait for a change before you take a position.

Once you are in the market, stick to your objectives. Ride out favorable trends until they turn the other way. Don't add to your commitment unless you have a profit on your original position. Don't add a second time unless you have a profit on the first addition. Additional positions should be added in pyramid fashion. Be prepared to accept numerous small losses. Remember it is possible to lose a number of minor skirmishes and still win the major battle. Do not risk most of your trading capital on any single trade. Generally, 5 to 8 percent should be the maximum. Use stop-loss orders to help protect your positions against trend reversals."

Do you think you can consistently follow this advice? Then size up your financial situation. Merrill Lynch will take you on as a customer if you have at least $50,000 in liquid assets and $2,000 in risk capital. You need at least $1,000 to open a margin account with this firm. Other brokers have similar policies.

If you think you need to know more before plunging into the futures markets, you can take a fourteen-lesson correspondence course in commodities trading. Write to the Association of Commodity Exchange Firms, Incorporated, Correspondence Course Director, 1 World Trade Center, Suite 1007, New York 10048.

14

Some Tropical Bonanzas

THE TROPIC regions of the world produce more than revolutions and cha-cha-cha. They also turn out such staples as coffee, the sugar to put in it, and the cocoa to drink when you get an attack of coffee nerves.

All three of these staples offer you a chance to make money. They are sold in active futures markets where the prices change from day to day. Every price change can mean a profit for the investor who has guessed right—and, of course, a loss for one who guesses wrong.

Although it is easiest to make money on these staples, the tropics also produce such extremely exotic commodities as frangipani and ylang-ylang oil for perfumes and coconut oil, which goes into artificial milk. You would find it hard to buy a barrel of ylang-ylang and even harder to sell it later, but there is a futures market in coconut oil.

First, however, let's talk about the three big staples—coffee, sugar, and cocoa. One great advantage of all three is that there is no United States government stockpile of them. Stockpiles are a constant threat to any market because the government can order sales from the stockpile when prices go up. That means prices go down, even though the investor has guessed right about shortages.

Coffee

The coffee market is a good place for the novice speculator to start. Sugar dealings are complicated by the fact there are two prices, the internal United States price and the world price paid by other countries. Cocoa recently has been more noted for the money lost in it than for the money made in it.

The coffee trade, on the other hand, is one of the simplest in the world. There are only a few big producers, so it is easy to keep an eye on supply. Consumption is almost entirely in two areas, so it is equally easy to keep up with the demand. One country, the United States, takes nearly half the world's coffee exports. Most of the other half goes to Europe, where market reporting is complete and quick.

Another factor that makes coffee speculation fairly simple is that the crop is nonseasonal — that is, coffee is coming to market all the time. Other commodities such as wheat are harvested only at certain seasons, so the price goes up and down according to the time of year. But the coffee supply is about the same all year round. This means that any price changes are due to other factors, which can be forecast in many cases.

However, there are a lot of these other factors. One, the most important, is frost in the Brazilian coffee areas. Although coffee areas are on the edge of the tropics, the coffee is mostly grown at fairly high altitudes. Coffee grows best at from 2,000 to 6,000 feet, and the higher it is grown, the better the quality. At high altitudes, frost can occur even in the tropics. Frost is generally reported in the newspapers but it does not show up in the shortage of supplies until several months later, when the frost-nipped flowers have failed to turn into coffee beans. This delay gives an alert investor time to buy coffee futures before the price goes up.

Another factor is drought in the coffee-growing areas. This is not as spectacular as frost and is not as certain to be reported. However, any news stories about drought in southern Brazil would be a buy signal for coffee futures.

Government action also has a strong effect on prices. Brazil produces more than a quarter of the world's coffee exports, and the Brazilian government has been very active in controlling its trade. It has a variety of ways of doing this, concerning foreign exchange values for coffee, but the most common is in granting (or withholding) export licenses. Thus any report that the Brazilian Coffee Institute is cutting down on licenses is a buy signal.

Another factor has been the International Coffee Agreement, or ICA. This agreement was drawn up jointly in 1962 by the growing countries and the drinking countries to keep the price of coffee fairly steady. In semiannual meetings, demand was balanced against consumption and the producing countries were given quotas — the number of bags they could export. The total of these quotas was supposed to be equal to the estimated demand. However, sometimes a country was unable to fill its quota because of crop failure, strike, or some other unpredictable event.

In such cases, the ICA divided the unfilled quota among other producing countries. The system has shown signs of breaking down since 1972, due to growing discord between producing and consuming countries, and it hasn't kept coffee futures prices from going up and down. For instance, in one year in the mid-1960s, coffee prices went up from 60 to 70 cents per pound (wholesale for "green" or unroasted coffee). This increase of 16 percent can be compared with the cocoa price movement during the same period: cocoa went up from 34 to 77 cents, an increase of 136 percent.

As this book was going to press, efforts were being made to revive the practically defunct ICA. Meanwhile, however, the producing countries were taking matters into their hands Some Central American countries had suspended coffee

exports to force prices up. Another group of producers—
Brazil, Colombia, the Ivory Coast, and Portuguese Angola—
had also banded together to push world prices higher. They
too proposed to do this by withholding supplies from world
markets. Their aim was to emulate the achievement of the
Organization of Petroleum Exporting Countries, which succeeded in quadrupling the world price of petroleum in 1973—
74.

The producing countries taking these actions accounted
for about 90 percent of world coffee production, but the success of their strategy was by no means assured. Coffee, after
all, is not as essential to the world economy as petroleum.

However, the demand for coffee is surprisingly constant,
whatever the price. The price of green coffee does not have
much effect on consumption in the United States: people
keep drinking coffee whether they are paying 70 cents or $1
a pound. Merrill Lynch comments that coffee-drinkers are
"reluctant to give up coffee even when prices rise sharply—
coffee consumption does not respond greatly to price
changes."

The New York Coffee and Sugar Exchange is one of the
oldest futures markets in the United States. It was founded in
1882 for coffee only; sugar was not added until 1916. This
well-established futures market shows that the trend in coffee
values, as in most other commodities, seems to be upward.
One reason is the constant devaluation of money due to inflation in nearly all countries. When money is worth less, it
takes more of it to buy a bag of coffee and the price of coffee
goes up.

Another reason for the rise in prices, however, may be
the rising standard of living, particularly in the industrialized
countries. In Europe, increasing prosperity has increased coffee consumption. Even Russia, as life there gets easier, is im-
porting more coffee. Proof that coffee-drinking follows the
standard of living is shown in the comparative import figures
for the United States and Europe. During the early 1960s, the
United States took 52 percent of world coffee exports. Ten

years later, the rising ease of living in Europe had increased that area's imports and Europe was taking more than half of all exports. The United States was down to 37 percent. However, coffee was still America's largest agricultural import and was right up there with oil among all imports of any kind.

Another bullish factor in the coffee trade is the more widespread use of instant coffees. By making coffee easier to use, it increases consumption. The United States uses about a fifth of its coffee imports in the form of instant coffee. Europe is lagging behind in this field. It takes fewer coffee beans to make a cup of instant than to make a cup of brewed coffee, because commercial brewing (to make the coffee that is freeze-dried) is more efficient than home brewing. As a result, a 10 percent increase in the consumption of instant coffee does not necessarily mean a 10 percent increase in the amount of coffee imported.

Coffee production in Africa and Asia is increasing, but not at a rate that threatens to lower prices. Latin America still grows 65 percent of the world's coffee. Africa turns out 30 percent. But the African coffee is a "robusta" type, with a stronger flavor than the "arabica" coffees grown in the Americas. The African variety is used largely for soluble coffee, where the "robusta" flavor can be toned down.

Still another bullish influence on the price level is the spread of coffee leaf blight in the Brazilian coffee plantations. The blight originated in Africa, but the robusta trees are more resistant to it than are the arabica bushes. Brazil is fighting the blight as well as it can, and seems to have it under control. But the blight still remains a threat to production in some of the coffee regions in central Brazil.

There seems to be little danger in the foreseeable future that production will increase so much that the price structure will be undermined. It takes four or five years for a coffee bush to get into production. It produces at a peak for ten years and then gradually declines. This means that a coffee shortage cannot force growers to plant more and so cause a glut in the next year.

The New York Coffee Exchange standard contract is for 37,500 pounds of Central American or Colombian coffee or for 32,500 pounds of Brazilian coffee. The first is called "C" contract (for Colombia) and the second the "B" contract (for Brazilian).

Most futures contract trading activity in recent times has been in the C contract. The coffee futures market hit a high in 1955, when 67,000 contracts were traded, but activity dwindled later, and between 1968 and 1971 only a few hundred lots were traded annually. This was because the ICA was keeping prices fairly steady, and the small price fluctuations did not offer speculators attractive profit opportunities.

But in 1972, some speculators noticed a possible shortage of coffee. Trading revived to a level of about 5,000 contracts outstanding at any one time. Usually about 500 are traded in one day.

In the coffee futures market you usually only have to put up about 5 percent of the total value of your contract to buy or deliver 37,500 pounds of coffee. In other words, at 70 cents a pound, you must put up about $1300 in cash. If the price goes up 10 percent, to 77 cents, you double your money.

There is a special way of dealing in coffee futures to take advantage of long-continued price trends. Merrill Lynch claims that it first called attention to this method in 1951 and "one would have made a profit on this program even if, at the end of the period, coffee's value had sunk to zero." The system is complicated and it is necessary to know the special vocabulary involved.

"One factor of great importance to any coffee trader is the existence of premiums or discounts in futures relative to 'spots' (the price for actual coffee for immediate delivery)," Merrill Lynch explains.

In a premium market, the price of each successive futures contract steps higher as one goes farther away from a spot position. (This means that a December delivery contract, for instance, is higher than an October one.)

Although premiums in futures have been considered the norm, the fact is that on certain commodities, including coffee, discounts of futures under spots have been more the rule than the exception. . . If the outlook seems bearish, distant months can trade at discounts—sometimes very appreciable ones—under spots.

In either case, as a futures contract reaches maturity, its price moves closer to the spot price. Thus any initial discount (or premium) relative to spots tends to disappear as that futures contract expires. . .If one can "buy the discount" often, the gain may be enough to outweigh any spot price decline.

Thus, the firm says, a steadily falling or rising price can make a profit for an investor who uses the system. Merrill Lynch commodity brokers are in a position to explain the system more thoroughly.

Cocoa

The first thing to remember about cocoa is that it has nothing to do with coconut. You can invest in futures deliveries of both coconut oil and cocoa, but that's the only similarity.

The second thing to remember about cocoa is that prices don't always come down after they go up. In recent market developments the experts, who remembered price falls after previous price peaks, lost millions of dollars by knowing too much. When prices hit a peak, they sold short. Small investors, who didn't know as much of the commodity's history, thought prices could keep going up. The little guys were right and the experts wrong.

Early in the 1970s, the cocoa market was chiefly notable for the amount of money lost in it. Rowntree, the big English chocolate maker, lost $48 million in six months. The Swiss subsidiary of a California bank lost $40 million the same way.

Most of these dollars were gained by investors who were either lucky or had a better idea of how cocoa prices were going.

Early in 1973, cocoa climbed to the highest price on record, 64 cents a pound, which matched the previous level set in 1954. The "experts" remembered that two years after the 1954 record was set, the price was back down to 20 cents a pound. Therefore these "experts"—one of them was the head of the cocoa supply department of the British candymaker—began to sell cocoa short. That is, they agreed to deliver cocoa in three months or six months at a price below the 65-cent level.

But cocoa prices did not go down. Instead, heavy rains in Ghana and Brazil, the two big producers, cut the crops way down. Prices went way up and the dealers had to deliver cocoa for 65 cents a pound when it cost them 80 cents or more to buy it. Since a cocoa contract is for 30,000 pounds in New York (it's only 11,000 in London) a change of 1 cent in the New York price means a change of $300 on one contract. Multiply that by the 16-cent loss and it's $4,800. Multiply that again by 1,000 contracts and it's nearly $5 million. So you can see where the money went.

And who got it? The man who bought 10 contracts for three months delivery picked up $48,000. If his broker had wanted a 15 percent margin, he would have had to put up just under $20,000, so his profit would have been 120 percent. Imagine that happening on your IBM stock in only three months. (Of course, if the experts had been right, cocoa would have gone down and the speculator would have lost most of his $20,000.)

Remember, in commodities, for every dollar lost by somebody, somebody else gains a dollar. However, because both sides pay commissions to the broker, he *always* comes out ahead (unless he gets the fever of speculation—and some of them do).

Cocoa grows all over the world and is consumed all over the world, so you might think it would be hard to keep up with the supply and demand. Luckily for traders, however, there are a couple of bottlenecks where cocoa activity is concentrated, and these make it easy to keep track of what is going on. The bottlenecks are the grinding centers. Most of them are in Europe but some are in America. Holland is the biggest such center, and the Dutch grinding figures, announced regularly, are a major factor in moving prices up or down. There are twenty-two growing countries, a hundred consuming ones, but only eight grinding ones. Those eight are the bottlenecks which show how much cocoa is coming in and how much is going out to the world's candy-makers, ice-cream makers, and chocolate-cake bakers.

What is grinding? To find out, let's follow the cocoa bean from the Ghana farm to the Hershey bar. In Ghana (or Nigeria, Brazil, Ecuador, or the Togo Islands in the Pacific) there are groves of spindly looking small trees. Growing out from their trunks are large fruits that look like melons. Unlike most fruits, these grow directly from the trunk and do not hang from branches. A man with a machete comes along and cuts the red or yellow ripe fruit. Technically, it is a berry. It contains from thirty to forty cocoa beans and is about ten inches long. Still using his machete, the worker cuts the fruit open and scoops out the seeds. They are piled high and covered with palm leaves and then left to ferment. This fermentation, called "curing," frees the cocoa beans from the pulp around them. The beans are dried in the sun, packed in burlap bags, and sent to the grinding centers.

At the grinding centers, the beans are winnowed with a current of air to blow away the leaves and other litter. Then they are passed between steel rollers to break them into pieces. After further cleaning, the pieces, by now called "nibs," go to big presses that squeeze out the oily substance in the beans. This is the cocoa butter of commerce. Once free of this fatty material, the nibs are dried again and ground fine into the cocoa you buy in the supermarket. To make chocolate, the finely ground powder is mixed with sugar and some of the cocoa butter and cast into cakes. To make milk chocolate, milk powder is added to the mix before casting.

Incidentally, don't try to calculate cocoa statistics by bags. A bag means different weights in different countries.

Ceylon, for instance, uses a 112-pound bag, while Jamaican cocoa comes in 196-pound bags. To make things more complicated, United States figures are usually given in pounds and European ones in long tons, 2,240 pounds. You may even see occasional figures in "tonnes," which are metric tons of 2,204 pounds.

Even though grindings are a reasonably good index of consumption, it is also useful to know how production is coming along. If the head cocoa buyer for the British company (he's the ex-head now) had paid more attention to the Ghana rainfall figures, he might have saved his company's money and his own reputation.

Rainfall is one of the two major factors in production. Cocoa needs plenty of moisture, from 50 to 200 inches of rain a year. The exact amount needed depends on soil drainage. But if the cocoa area gets too much, production is off. The other major factor in prices is the amount of insect damage and plant disease. Too much rain increases the danger of black pod, a fungus disease that attacks the melonlike fruit and ruins it.

There are still more threats to the cocoa farmer. One is "witch's broom," another fungus that makes the shoots from the trees hang down like the straws in a broom. The most dangerous is "swollen shoot" disease, caused by a virus. Plant pathologists say a tree stricken by black pod or witch's broom can be saved by spraying, but nothing can save a tree hit by swollen shoot disease. The leaves curl, the tree stops growing, and it dies within a couple of years. Then there is the capsid bug, which feeds on the cocoa pods themselves. These insects can be controlled by spraying, but sprayers are expensive for people who own on an average only three acres of cocoa trees (Nigeria) or five acres (Ghana).

Cocoa consumption is considerably steadier than production. One authority estimates that a reduction of 25 percent in the price of cocoa will increase consumption by only 10 percent. Even when the price does change, there is a lag of 6 to 9 months before it shows up in consumption figures. That is because the manufacturers generally have a stock of cocoa on hand and sell chocolate at the old price, not changing the retail price until they begin using the new supplies.

Furthermore, change in the price of the raw bean does not always mean a change in the price of chocolate itself. Other vegetable oils—coconut oil, for example—can be substituted for cocoa butter in making chocolate bars. The flavor is not quite as rich but the price is not as high, either.

One more important factor in cocoa price changes is the position of the government in the cocoa-growing countries. In all the major growing areas, the governments have set up cocoa marketing organizations. In Ghana it is the Cocoa Marketing Board; in Brazil the organization is Cacex, the cocoa department of the government's Bank of Brazil. These government bureaus buy the cocoa from the planter and then sell it overseas. The purpose is to smooth out changes in the prices received by the grower. In good times, when world prices are high, some of the prosperity is passed along to the planter in the form of slightly higher prices. The rest the government squirrels away for a time of need. Then, when world prices fall, the government is in a position to pay the grower more for his cocoa than it is sold for overseas.

These departments also restrict their cocoa sales in an effort to keep prices more steady. The amount of actual cocoa that is stored every year is the "carryover" from one season to the next. The carryover is as important as the actual production in fixing prices, since a short crop can be made up by the carryover. This also steadies the price of cocoa in the world market.

Since 1960 efforts have been made to set up a controlling world body to balance cocoa production against demand, as has been done for the coffee market. Early in the 1970s there was tentative agreement on quotas and the prices to be sought, through the International Cocoa Organization. But the short crop drove prices up far beyond the agreed range and further talks became necessary. Nothing was decided because 80 percent of the producers and 70 percent of their customers must agree, and this can't happen when prices are high. Furthermore, the United States, the world's biggest consumer, is not a member of the organization.

There is another way besides buying futures to make money in the cocoa market. It is quite complicated, however, and should only be undertaken under the guidance of a good broker. It consists of watching for differences between the price of cocoa in London and in New York. When New York cocoa is cheaper, it is sometimes profitable to buy it in the American market, at the same time selling in London. But the differences are always small, the amounts of cocoa involved to make a noticeable profit are huge, and there are a lot of very smart cookies in the market looking for the same difference. The number of people who get rich from this practice, called "arbitrage," is very limited.

Sugar

While copper may be the commodity most affected by world politics, sugar is not far behind as a political football. Almost all the major consumers of sugar and many of the producers have special price-fixing machinery. As a result, it takes more than a short crop or a longshoremen's strike to affect the price you pay for sugar in the supermarket.

However, prices in the futures market do swing widely over a short enough time to make sugar futures an attractive speculation. After all, if you buy futures for 2 cents a pound and the price goes to 3 cents, that's a 50 percent profit, even without the leverage of operating on margin.

One thing must be explained here: there are two different kinds of futures prices. One is the United States price, which is generally about twice as high as the world price. The other is the so-called "world price," which is what sugar would bring if it had to be sold for use outside the United States or the British Commonwealth or one of the other special groupings of producers and consumers.

The normal situation since 1950 has been for sugar to sell at a higher price in the United States market than in the world market. World sugar has been at a lower price level except on a few occasions in 1950, 1957, 1963, and 1972—74; the exception has never held for longer than eighteen months at a time. When world sugar is selling at a higher price than United States sugar for several months, you might therefore conclude that you have good odds of making money by betting on a return to lower world prices. You could do this by selling one world contract while simultaneously buying a domestic contract.

Both are traded on the New York Coffee and Sugar Exchange, where your minimum margin for a contract of 112,000 pounds is $2,500. Every time sugar goes up or down one cent a pound, you have a $1,120 gain or loss on your contract. Most of the action is in the world contract—the domestic futures contract is a small, thin market.

The domestic sugar market is directed and controlled by Washington. The sugar price is highly volatile in world markets—during the six years from 1968 to 1974, it went from 1.5 cents per pound to more than 30 cents. (The lowest price on record was 0.8 cents in 1934 and the highest was 31 cents in 1920.) In order to protect consumers and producers from these wild gyrations, Congress passed the Sugar Act, which for many years has given the government power to maintain steadier prices.

The government makes an annual estimate of how much sugar the country needs for the coming year. Washington knows how much the United States cane and sugar beet growers will produce, usually about 60 percent of the country's needs.

In 1973, for instance, the government set a quota of 11.7 million tons —its estimate of total United States consumption. The domestic producers were assigned a quota of 6.4 million tons and the other 5.3 million was assigned to thirty-two other countries. As the year progresses, these foreign quotas can be readjusted so that the right amount of sugar will come to the United States market.

The foreign quotas are eagerly sought for in normal times, when world prices are lower than domestic ones. That is because sugar prices in the United States are kept high enough to make cane and beet profitable for United States farmers and plantation owners. Nobody is going to sell his sugar for 3 cents a pound if he can get a quota to send it to the United States and sell it for 8 cents.

Thus, the United States has a special relationship with its suppliers. Britain has a similar relationship with the Caribbean islands and India; France and the Common Market have arrangements with their suppliers. Russia, the world's largest sugar producer, controls the price of sugar in eastern Europe. All Cuba's crop, once the controlling factor in world prices, now goes to Russia and its friends. This means that about 90 percent of the world's sugar is sold under some fixed-price agreement.

The other 10 percent goes to the world market, which handles about 8 million tons a year. Since world production can vary by that amount from year to year, the price swings can be very wide. Therefore, the state of carryover stocks from previous years becomes highly important in figuring which way the world market will go.

Because sugar doesn't spoil, any surplus can easily be stored. These carryover stocks can be huge enough to supply the entire world market demand for a year even if short crops mean no new sugar is sold at world prices. For instance, the carryover in 1964 was 11.1 million tons, while in 1972 it was 15.7 million.

"Changes in total production, aggregate world demand and visible stock levels (carryover) ultimately become the arbiters of world sugar prices," says a report by Merrill Lynch.

> The world market is not as all-encompassing as its name might suggest, but deals with approximately 10 percent of annual sugar outturn.
>
> A change of 2 million tons in a total sugar production figure of 66 million tons might appear to be relatively insignificant. Yet when taken in the perspective of the world or free sugar market of some 6.6 million tons, such a change can have a tremendous price impact.

Judging by the carryover figures, the price of world sugar

should increase for at least a few years. Commenting on the fact that world prices in 1973 were above United States domestic levels, Bache and Company, another broker active in sugar explained:

> It may seem surprising that futures managed to embark on a major bull move in the face of the tremendous (6.1 percent) increase in world production. Changes in consumption, however, explain this apparent disparity.
>
> The long term trend of sugar consumption has been quite stable, with the combined effect of population and income causing usage to increase by 3 to 4 percent per year. . .Because of its universal appeal, lack of substitutes and relatively low price, a rise in the price of sugar has as yet not acted as a serious deterrent to consumption. As a result, the past few years have seen the gains in consumption far surpass production increases, with the result that available supplies have dwindled.

Since the world-market tonnage is so small, the report continued, "the reduction of reserve supplies has been magnified almost tenfold with respect to quantities available for export, contributing to the substantial rise in sugar futures prices."

We have seen that sugar prices were high early in the decade of the 1970s and why they rose. The logical next question is whether the prices are going to continue to rise. In other words, should you plan to buy or sell sugar futures? We can't tell you the answer, but we can give you some symptoms to look for if you want to go into the sugar market.

First of all, government actions around the world are one of the key factors in the sugar market, and they are unpredictable. As this book was going to press, for example, the United States House of Representatives voted to kill the 1934 Sugar Act. The decision meant that the law that has fixed quotas and subsidies for sugar production for the past forty years would expire December 31, 1974. Congressmen were strongly influenced by consumer advocates and soft drink manufacturers, who claimed the Sugar Act subsidies were costing American consumers about $500 million a year. They were also angry about paying subsidies to big Southern sugar growers at a time when the sugar price was going through the roof.

However, the bill still had to get through the Senate, where the sugar-growing interests could count on strong support for keeping some form of the old quota and subsidy system in force. And a third unknown quantity was the attitude of the Nixon administration. Even if the Senate went along with the House Bill to kill the Sugar Act, the President still had authority under other legislation to set quotas on sugar imports and to extend price supports to domestic sugar producers under a 1949 farm law. If the old system expired, the President could thus recreate something very similar to it if he had a mind to do so.

Do you know what is in a politician's heart? Can you predict what Congressmen, Senators, and Presidents will do? Can you foretell what actions foreign political leaders will take? If so, you could make a killing in the sugar futures market.

But there is still one skill more you will need. You must be able to anticipate how the market will react to these political measures. The House of Representatives voted to kill the Sugar Act on June 5, 1974, because it wanted to bring the price of sugar down. On June 6 the price of sugar shot up on the world sugar futures market. Speculators figured that the end of the Sugar Act meant that American buyers would have to compete with other buyers on the world market and would then drive the price up.

By the time you read this book, some of these political uncertainties will have been cleared up, and other new ones will be looming ahead to make the sugar market still one big political question mark. The uncertainties also affect the sugar growers very strongly.

There is a strong possibility that the high price early in the decade will persuade major producing countries to increase their plantings, Cuba, Brazil, and India all need foreign exchange and all are important sugar producers. However, because it takes sugar cane fourteen months and sugar beets six to eight months to grow to maturity, any increase in planting will not show up in the market for six months to a year and a half. This time lag gives you enough warning so you could get out of buying futures and sell them instead.

Another trend to watch is growing consumption. Luckily, that is fairly simple. Sugar use has levelled off pretty much—in the United States it is 97 pounds per person per year—so any increase in American consumption will be due primarily to population growth, which is 3 or 4 percent per year.

The accuracy of this forecast can be borne out by comparing estimates made in 1968 of future consumption, based on a 4 percent world population growth. This estimate showed that consumption in 1973 would be 82.7 million tons. The actual consumption was 78.4 million. The difference between the estimate made five years before and the actual figures was only 5 percent, a very low difference for such a long period. The lower consumption might have been due to the higher prices at the end of the period. Had prices remained stable, the difference between prediction and reality would have been even smaller.

There is an outside chance that factors other than population growth might increase the demand for sugar. Such factors would include the development of nonfood uses for sugar and the use of sugar cane as a cattle feedstuff. Sugar is already used to produce alcohol. Research is underway to find a means to use sugar as a raw material for the chemical industry. With oil, formerly the most important chemical feedstock, in short supply, the demand for a substitute will grow. Sugar is a possible alternative. Should sugar be used in this way, the price should stay high.

Efforts to use the cane as cattle feed are underway in Barbados on an experimental basis. Tony Crozier, a Barbados editor, says that cane feed will produce beef at a food cost of only 25 to 30 cents per pound. Furthermore, an acre of cane will support five beef cattle, compared to two animals per acre on normal feeds.

The exact economics of the system are not yet clear, because the pith, the soft inner part of the cane, must be separated from the hard outer skin before the pith can be fed to cattle. The cost of this separation is not yet certain. But the Barbados government, uncertain of future sugar prices now that Britain is in the European Common Market, has converted one sugar mill into a separation center.

If the process is feasible and its use spreads, the effect would be a further support for sugar prices. Plantation owners could make more money turning their cane into beef than they could making it into sugar. This would reduce the flow of sugar to the world market and thereby keep prices high.

Another factor might operate to make sugar scarcer and therefore more expensive. This would be a ban, now being discussed in Washington, on saccharine because of supposed cancer-producing properties. The withdrawal of cyclamates, another sugar substitute, sharply increased the demand for sugar.

These are the factors that the sugar investor should watch for in planning his course of action.

Coconut Oil

Coconut oil is one of the newest commodities to be regularly traded on a futures market, but its price has risen sharply in this decade. Formal oil futures trading only began early in the 1970s. The reason for the late arrival of oil is that copra, the raw material, was once imported instead of the finished oil. A few years ago, however, the Philippine government ruled that copra must be processed in the islands and only the oil could be exported. The idea, of course, was to make more jobs for the Filipinos.

If you take the white meat out of a coconut and dry it, you have copra. If you squeeze the copra, the coconut oil comes out. The dry white mass that is left is coconut meal, used for cattle feed. Coconut oil is shipped overseas where it is used for food, to make complicated chemicals, and for soap.

The oil is used more in Europe than in the United States, and Rotterdam, Holland, is the big market for spot sales. However, coconut oil futures are traded on the Pacific Commodity Exchange in San Francisco. The standard contract is for 60,000 pounds of oil, and there are usually only about 1,000 contracts outstanding. This means the market is pretty small and a tiny change in supplies can cause a big change in prices.

Like most other tropical products, coconut oil has gone up sharply in price in recent years. The change from the end of 1972 to the end of 1973 was about 300 percent, which means that the value of a contract went from $6,000 to $24,000. The margin on one contract at the beginning of the period might have been only $600, producing a profit of $18,000. Later, of course, when the price went up, the margin would also have increased, to some $2,500.

What makes coconut oil dealing fairly simple is that almost the whole world market is fed by the Philippines. And Philippine output is almost entirely controlled by the weather there. So if you watch the meteorological reports from Manila, you can make a shrewd estimate of which way prices are going.

The United States Department of Agriculture has figured out that you can predict Philippine coconut production with reasonable accuracy by watching the rainfall figures in the Islands. For instance, the total rainfall between January and June, 1974, will give an indication of what the coconut crop will be in March, 1975. This is because the coconut ripens all year round, about one year from the time of flowering. And flowering comes in the time of best rainfall. Armed with this information, you can foresee that a drought in 1974, for instance, will result in a short crop in 1975, and that should mean higher prices in 1975.

You should also be alert for news of typhoons in the

Philippines—they are the Pacific version of Atlantic hurricanes. A bad typhoon hitting the coconut plantations will blow down many trees, reducing the crop. New trees will be planted, but it takes 5 to 7 years before they come into production. Therefore, a bad storm could mean higher oil prices for the next 5 to 7 years.

There are other factors in the market, of course. Indonesia is a big producer but sells almost all of its oil under contract to Japan and the rest of Asia. However, a bumper crop in Indonesia, if coupled with a short crop in the Philippines, could attract Indonesian oil into the world market.

Also, coconut oil has many competitors—the oilseeds such as Canadian rapeseed, palm oil from Africa and Malaysia, and peanut oil. If coconut oil prices go too high, some of these others can be substituted. Or if there is a shortage of the other oils, coconut oil can go into those markets, thereby raising the price of the Philippine product.

American consumption of coconut oil has increased from 287,000 tons in 1960 to about 400,000 tons in the 1970s. The increase was mostly due to the growing use of coconut oil for food: margarine, cooking oil, cookies, and other bakery goods, and even to supply the creamy part of artificial milk.

For many years coconut oil was sold on the spot market for 8 to 10 cents a pound. In times of scarcity it went to 13 cents. But in the soaring market of 1973-74, it went to more than 60 cents. The reasons were a drought in the Pacific, a shortage of ships due to the fuel shortage, the higher cost of other foods, which made people turn to coconut oil, and the devaluation of the dollar, which raised prices 18 percent.

Meanwhile, however, the Philippine coconut industry—which exports to the tune of nearly $1 billion a year—was well on the way with a fifteen-year planting program. This was expected to bear fruit with sharply increased production in 1975.

15

Some All-American Products

T HE BIGGEST year so far for the commodity speculator was 1973 — but that doesn't mean there aren't bigger years in the future. Trading volume grew spectacularly in that year, and so did prices. For the first time, the dollar value of all commodities futures traded on United States exchanges exceeded the value of securities traded on the stock exchanges. Another indicator of this boom was provided by Reuters, the British news service, which keeps a commodity index. It was set up when Britain had an empire, much of it in the tropics, so the index is heavily weighted toward tropical goods. Ten of the seventeen items on the index are such tropical products as cocoa, coffee, and sugar. This index rocketed during 1973 and made new highs day after day. There were many reasons — inflation, which made the same goods cost more in devalued currencies; bad weather, which caused crop shortages; and rising standards of living, allowing many formerly austere countries to afford more of life's good things.

Prior to the seventies, the Reuter index peak was 630,

reached during the shortage period of the Korean War in 1951. The index takes the 1931 price of all seventeen items on the list and weighs them together to make a 1931 total of 100. So any price comparisons are with the depressed 1930s. Anyway, by 1951, when the Korean War broke out, the index had gradually gone up more than 500 percent. The Korean fighting shot it up sharply to 630 — a peak that stood for the next twenty-one years.

Rising costs of more raw materials pushed the index up to 762 at the end of 1972. That's where it was at the start of 1973's big rise. But 762 was just a way station on the road to the top. By the middle of 1973, the index had jumped another 50 percent and it broke through the 1,000 mark for the first time in history. By May, 1974, it was up to 1,400. In fact, in one eleven-day trading period it rose 5 percent. In July, 1974, the Dow Jones index of futures prices, an index oriented toward the United States economy, fluctuated above the 300 mark, more than double its level two years before. Nobody yet can see where the top will be as long as the world's governments keep churning out more and more paper money from their inflationary printing presses. Unless a worldwide depression knocks the bottom out of world markets the chances are that the indexes will continue to rise.

Cotton

Cotton is a product in which prices are controlled almost entirely by United States production and consumption. Although it is an important commodity in world trade, the United States is the major exporter and consumer.

For years the cotton market, once among the most active in the United States, had fallen on quiet days. Government support measures had evened out price fluctuations. Mills bought what they needed ahead of time, production was geared to demand, and if production did rise, the capacious government warehouses yawned to take in the surplus at the going price. "So why speculate in cotton?" asked a lot of people. And they didn't.

But the jump in commodity prices in 1973 was so great that it shook the somnolent cotton futures market out of its doldrums. Cotton prices started up and rose and rose and rose. While they didn't break the old price record of a dollar a pound, set in Civil War days when southern cotton was cut off from the British market, the price levels rose nearly as high. Cotton men used to say that 10-cent cotton was profitable—that is, if you could get 10 cents a pound for it you could make a living. Of course, that measure is now out-of-date, what with the price of fertilizer and taxes on cotton land and the cost of machinery to replace manpower in the cotton harvest. But there are still large profits to be made.

The rise started soon after the beginning of 1973. The United States and mainland China had been reconciled politically, and the Chinese were looking for raw materials. They came back to their traditional supplier, America, with their orders in hand.

Cotton had been as low as 31 cents in August, 1972, but soon after the first of the year Chinese buying reports had it up to 40 cents. And that was only the beginning. By July it was 56 cents, by August 75 cents, and by the end of September 86 cents. That meant that anybody who owned a bale (500 pounds) of cotton had made $230. And since the standard futures contract is for 100 bales, that means a profit of $23,000 for anybody with a single contract.

That's wonderful for 1973, but what of the future? The same factors that pushed the price up to 86 cents are still operating. Of course, there are other exporting countries that can supply the world market, such as Egypt and Pakistan. But the United States has one big advantage over them—the United States dealers will sell cotton on a two-year futures basis. No other country will sell cotton that far ahead. The user countries—Japan is the biggest importer—realize that cotton may be scarce in the coming years so they want to make certain of future supplies. The two-year contracts ensure those supplies. (These are not the kind of futures contracts you can buy if you deal on the regular exchanges—they are contracts between exporters and foreigners to buy and sell cotton within a certain price range.)

In 1973, Japan contracted for 1.2 million bales of United States cotton, about 10 percent of the total crop. China bought another million bales. In other words, nearly a fifth of the total American crop can be expected to go to the Far East.

"We expect that China will be buying a million bales of cotton or more from the United States for many years to come," said William Dunavant, one of the country's biggest cotton dealers. "It will make cotton very expensive and very tight."

Dunavant said there is another reason besides the two-year futures contracts that makes foreigners want to buy American cotton. That other reason is that they are certain the United States will be able to meet its commitments to ship the commodity; they fear that smaller countries would not honor even a one-year futures sale.

Another reason for the general bullishness in the cotton market was that the Japanese were not only buying cotton futures but they were also actually buying and storing bales of cotton—what the trade calls *physicals*. If that cotton is bought and shipped to Japan to be stored, even a United States embargo on exports would not affect its future price. The United States did forbid exports of soybeans when the price rose too high, and that has made foreigners suspicious of similar action in other commodities. In fact, the American cotton mills regularly ask for such an embargo when the price rises.

The Japanese could buy and store cotton because of the unfavorable United States trade balance with Japan. In order to pay for the Datsuns and Toyotas and Sony radios and Panasonics and so on, the United States sent more dollars than usual to Japan. Japanese exporters could sell the dollars to the Japanese cotton mills at a low price. The mills then used these cheap dollars to buy cotton in America.

There are still other factors pushing up cotton prices. The Japanese, particularly the more prosperous ones, are wearing more clothes than they once did. They have more spare shirts and they are consuming more cotton textiles.

Since cocoa prices are way up, the cocoa farmer in Ghana has more money to spend. Some of it will go on extra cotton goods for his wife's dresses. All over the world the growers of tropical crops are getting more money for their harvest and, because they are in the tropics, they are buying more cotton goods.

Cotton prices also depend on the availability of other commodities. Cotton and soybeans grow in the same climates on the same kind of soil. With soybean prices rocketing up from $2.50 a bushel to $12 in 1973, a lot of cotton land was being planted to soybeans. That means United States cotton crops will be lower as long as soybean prices are high. The same thing happens in Brazil, which has a lot of cottonland. Brazil's soybean output is leaping in the early 1970s because of the high prices; that means less Brazilian cotton to help make up for any world shortage.

The movement to conserve natural resources may have its effect as well—cotton could easily become a favorite textile of the ecology crowd. The Cotton Association bills cotton as "The Ecology Product" in a series of big billboard advertisements. Cotton, they say, is a purely vegetable product, produced directly from the soil. That means its production per acre is higher than wool, since a sheep requires a good many acres of grazing land. Unlike synthetic fibers, cotton does not need any processing in odoriferous chemicals (you can smell some rayon factories for miles). Cotton is self-destructing when exposed to the weather, unlike many plastics and other synthetic fibers. Therefore it is non-polluting. Since cotton is a plant, it gives off oxygen when it is growing. Sheep, on the other hand, breathe in oxygen and breathe carbon dioxide. That may seem to you like a small thing but to a devoted ecology fan it's a big one.

On the other hand—the Cotton Association doesn't say this, but the sheep people do—the cotton plant takes nourishment from the soil. The sheep do, too, but they return some of it in the form of manure. However, none of this advertising and counter-advertising was able to affect cotton prices as they made their big 1973 jump.

There was one special factor in 1973 that cannot be counted on in the future. That was the bad weather—rain and floods—during the cotton planting season. These cut almost two million bales from the 1973 United States harvest, thus contributing to the higher prices. The chances are that won't happen again, at least not on such a scale. But the possibility is always there and that helps support prices.

In fact, if you hear about heavy floods along the Mississippi River any spring, that could be a buy signal for cotton futures. Of course, all the big investors will get into the act on the same information, but if you act fast, you should be able to pick up a few futures contracts at a price that will give you a nice profit by fall.

Since the regional markets closed, most cotton is traded on the New York Commodity Exchange. A futures contract for cotton is 100 bales, or 50,000 pounds. The price is quoted in cents per pound and moves in hundredths of a cent. That means the minimum move is $5 per contract, and price fluctuations are limited by the Cotton Exchange to 2 cents from the previous day's close or 4 cents from a day's high to its low. This limits your gain to $1,000 per contract per day, but it also limits your loss to the same amount.

When cotton is high, the margin your broker demands will probably be higher than in times of steadier prices that are close to the ten-year average. However, you should figure on not less than $1,000 margin, plus your original deposit with the broker.

Lumber and Plywood

As in the case of cotton, timber prices are largely controlled by American production. The lumber industry is probably the only one in the world that plans for a hundred years in the future. Forest companies cut down trees and replant seedlings that will probably not be harvested for 100 years or more. That is the planning program in the western and northwestern timber states. In the South, where the easy climate makes pine trees grow faster, the interval is down to thirty or forty years. And modern genetic research is now producing "super-trees" that will mature much faster than that.

Canada and the United States together have about a billion acres of commercial forest land, with about half that in the United States. America also has another 250 million acres of forest land that is not available for commercial timber cutting or that would be uneconomical to use.

The depletion of the available forest land as well as other factors could produce a serious shortage of sawtimber in the years ahead. This could mean a price rise of 60 percent in the kind of lumber used for building within the next thirty years, according to a 1973 United States Forest Service forecast.

The government is a major factor in the lumber and plywood market because it owns about a quarter of the United States commercial forest land and controls about half of the total sawtimber available. Thus what the government does about controlling the cutting rate has a big influence on timber prices.

What other factors will affect supply and demand for timber and make its price go up and down?

Population growth means great need for housing. Watch the national census figures and the figures on formation of new households. New housing starts — the figures are released regularly by the government — will show how many houses are being built. Most of the remaining new households will move into apartments. The difference is important: a house takes 10,500 board feet on an average and an apartment uses only 1,000 board feet.

An economic boom means a greater demand for lumber from industry and industrial consumption. If a slump is coming, demand will taper off and push lumber prices down.

There are also competing materials. Are lumber prices getting so high that some competing materials might be used? Higher prices for wood could mean that steel, aluminum, or plastics might be substituted for wood in house-building. But, as the Forest Service pointed out, these substitutes use energy that is in short supply, cause pollution, and use up resources that cannot be renewed. Timber, on the other hand, will replace itself over a period of years.

What about foreign demand for United States lumber? If there is a housing boom in Japan, a major importer of American wood products, this will take lumber out of the United States market and tend to drive prices up. If there is a housing boom in the United States at the same time as in Japan, and the coincidence drives the cost of home-building too high for Americans, Washington might decide to protect its own people by limiting or banning exports.

The lumber industry is one of the oldest in the United States. The plywood industry is one of the newest, and it has had a spectacular growth.

Futures trading in both commodities began in 1969. Lumber is traded on the Chicago Mercantile Exchange. Plywood is traded on the Chicago Board of Trade and the New York Mercantile Exchange. The Board of Trade has a small business in lumber, which concerns only a few hundred contracts. Prices are set by the larger-scale dealings on the Chicago Mercantile Exchange.

Timber sold on the futures market is always soft wood, mostly fir. Hardwood timber, which is usually used only for flooring, is sold only on a spot basis. Lumber is measured by the board foot, a board 12 by 12 inches by 1 inch thick or its cubic equivalent. Plywood is sold by the square foot of three-ply board 3/8-inch thick.

The lumber contract is for 100,000 board feet of 2 by 4 fir timber in random lengths from 8 to 20 feet. Trading is usually active, with some 3,500 contracts outstanding, and daily dealings of $5 million. The plywood contract is for 69,120 square feet. There are usually about 5,000 futures contracts outstanding. The price is quoted in dollars and cents per thousand square feet, with the minimum fluctuation 10 cents per thousand feet. That means that a rise of 10 cents means a profit of almost $7 per contract.

In 1970, lumber was trading at between $75 and $90 per thousand board feet. By March, 1973, it was up to $195. The cyclical nature of the building industry can produce dramatic price swings, with a potential for doubling or more in a couple of years. The profit possibilities, of course, are huge. They are magnified ten times or more by the fact that you only have to put up perhaps 10 percent of the value of the lumber you are buying.

The construction industry is the major market for timber. About a third of the United States consumption goes into private home building; another third goes into non-residential construction. Obviously, if you watch the construction industry you are going to have a pretty good idea of lumber and plywood demand. A building boom means a soaring demand and a slump means slack demand and falling prices. So watch how mortgage rates are going—high mortgage interest means a housing slump, while low interest rates for home-buyers fuels a housing boom.

Per capita consumption of lumber has been declining in the United States since 1904, when it was more than 500 board feet. In the 1970s it is less than 200 board feet per person per year. The total market, though, has expanded, due to the growing population.

Inroads have been made into the lumber market by plywood, brick, steel, and other substitute materials. Statisticians have even worked out a formula that shows the demand for lumber or plywood declining by 0.1 percent for every 1 percent rise in timber prices. In contrast, plywood consumption has been rising at an average of 11 percent per year since 1925.

Although the United States is self-sufficient in timber (except for some hardwoods used for plywood, veneer, and furniture), foreign demand is a big factor in setting prices. Japan is a major importer of both logs and finished timber, most of which comes from Canada and the United States.

Japan has suffered a severe housing shortage since World War II. It has sought United States timber to correct this, and the recent increase in Japanese foreign trade has permitted the purchase of more United States timber. For instance, imports in 1972 were 40 percent higher than in 1971, for a total of 2.78 billion board feet.

What all this adds up to is this: Watch the housing starts for probable domestic demand. Watch the Japanese trade figures for probable Japanese demand. Watch the newspapers for word of strikes or fires in the United States or Canadian forests. Fewer than 200 mills produce plywood in the United States. If one of them burned down, production could be affected enough to influence the price.

Here are some further likely sources of information that could help you in the lumber and plywood futures market:

The Forest Service, United States Department of Agriculture, Washington, D.C.; Western Wood Products Association, Portland, Oregon; National Association of Homebuilders, Washington, D.C.; American Plywood Association, Tacoma, Washington.

Orange Juice

There are big fluctuations in the orange juice futures market, and they are almost entirely due to weather. Since all investors get the same weather information at the same time, it takes fast action to get into the buying line ahead of the opposition.

The contract in the New York futures market is for 15,000 pounds of frozen, concentrated orange juice. The price is quoted in cents per pound, so a typical contract might have a product value of $7,500 when the price was 50 cents per pound. Recent prices have ranged between 30 and 75 cents. On a single contract, your broker might ask for a margin of $900. A 1-cent price move could make you $150 if the move were upward.

A special group of brokers, called the Citrus Association, trades orange juice in connection with the New York Cotton Exchange. However, your regular broker can take and execute your orders for the juice.

What makes orange juice so comparatively simple a speculation is that two-thirds of it is produced in Florida and

222 THE SPECULATOR'S HANDBOOK

nearly all of it is drunk in the United States. That means that Florida weather is the main factor in supply and the demand depends entirely on American breakfast habits. There are no foreign markets involved, no problems of exports, imports or foreign exchange, no embargoes. It depends mostly on whether there is a frost in the Florida orange groves when the fruit is in a tender stage.

California weather is a minor factor. The non-Florida third of the supply is shared between California, Arizona, and Texas. However, California does produce a quarter of the total, so a freeze there does have some effect on the futures prices.

Cold weather is not the only meteorological fact to be considered in forecasting future price changes. A hurricane sweeping through the orange groves could injure trees or blow down fruit. Drought could reduce the juice yield even though the number of oranges themselves was not reduced.

There is also a longer-range possibility of a change in buying habits. The powders making an orange-juice-like drink have had some penetration of the market, since they are simpler to store and do not require freezing. The sale of fresh, pasteurized juice is also a competitive factor in some urban markets.

However, any of these changes would be gradual and would not affect a three-months futures contract. About the only thing that would help or hurt such a contract would be frost in Florida — and that would surely be reported in your local newspaper.

One thing to consider, though, is that a serious and prolonged energy shortage might make freeze effects worse than they have been in the past. Growers try to protect their trees against cold weather by burning gas flares or oil-fired smudge pots, or by using big windmill-like fans to blow away the cold air near the ground. If there is not enough energy for these measures, a freeze could do more damage than have similar ones in the past. This possibility could justify a flyer in orange juice the next time there is a threat of frost in Florida.

16

Some Food Staples

IN PREVIOUS chapters, we've taken a look at the ground rules for speculating in a variety of futures markets around the world. Now let's take a look at some food commodities that affect all of us. Most food commodities in the United States have a demand that is fairly constant, in spite of higher prices. Americans who are paying higher prices in the supermarket grumble about the cost of living, but they buy much the same products as usual and cut back on costs in some other area.

In the past few years, however, another factor has been growing in importance in the commodities markets—namely, international trade.

A quotation from a New York Times News Service dispatch, published by *The Times* of London on September 10, 1973, highlights the extent to which the United States has become the whole world's granary.

As the most closely watched harvest in the United States peace-time history gathers momentum a commodities 'numbers game' involving incredibly high stakes is being played by governments around the world.

The first numbers in this crucial lottery will be drawn tomor-row, when the Department of Agriculture announces its last 1973 crop estimates before the autumn harvest rolls into high gear.

At stake is not only what consumers will pay for foodstuffs during the next 12 months, but also whether countless millions throughout the world will have enough to eat.

American farmers produce about half the world's corn, and the United States accounts for about half the world's international trade in corn. The United States is the world's biggest producer of oats and a major producer of sorghum. All of these grains are indispensable to feed cattle, hogs, and poultry, which in turn feed people around the world.

The United States is also the world's biggest exporter of wheat, and has thus become the bread-basket for a large part of humanity. Massive shipments of American wheat in the 1920s and 1970s have saved the Soviet people from famine.

American agriculture is also far and away the world's biggest producer of soybeans, turning out around one billion bushels a year—two-thirds of the world total. Its nearest competitors are China and Brazil, with about 250 million bushels. Nobody else comes anywhere close in growing these beans, which are the cheapest source of protein for both humans and animals.

It is small wonder that governments and traders in London, Tokyo, Moscow, New Delhi, and other capitals watch every development through the year as American farmers plant and reap their crops. Such vast worldwide interest has spurred the growth of great commodities markets in Chicago and elsewhere, in which the volume of trading grew about fifteen-fold from 1963 to 1973. The dollar value of commodity trading in Chicago far surpasses the activity in the New York stock market (although, of course, on 10 to 15 percent rather than 50 to 60 percent margin). On the Chicago Mercantile Exchange, trading totaled $100 billion in 1973. The figure for the Chicago Board of Trade was $260 billion. Shares worth a total of $146.5 billion were traded on the New York Stock Exchange in 1973.

Curiously, though, only about 500,000 people are active traders in the commodity futures markets compared with 30 million or so who have invested in United States stocks. It is not that the stakes are high. You can get into the commodity markets with only a few hundred dollars or so. It is probably public ignorance of the futures markets and fear of their riskiness that have kept more people from going into them as speculators.

The essential thing to keep in mind is that for you these are markets in which you *speculate* — you take big risks, though not necessarily with big money, in the hope of making large gains.

There are other people in the commodity markets who want *safety* and they look to you to provide it for them. They are the *hedgers*. They are mostly big fish and include mainly grain elevator operators, manufacturers of grain products, importers, and exporters. These people all have one thing in common: they want to minimize their risk and, if possible, to eliminate it entirely.

A grain elevator owner in the Midwest who holds millions of bushels of corn that he bought at $3 a bushel runs a terrible risk of loss if the price should drop to $1.50 a bushel in the next few months. In fact, he will probably be unable to function at all, because he will not be able to get any bank to finance him unless he hedges his risk by selling contracts for an offsetting amount in the futures market. Once he has done that it makes no great difference to him whether the market rises or falls, since the contracts he sold will balance out the corn he holds.

What you are in fact doing, therefore, in the futures markets is assuming the risks these businessmen want off their shoulders. As a speculator you are performing a useful economic function, and in return for your risk the market offers you the possibility of great rewards. It allows you to put up very little cash for a big investment and enables you to make a great deal of money very quickly if you are shrewd and lucky.

It is obviously an efficient system, because the United States, which allows a relatively free hand to private farming and private speculating, invariably has huge farm surpluses, whereas the Soviet Union and other countries that allow neither frequently have to import American grains to feed their own people.

Pork Bellies

Before we get involved with the international food market, however, let's see how much money can be made in an All-American commodity — pork bellies. Pork bellies are just about the most actively traded commodity on United States exchanges. They are produced by American farmers for the American breakfast table. They are almost unaffected by foreign buying or selling in international trade, so you don't have to keep an eye on what the foreign traders are up to.

Practically everything of interest to you as a pork-belly speculator is happening right in the United States, mostly under the supervision of United States government inspectors, who provide a wealth of statistics for your guidance.

Pork bellies are also a commodity for which there is really no competing substitute. When you trade in corn futures, you always have to keep an eye on the oats and barley markets because they are possible substitutes if the corn price gets too far out of line.

The reason there is no substitute for pork bellies is that they are the raw material for slicing bacon rashers, and people either eat bacon or they do not. When the price of bacon rises sharply, people do not usually eat steak or lamb for breakfast instead. In fact, a more important influence to watch on the pork-bellies futures market may be the price of eggs. If bacon and eggs both get too expensive, housewives across the nation might switch to cereals for breakfast instead. This will obviously be bad news for the pork-belly market.

However, the demand for bacon is surprisingly constant, because people who are addicted to bacon and eggs do not like to do without them, no matter what the price. Bacon is an expensive and inefficient food that mostly dissolves into fat on being fried, so these people are not too rational about the price of their rashers. This is what economists call an *inelastic demand*, which means that consumers are going to buy just about the same amount of bacon whether the price is high, medium, or low. This in turn means that prices are going to depend on variations in the supply. Even a small change in the amount of bacon coming on the market may have a large impact on prices.

Another thing that simplifies the pork-belly futures market is the lack of carryover from one year to the next. From October to May, some pork bellies are frozen and stored for use until the following September. But they are perishable and are not kept too long in storage. This means that, unlike in some other commodity markets, you do not have to worry too much about stocks from former years overhanging the market.

Now let's get down to facts. A pork belly is the layered section of meat and fat under the rib cage of a hog. It is split down the middle into two halves that weigh as much as eighteen pounds each. Pork bellies are cured and smoked to produce bacon. The belly is only about 12 percent of the hog's weight, so the bacon produced from it can be considered a by-product of the pork and ham that comes from the rest of the hog. The price of bacon therefore is only a minor factor in the farmer's decision to raise more or fewer hogs. He has to consider what profit he can make out of the whole animal. Bacon production, consequently, is not fully responsive to demand. And this is where things get out of line, with the resulting big price swings creating chances for big gains.

In the pork-belly futures market, you can usually trade

on a margin of $900 to $1,000. With this leverage, the gains or losses on small price swings are multiplied many times over and can thus have dramatic effects for you in a matter of days or even hours.

You buy and sell frozen pork-belly futures on the Chicago Mercantile Exchange. Each contract is for 36,000 pounds of what is in fact uncured, unsliced bacon, stored after December 1 of the current crop year in a warehouse approved by the exchange. This is deliverable in the prime weight range of ten to fourteen pounds per belly, inspected by a grader of the United States Department of Agriculture. Not that you care personally about these details really, except as a general guarantee, because you are never going to take delivery.

Here is the table you will be looking for in the newspaper:

	Open	High	Low	Close	Prev. Close	Life of Contr. High	Low
FROZEN PORK BELLIES							
Feb.	80.37	80.37	78.30	80.37 — —	77.87	83.40	45.00
Mar.	78.50	79.20	76.70	†79.20 — —	77.75	81.85	47.05
May	77.95	78.50	76.15	†78.50 — —	77.00	81.00	47.50
July	76.60	76.60	76.05	†76.60 — —	†75.10	79.20	64.20
Aug.	73.90	73.90	72.80	†73.90 — —	72.40	76.10	64.10

Total sales, 3,149 lots; Feb., 2,105; Mar., 665; May, 290; July, 149; Aug., 40.

The prices are quoted in cents per pound. At 80 cents, each contract of 36,000 pounds is worth $28,800. If you are only putting up $1,000 of this, you obviously have very high leverage. For every cent per pound your contract goes up or down you are ahead or behind $360. Your brokerage commission for one contract is about $45.

Before there are any pork bellies to trade there have to be hogs to get them from, and there have to be farmers producing hogs. Every three months, in December, March, June, and September, the United States Department of Agriculture issues its *Pig Crop Report,* in which you will find estimates of the United States hog population as well as the farrowing intentions (breeding plans) reported by farmers. The report lists the hogs kept for breeding, and those intended for market, divided into animals under 60 pounds, 60-119 pounds, 120-179 pounds, 180-219 pounds, and over 200 pounds. The report also estimates the number of pigs to be farrowed in the next six months. Hogs gain about 1.5 pounds a day and are ready for market six or seven months after birth, when they have reached their optimum weight of 200 to 250 pounds.

You will find up-to-date information on hog marketing and slaughter in *Live Stock Market News,* another publication of the United States Department of Agriculture. This weekly report gives you the latest figures on receipts of hogs at terminals and markets throughout the United States as well as data on hog-slaughtering under federal inspection. It also gives you the hog-corn ratio, a significant indicator of the profitability of raising hogs for the average farmer. The ratio represents the number of bushels of corn required to buy 100 pounds of live hogs. When the ratio is high you know that conditions are favorable for expanding hog production.

The Chicago Mercantile Exchange makes daily and weekly reports on the movement of pork bellies into exchange-approved warehouses, and the United States government reports monthly on total pork bellies in storage in the country. The government also releases weekly figures on the quantity of bacon sliced under federal inspection in the United States. This amount represents about 65 percent of total bacon consumption, the remainder being produced for intrastate consumption or for other purposes such as canned soups, which are not subject to federal inspection regulations.

From these sources you can form a fairly clear picture of the entire cycle of production, from the time that Farmer Jones in Missouri decides to raise 200 hogs this year instead of 150 like last year to the day that Mrs. Smith serves her family bacon and eggs instead of oatmeal in New York City.

You can get many of these statistics, as well as the daily prices and trading volume in the futures market, from the exchange's *Daily Information Bulletin.* In order to make a comparison with previous years, you should obtain the Chicago Mercantile Exchange Yearbook. Many of these details and related news items are also available in the commodities section of major newspapers.

With the facts in your head, all that remains is to interpret them, and decide whether they mean prices are going up or down. There are some important indicators to help you here. In Chicago and other hog markets, government officials report daily on the average weight of hogs sold through those yards. If the average weight goes up, you might well deduce that farmers are holding hogs back from the market because prices are too low or for some other reason. Sooner or later, they will have to sell them, and this will push prices down. If farmers are going to the other extreme and are actually marketing pregnant sows, you know that they are in a state of panic and are trying to get rid of their livestock at any price. This might well mark the climax of a bear market and signal the beginning of a bull market, caused by the wholesale liquidation of breeding stock.

You should be aware, of course, that all these facts are available not only to you but also to everybody else who takes the trouble to study pork-belly futures. There are a lot of speculators in this market, and what they are thinking is an important market factor.

This is the psychological factor. Put it this way: the fundamentals of the market are supply and demand, and you may succeed in predicting them quite accurately. But if most of the market thinks otherwise, the fundamentals will be ignored, and prices will respond — at least for a time — to that erroneous majority belief. If your futures contract expires within that period, it will be just too bad for you. It will do you no good at all to be basically right in the end if the market turns too late for you to profit by your foresight.

That is why the technical aspects as well as the fundamentals of the market should be kept in mind. For a certain time prices may be dictated not by the reality of supply and demand but by people's *expectations* of supply and demand. This is obviously a subjective and highly unreliable factor, because it can change overnight if most traders switch from pessimism to optimism or vice versa. But you can keep track of it nevertheless, by means of charts.

There are traders who even ignore fundamentals altogether and operate entirely on the basis of charts that show them what the prevailing *opinion* is in the market rather than what the real *situation* is.

You can subscribe to a charting service or you can make up charts yourself once you see how it is done. One firm that offers weekly charts on pork bellies and many other commodities is Commodity Research Bureau, 1 Liberty Plaza, New York 10006. This firm also publishes a Commodity Yearbook with the essential statistics of all major commodities traded in the United States.

Now that you know where to get a good part of the information you need to be an informed speculator in pork bellies, you can spend a few weeks testing your aptitude in the futures markets without risking a penny. You won't make any money, either, but you will be able to decide whether pork bellies (or any other futures market) is for you.

Write to the Chicago Mercantile Exchange, 10 North Franklin Street, Chicago, Illinois 60606 and ask for the exchange's *Commodity Trader's Scorecard*. This booklet gives you the basic facts on all major commodities traded on the exchange, including pork bellies. It also provides a worksheet for you to use in noting the details of your imaginary trades.

When you have learned how to keep track of important facts and have some experience in predicting trends, you will be much better equipped to make your own buy and sell decisions. As exchange president Everette Harris says in the *Scorecard,* "After you've used the *Scorecard* for a while you may decide futures trading isn't for you." But if you decide it is, your experience with pork bellies gives you a great deal of the background you need to trade in a couple of other commodities.

Live Hogs and Frozen Hams

Most of the sources of information we mentioned with regard to pork bellies, such as the government's *Pig Crop Report,* are of equal value to you in trading live hog futures.

This is also a lively market in which the volume of trading has been around $50 million a day. The Chicago Mercantile Exchange contract calls for delivery of 30,000 pounds of live hogs with an average weight of 200 to 230 pounds per hog.

Frozen hams are traded on the same exchange in lots of 36,000 pounds. The contract specifies 14- to 17-pound skinned hams from federally inspected packing plants. This is a much, much smaller market that is not worth bothering about until it grows big enough to offer you more liquidity.

Cattle

Pigs are not the only livestock in which you can deal, however. You can also speculate in cattle, and thanks to the low margins required in commodity futures, the potential profits can be astounding. In August, 1972, for example, cattle future contracts for February, 1973, delivery were trading at about 34 cents a pound. The price advanced to 44 cents a pound in the following months. If you had bought a contract in August and sold it in January, you could have made a profit of more than $12,000 on a margin of only $1,200 — over 900 percent in just five months.

There are several ways you can speculate in cattle. On the Chicago Mercantile Exchange there are contracts in feeder cattle, Midwestern live cattle, and frozen boneless beef. On the New York Mercantile Exchange, you can deal in Imported boneless beef. The most recent addition is the Pacific Commodities Exchange in San Francisco, which in October 1973 started trading in western live cattle futures.

Live cattle contracts are for 40,000 pounds of live animals graded "choice" or better by the USDA. Since a steer weighs about 1,000 pounds, when you buy one contract you are buying the equivalent of about forty head of cattle. Feeder cattle contracts are for 42,000 pounds. Frozen boneless beef contracts are for 36,000 pounds of American beef; imported boneless beef contracts are for 30,000 pounds.

Minimum margins on all these markets are usually about $500 to $1,500. At the time of writing they were all small markets with thin trading, with the exception of the Chicago live cattle futures market, which is big and active, with an open interest of about 30,000 contracts or more. This means there may be 30,000 contracts in existence at any one time, and you thus have plenty of people with whom to trade. Daily trading in Chicago live cattle futures might come to $250 million or so on a typical day. This gives you a high degree of liquidity compared with the imported boneless beef market, where only fifty contracts or so may exist at one time and buyers or sellers may be scarce indeed.

The basic situation in all these beef futures markets is that, although the United States has a lot of cows on the range, which produce about 22 billion pounds of meat a year, the country still has to import another 1.5 billion pounds or so, mainly from Australia, Mexico, and Central America. There were 37 million cows grown in the United States for beef production (excluding milk cows) in 1970, and they are expected to number 46 million head by 1980. By that time imports may total 2 billion pounds, according to the experts.

The main sources of information in the cattle futures market are the USDA Crop Reporting Board and Economic Research Service. These two sources provide you with figures on total cattle and calves on United States farms, commercial slaughter of cattle and calves, the number of cattle and calves on feed in the United States, the condition of American pastures and ranges, the average prices of cattle and calves received by farmers, and the number of cattle delivered at the Chicago and other markets.

Many of these facts are also reported in major newspapers, where you should also keep an eye open for United States government measures affecting the meat industry, such as restrictions on imports. Argentina, for example, a nation of 24 million people, has about 48 million cows. In spite of this surplus, Argentina's exports of fresh beef to the United States are practically zero because of sanitary precautions. Foot-and-mouth disease is widespread among Argentine cattle, and to avoid contagion of American cattle, the United States will not allow Argentine beef into the American market unless it has been cooked. If Argentina should clean up its herds, the situation might change drastically.

Statements by the American Meat Institute, the Secretary of Agriculture and the American National Cattlemen's Association reported in the press may also have a major impact on the cattle futures markets.

Iced Broilers and Tom Turkeys

Iced broiler chickens are a fairly active futures market on the Chicago Board of Trade. Turkeys offer a very small, seasonal futures market on the Chicago Mercantile Exchange.

The turkey contract is for 36,000 pounds of frozen, eviscerated U.S. Grade A turkeys. It is not worth bothering with unless it grows considerably bigger.

The iced broiler contract is for 28,000 pounds of chicken. Here again, the USDA is the main source of data. The main factors to watch are the prices of broiler feed, whether competing products such as beef and pork are priced high or low, military purchases, exports to other countries, and of course, the main item — consumption by John Q. Public.

A commonsense approach is to watch prices when you shop at your supermarket. Do you think the price of chicken is too high, and that you would rather eat pork? Or do you think that chicken is dirt cheap compared with beef and lamb? This could give you a good practical basis for taking an interest in the futures market and looking for further information.

Pigs, cattle, and poultry all have one thing in common — they are fattened on soybean meal, corn, and other grains, which you can also buy and sell in the futures markets. You can be sure that the prices of beef, pork, and chicken will rise when the prices of these feeds rise and fall when they fall.

Corn

Corn futures are traded on the Chicago Board of Trade, the Minneapolis Grain Exchange, and the Kansas City Board of

Trade. Contracts are for 5,000 bushels each, which at $3 a bushel means a total of $15,000 per contract, and at $1.50 would come to $7,500. Margin requirements vary on the different exchanges at different times and depending on the brokerage firm with which you are dealing. Most margins, however, are in the range of a few hundred dollars.

You may want to make a "dry run" before you risk any money on corn futures, as we suggested for pork bellies. Or, perhaps you have found a broker whose advice you value. There are other advisory services you can turn to. One such is *Futures Markets Services,* published weekly by Commodity Research Bureau, 1 Liberty Plaza, New York 10036. It analyzes fundamental developments affecting price trends in corn and other feed grains.

Now let's see how corn flows into the world market as crops are planted and harvested around the globe. About midwinter in the northern hemisphere, the first production forecasts are published on the coming corn crops in the southern hemisphere (Australia, Argentina, and South Africa), where the seasons are reversed. These three countries and the United States, Canada, France, Mexico, and Thailand are the world's major corn producers. A bad crop in Argentina or Australia may mean a bigger demand abroad for United States corn and thus lead to higher prices also in the American market.

Through its embassies abroad, the United States government keeps an eye on production in these countries and issues periodical crop estimates. You can obtain this information by subscribing to *Foreign Agriculture,* a weekly magazine published by the USDA (subscription $10 a year, single copy 20 cents). Write to the Superintendent of Documents, Government Printing Office, Washington, D.C. 20402.

The first indication of the coming United States corn crop is found in the Planting Intentions Report issued about the middle of March by the USDA. You will find the gist of it in most major newspapers' commodities section. This gives you an idea of what farmers across the nation are planning to do with their land in the coming year.

About 75 percent of the United States' corn grown for market is raised in the so-called corn belt states, of which Illinois and Iowa are the most important, followed by Indiana, Minnesota, Nebraska, Ohio, and Missouri. Corn planting in these states is usually finished by the first days of June, and harvesting is over by the end of November or beginning of December. Bad weather, however, may alter this pattern. Within this period the growing corn needs hot sun and sufficient rainfall at regular intervals. Weather conditions are of critical importance. You can keep yourself informed on growing conditions through the weekly Weather and Crop Bulletins issued every Tuesday by the United States Department of Commerce.

The USDA's Crop Reporting Board issues production estimates at intervals, which give you constantly revised ideas of the size of the growing crop as the season advances. They start in July and continue until the final report in December. As we have seen, these reports attract worldwide attention and they have a major impact on the futures markets as they appear. You should be watching for them in the commodity news section of your newspaper.

A number of private sources also release their own estimates, usually a few days ahead of the government reports. Once the corn has been planted, the estimated size of the crop varies because of drought, frost, and other weather hazards as well as dangers such as insect pests, which can take a heavy toll.

While the crop is coming in, the USDA also keeps you posted on corn consumption. The major part of the crop is used to feed cattle, hogs, and poultry. Industry also uses a minor part, mainly to produce starch, sugar, and liquor. The percentage of the crop that is exported varies from year to year, depending on prices and the competition of other producing countries.

The USDA issues quarterly reports on the disappearance of corn stocks, which give you an overall picture of the

available supply. The *Feed Situation* report is issued five
times a year—in November, February, April, May, and
August—and gives a complete rundown of all feed grains
available for livestock, with statistics and informative articles.

Official United States corn export figures, based on
weekly customs inspections, are also published every Monday
afternoon. The main buyers of American corn are usually
Japan, Holland, Great Britain, and Italy. The corn is shipped
out to them mainly through ports in the Gulf of Mexico. Any
dock strikes there or rail stoppages in the midwest will certainly have a big impact on the futures market. For up-to-date
information on United States foreign trade in corn and other
farm products, write to the United States Department of
Agriculture, Economic Research Service, Washington, D.C.
20250, and ask for the monthly publication, *Foreign Agricultural Trade of the United States.*

With all this background information to guide you on the
probable future course of corn prices, you should be watching
the table in the commodities section of your newspaper which
gives you the anticipated prices of corn for about a year into
the future:

CORN
Friday, August 17, 1973
CHICAGO BOARD OF TRADE

	Open	High	Low	Close		Prev. Close	Life of Contr. High	Low
Sept.	3.30	3.30½	3.11	3.11	3.12	3.19	3.47¾	1.35½
Dec.	3.08	3.13	2.99	2.99	3.00	3.04	3.33	1.32½
Mar.	3.09	3.11	2.97	2.97½	2.98	3.02	3.30	1.33¼
May	3.07	3.07½	2.93·	2.93	2.93½	2.98	3.20	1.56
July	3.00	3.03	2.90	2.90	—	2.93	3.15¼	2.30

Another table shows how much trading there is daily in
each delivery month (the figure represents thousands of
bushels):

Sales

FRIDAY AUGUST 17

Chicago

	Corn
Sept.	17,115
Dec.	62,730
Mar.	18,945
May	6,725
July	3,940
Total	109,455

A third table shows you how many thousands of bushels there are in all the futures contracts there are in existence in the Chicago market:

Open Interest

FRIDAY AUGUST 17

Chicago

	Corn
Sept.	68,315
Dec.	176,560
Mar.	81,505
May	53,310
July	9,295
Total	388,985

It will also be helpful—in fact, it is essential—to know what other speculators and hedgers are doing in the futures market. The United States Commodity Exchange Authority, a section of the Department of Agriculture that acts as watchdog over the commodity markets, issues monthly reports on *Commitments of Traders in Commodity Futures.*

Now what is the possible profit for you in all this? Turn to the price table above, and look at the last line. Suppose you had bought the July, 1974, corn contract and were lucky enough to get it at the lowest price it ever reached in the previous year—$2.30 a bushel (the very last figure in the table). You would have put up perhaps $1,000 of your own money as margin and would thus have acquired a 5,000-bushel contract worth $11,500 at the price you paid. Suppose that on Friday, August 17, 1973, you sold this contract at the opening price of $3.00 a bushel (the first figure in the last line). You would thus have sold the 5,000-bushel contract at

$15,000. Your profit is this $15,000 minus the $11,500 you paid, or $3,500. To get back $3,500 on a $1,000 investment in less than a year is not a bad deal at all. Your brokerage commission would have been $30.

You would of course have been very lucky to get the contract at the lowest possible price of $2.30 a bushel. But this was by no means the most profitable example we could have taken from the above table. You can work out for yourself how much you would have made by buying the September, 1973, contract on the first line of the table at $1.35½ a bushel and selling it at $3.30.

But before we start adding up our hypothetical future profits let's glance at some traps for the unwary and see how we can get around them.

Suppose the weather is bad in the midwest and you think the corn crop is going to be ruined. Do not be too hasty about rushing to buy corn futures. Find out first the size of the stocks carried over from the previous crop. How big are the other feed grain stocks? They might be sufficient to tide consumption over a couple of bad crops in subsequent years. In recent years, the carryover corn in commercial hands (not in government stocks), which is known as the *free supply,* has been a factor to be reckoned with. And if this free supply is not enough to satisfy consumption, you still have to anticipate that whatever stocks the government has in hand may come on the market.

All these factors have to be juggled at the same time, and it is obvious that nobody can come up with exactly the right prediction every time. There are just too many variables and imponderables to be absolutely sure of anything.

That is why you should cut your losses immediately and abandon your positions in the market as soon as you see the situation turning against you. Perhaps the weather damage to the crops was not as bad as anticipated. Perhaps you underestimated the free supply. Perhaps various other unanticipated things happened, such as a locust plague ravaging the corn crop in Argentina. This is no place to be stubborn. Cut your losses and run. As we saw in chapter 13, the futures market is not for the rigid, doctrinaire, unbending person who always wants to prove he is right every time. It is for the agile, quick-thinking, unprejudiced person who is quite willing to admit he is wrong most of the time and then acts at once to eliminate the consequences of his mistakes before they overwhelm him.

Grain prices, like the prices in all commodity futures, can be affected drastically from one day to the next by news developments. But the interpretation of these developments can be very tricky. For instance, on July 10, 1973, the USDA predicted record grain and soybean crops for the year. In normal times it would seem logical to conclude that if the harvest were to be so abundant in a few months' time, the prices of corn, soybeans, and wheat would drop. The government report should have been a bearish factor in the futures markets for these products, as well as for cattle, hogs, poultry, and eggs, which are obviously going to be cheaper to raise and produce if feed grains become cheaper.

But what happened? The following day every single one of these commodities, from corn to eggs, shot up the daily allowable limit on the Chicago exchanges. Why? Because many commodity traders felt that the prospects of huge United States grain and soybean production would eliminate the need for extending United States export controls currently in force for those products. Speculators also thought that the abundant crops might also lead the government to relax or abolish price ceilings then in effect for these commodities. So they did not sell—they bought.

Were the speculators right in this assessment? At the time things happen, who knows? Every decision is essentially a step in the dark when it involves predicting the future. The decision could seem correct and then be nullified by some new development in the world, such as bumper grain crops in Russia and a severe curtailment of American grain exports to the Soviets, which would cause a grain glut on the United States market.

What in fact happened on this occasion was the announcement the following day of large United States grain purchases by both Russia and China. Futures shot up once again.

To be a successful commodity trader, you must keep abreast of such developments in the world through your newspaper, government data, market letters, and trade journals. You are in the market together with some very smart operators who have these facts at their fingertips.

But once you have taken the trouble to keep yourself informed, you and everybody else are competing on equal terms in the futures markets. The shrewdest assessment of the current situation in the corn futures market can be upset next week by floods in the Mississippi Valley, hailstorms in Nebraska, drought in Indiana, or frost in Minnesota.

Farmers have always known this, from frequently grim and bitter experience. Just consider one big risk the farmer is trying to avoid and that the futures speculator is trying to evaluate as he assumes that risk by undertaking to buy the farmer's crop in the futures market. The risk is the weather, and it can make or break both farmer and speculator with almost complete unpredictability. We now have weather satellites up in the sky, a network of meteorological stations girdling the earth, computers, radar, and rain-seeding techniques. With all these gadgets available to predict and control the weather, how far ahead can we actually see it coming?

For a period of about two to three days the weather can be forecast for a given area with an accuracy of about 85 percent. In the early 1960s this predictable period was only twelve hours. The United States Committee on Atmospheric Sciences says the highest priority should be given to improving forecasts for a twelve-hour to two-week time span. "While individual forecasters may make claims for longer periods," says Cargill Investors Services, a Chicago commodities broker, "the most

realistic view for long-range forecasting in the next decade undoubtedly lies within the government's two-week scope."

And nobody can raise a corn crop in two weeks. In this
area, at least, the futures markets play no favorites — the farmer, the big-deal grain exporter, and the small individual
speculator are all in the same weather-battered boat.

Oats, Sorghum, and Barley

Much of what we have said here about corn is also applicable
to oats, sorghum, and barley, which are also used mainly to
feed livestock in the United States. Together with corn they
are known as the feed grains.

They are closely tied to corn by the very fact that they are
all used as animal feed. In fattening cattle, for instance,
sorghum is considered to have a feeding value of 92 percent
of that of corn, while in feeding hogs, oats is estimated to have
a value of 90 percent of that of corn. If any of these grains gets
too far out of line in price it will soon be substituted by another, cheaper grain down on the farm.

Oats futures are traded on the Chicago Board of Trade.
Each contract is for 5,000 bushels.

The world's biggest producers of oats are — usually in this
order — the United States, Russia, Canada, West Germany,
Poland, France, and Australia. You can obtain information
on production figures, United States government price support programs, oats stocks in the United States, prices, and
farm parity prices, from the Foreign Agricultural Service,
Crop Reporting Board, Agricultural Marketing Service, and
Economic Research Service, all of the United States Department of Agriculture.

Grain sorghum is traded on the Chicago Mercantile Exchange. Each contract is for 400,000 pounds. The United
States government sources given above also provide information in this market.

Oats and barley futures were traded on the Winnipeg
Grain Exchange until December 1973 in contracts of 5,000
bushels each. The Exchange then ended operations in these

markets, except for the liquidation of existing contracts, which were sporadically traded early in 1974.

Wheat

Wheat futures are traded on the Chicago Board of Trade, the Kansas City Board of Trade, and the Minneapolis Grain Exchange. The crop year is from July 1 to June 30 of the following year. The futures contracts run a year into the future.

Actually, in Chicago there are now two different wheat futures contracts. One, known as "wheat" or "Chicago wheat," has been traded for many years and is one of the biggest and best established futures markets, with a volume of thousands of contracts.

Another futures contract, known as "Gulf hard red winter wheat," was set up by the Chicago Board of Trade in April 1974. At the time of writing it is still a small market with thin trading. Both the old and the new wheat futures contracts in Chicago are for 5,000 bushels each.

The difference between them is that the traditional Chicago wheat contract is oriented towards the domestic United States market. Since it no longer reflected the predominant world price due to the growth in the world wheat trade, the Board of Trade decided to set up an export-oriented wheat futures market.

Hard red winter wheat is grown throughout the plains states and represents more than half of all United States wheat production. About two-thirds of the hard red winter wheat grown in the United States is exported. The new Gulf hard red winter wheat futures contract is therefore designed for the wheat exporter. It is more closely tied to trends in world trade than the old wheat contract. The word Gulf in the contract's name is due to the fact that most of this wheat is exported through ports in the Gulf of Mexico.

Harvesting of winter wheat begins in May in the Southwestern United States and then advances northward into the central and northwestern states by July. By this time, the spring wheat harvest is starting and continues into September. The price of wheat therefore has a seasonal trend, declining from May when the first wheat starts coming on the market as the harvest begins, reaching a low in July and August, and then advancing through the next winter and spring. This schedule, of course, depends on how other factors hit the market at various times of the year. American farms produce several varieties of wheat known as hard spring wheat, durum, hard winter, red winter, and white wheat, which are planted and harvested at different times of the year.

The United States exports a large part of its wheat crop. Therefore, a decisive factor in the price of wheat is the world export market. Thus, you must watch not only production and consumption in the United States, but also crop failures in the Soviet Union, droughts in China, and the state of the crops in Australia and Argentina.

The world's main wheat exporters are the United States, Canada, Australia, Argentina, and the European Economic Community, which together account for about 80 percent of the world's wheat exports. In the last few years, world wheat production has ranged from 7 to 11 billion bushels. However, a great part of this total is consumed in the producing countries and so does not get into international trade.

The Soviet Union usually produces from 1.7 to 2.8 billion bushels a year. In bad years, it has to import massive quantities of wheat from abroad. Other major producers are the United States (with a crop running from 1 to 1.7 billion bushels), Canada (400 to 800 million bushels), Australia, France, West Germany, Italy, and Argentina (200 to 250 million bushels each).

The major exporters are the United States, which has shipments ranging from 400 to 800 million bushels a year; Canada, which has exports running from 300 to 600 million bushels; Australia, with 200 to 600 million bushels shipped abroad; and Argentina, with 70 to 230 million bushels usually exported. Official crop forecasts are none too accurate in some of these countries. Argentina, for instance, sometimes finds itself obliged to *import* fairly sizable quantities of wheat because it has taken on excessive export commitments as a result of over-optimistic crop estimates.

You can keep abreast of the foreign and United States wheat crops through the same USDA reporting services that were mentioned in connection with corn, as well as through the United States Department of Commerce (for international trade figures), and the Chicago Board of Trade (for futures market data).

The USDA's Crop Reporting Board turns out crop production reports as of June 1, July 1, August 1, September 1, October 1, December 1, and finally when the crop is all in.

Just as with the corn crop, an important factor in the wheat futures market is the amount of stock unsold and the carryover from the previous year. Some of this is held by private grain dealers or farmers' cooperatives, but a greater or lesser part may be in government hands as a result of the price support program. This program is intended to help farmers get a fair price for their wheat. Farmers are obviously in a weak position because they all want to sell their wheat at the same time — as soon as the harvest is in. There is then a glut on the market. Most farmers, because they are too busy on the farm to pay much attention to marketing their product, don't trust the futures market too much. They suspect they are likely to get taken on complicated deals.

Under present legislation (which may be changed), the farmer can hand over his wheat in a government low-interest loan program and get, say, $1.25 a bushel for it. If the price goes up he can repay the loan, take back his wheat, and sell it on the free market. If the price should drop below $1.25 a bushel he can decide to let the government keep the wheat, which serves to cancel his loan.

It is always an open question, therefore, what these farmers or the government are going to do with this wheat under government loan, and the uncertainty always hangs over the wheat futures market.

The government intervenes in the market in yet another way, by subsidizing American wheat exports to foreign countries. The Department of Agriculture calculates the average price of wheat on world markets every day and compares it with the price of wheat on American markets. If the price abroad is $2.70 a bushel and it is $3.00 in the United States, the subsidy might be 30 cents or so. The effect is to draw wheat off the American market. Government policy can change, of course, and this is another factor creating uncertainty.

Government policy was especially criticized after the massive American wheat sale to the Soviet Union that followed the disastrous Russian crop failure in 1972. About 450 million bushels were sold, for which the Russians paid more than $1 billion. There were angry charges later that some big wheat exporters had used their inside knowledge of the monster Russian deal in a deliberate effort to push the home price up and the foreign price down so as to collect huge government subsidies running into hundreds of millions of dollars.

American farmers who sold their wheat cheap before the Russian deal became known felt cheated when the price of wheat shot up after the huge scale of it became apparent. Some American taxpayers also felt cheated by American government subsidies for the benefit of the Russians, and American government consumers felt cheated by the resulting increases in the price of bread when the price of wheat had just about doubled. The upshot was a clamor for an investigation by Congress and for a change in the laws.

Enormous deals on the scale of this Russian wheat sale come rarely, however, and consequently such opportunities for price and market manipulation by big dealers are not too frequent. The corn and wheat futures markets are usually just too big for any one trader to dominate. In the wheat futures market, the number of contracts in existence in Chicago is typically around 27,000 and the number traded in a given day might come to 10,000.

Soybeans and Soybean Products

The soybean futures market is even bigger. On July 2, 1974, for example, there were nearly 46,000 contracts in existence and nearly 12,000 were traded that day. The soybean complex has two other futures markets—soybean meal and soybean oil. These are substantial markets, and they are worth investigating for possible profits.

Soybeans are not much to look at—they look like overripe peas, a pale tan color. But that color could be gold and they still wouldn't be worth as much to some speculators. During the big soybean boom of 1973, gold went up only 300 percent or so, while soybeans went up 400 percent and offered far greater opportunities of operating on margin, thus multiplying those gains many times over.

Soybeans started out the year around $3 a bushel. By mid-year, they were above $12. Financial experts who follow the commodity markets think several hundred speculators in soybeans made as much as $3 million each.

Soybeans are traded on the Chicago Board of Trade in contract lots of 5,000 bushels each. The minimum margin in early 1973 was $750 per contract, although some brokerage houses required more than that. A 5,00-bushel soybean contract for delivery in July, 1973, bought in January, 1973, at $4 was worth $20,000. A July, 1973, contract sold six months later at $12 a bushel worth $60,000. The difference: a $40,000 profit on a margin investment of $750 to $1,500, in much less than a year. (Less commission charges of $30.)

A variety of causes made these glowing profits possible. The worst floods in history cut down farm production in the Mississippi Valley. An ocean current changed course in the Pacific, and anchovies practically disappeared off the Peruvian coast (fishmeal made from anchovy is the main competitor of soybeans as animal feed). The United States dollar was devalued, which made soybeans cheaper for foreign buyers. It is highly unlikely that all these things will happen at the same time again, but if you think you can predict when each of them will manifest itself once more, you have a great future as a soybean speculator.

Meanwhile, here are some facts about soybeans to work on as the basis for your first million. The United States is the world's greatest producer. It generally uses about three-quarters of its crop and exports the remaining quarter, mainly to Europe and Japan.

Most American soybeans are grown in Illinois, Iowa, Indiana, Arkansas, Missouri, Minnesota, and Ohio. The weather and growing conditions in these states are therefore of paramount importance. Crop production reports are issued by the USDA Crop Reporting Board as of August 1, September 1, October 1, November 1, December 1 and the final report when the entire harvest is in. Further details are available from the Agriculture Department's Agricultural Marketing Service and Consumer and Marketing Service.

As in the case of wheat, soybean farmers are helped by a government price support program. Unlike in grain production however, the amount of acreage planted is not controlled. There is thus a government floor under the price of soybeans, but huge price increases such as those in 1973 could swiftly lead to a big increase in United States soybean production.

Production abroad may expand very rapidly, too. Soybeans can be grown on land too poor for most other crops. They need little cultivation and they actually improve the soil by taking nitrogen out of the air and putting it into the ground through their roots. Brazil alone has thousands of square miles of otherwise unusable lands, and its soybean crop has been growing at the rate of 50 percent a year, rising to nearly 250 million bushels. Brazil could very soon become the soybean supplier to the world.

Other speculations you can make are in what is known in the futures market as the soybean complex. A bushel of soybeans weighs sixty pounds. From this one can extract forty-eight pounds of *soybean meal* and eleven pounds of *soybean oil*. The remaining pound is moisture that is lost in processing.

You can also trade soybean meal futures on the Chicago Board of Trade, where each contract is for 100 tons. You can trade soybean oil on the same Exchange, with each contract representing 60,000 pounds. Both these products also took off when soybeans started rising in early 1973. Oil prices doubled and meal prices more than quadrupled. You would thus have done much better buying meal futures at that time. The difference was due mainly to the diverse uses to which oil and meal are put.

Soybean meal is used to feed animals. It provides the protein in the feed mixes for hogs, poultry, and other livestock. Western European nations usually take about three-quarters of United States soybean meal exports, and in 1973 these countries were practically unable to buy fishmeal, the main competing product, because Peru, the world's biggest producer, had banned all anchovy fishing until its ocean stocks built up again. Cottonseed and linseed meal, the next best substitutes, have nowhere near the nourishment value of soybeans, which are 44 percent pure protein; in any case, they, too, were going up in price at the time.

Soybean oil, on the other hand, is mainly for human consumption. It is used for shortening and margarine, and for salad and cooking oil. The rapid growth of fast-food service restaurants has boosted the use of soybean oil for cooking. Its competitors are lard, butter, cottonseed, and peanut oil.

The United States usually consumes about one billion pounds of soybean oil a year, and its annual exports range from 600 million to 1.2 billion pounds. Foreign demand is therefore a powerful factor in the price.

When you speculate in soybean futures you are taking the general, overall picture of soybean production and consumption around the world. When you buy or sell contracts in the soybean *meal* or the soybean *oil* markets you are entering a more highly specialized field, where human or animal consumption is the important thing in each case.

However, this distinction may be increasingly blurred in

coming years, as soybeans are used more and more as human food. Already you can buy imitation bacon bits made of soybeans—salted, flavored and colored to look like bacon. Meat products "extended" with soybean products are already on the market. Ground soybeans make a passable milk substitute, and soybean oil may be used in the artificial milk that can be sold in some states. As protein foods such as meat, eggs, and fish go up in price, there should be an increasing demand for substitutes, and soybean products could fill that demand. There is even a prospect, although still little more than a dream, of a soybean steak that would look and taste like the real thing and cost only a quarter as much.

But don't bet on it on the futures markets, which only look a year to eighteen months ahead. People who are too far ahead of their time tend to lose fortunes while trying to sell their idea to a skeptical market.

Rye

Meanwhile, we still have to investigate the posibilities of speculating in one more grain, which is used not only to feed animals and humans but also to make liquor. This is rye, and it is traded on the Winnipeg Grain Exchange. It is a small market compared with wheat, corn, and soybeans, but can be followed through the same United States government reports on world and United States production, stocks, prices, imports and exports. Official United States crop reports are issued from July to December, but the United States produces only 27 to 41 million bushels a year. It is dwarfed by the Soviet Union, with 450 to 650 million, Poland with around 300 million, and West Germany with 100 to 150 million bushels a year.

Rye is used in the United States mainly for food (about 25 percent of the total), animal feed (about 40 percent), and alcohol (around 25 percent). The remaining 10 percent is used for seed or exported.

17

Some Dietary Luxuries

YOU MAY have to wait a while before you can sink your money into a futures contract for 5,000 cases of cashew nuts. Yet nuts may be one of the most exotic investments you can make during the 1970s. While there was no organized futures market for them as the decade started, there was a flourishing trade to help consumers hedge against their futures needs. Bache and Company started this restricted market late in 1972. Trade sources said nuts would be registered for regular trading on one of the recognized commodity exchanges in due course.

Robert E. Gould, manager of the Bache nut department, explained the move by saying that "while cashews and other nuts are not yet considered a basic food, they cannot be divorced from the total world food picture."

Nuts could be an exciting article of trading once they are registered. The market is big enough to be active—India alone shipped $110 million worth of cashews in 1972 and the volume is rising.

The nut supply situation is complex so there will be a lot of factors affecting prices. Most cashews are grown in Africa, with Portuguese East Africa the largest single producer. Guerrillas have been active in this region, and if they control any large part of it, this could affect the supply, which would drive prices up.

The harvested nuts are shipped to India for roasting and separating from the shells, the latter a skilled hand operation in which the Indians specialize. Any internal convulsions in India would affect the processing, also driving up prices. And India grows a lot of the nuts itself, so trouble in India could also cut down the total supply.

Another factor that will affect the market is the growing world consumption. Russia is a big buyer and promises to have enough money to take a large portion of future crops.

Cashews can also provide the wide price swings that make profits for the investor. For instance, when Bache started its nut market in October, 1972, cashews were selling for 70 cents a pound. Then came new figures on production, showing a probable shortage and the devaluation of the dollar, and in six months the price was up to $1.20 a pound. That's a rise of 71 percent, and when there is a formal futures market, it could mean a profit of 71 percent, leveraged perhaps by a factor of ten.

Wine—Judgment is Everything

Buying wine for investment, not ingestion, requires more good judgment perhaps than any other way of putting your money to work to make more money. Unlike copper futures, where you don't have to worry about the grade or national origin of the metal, wine presents you with a series of decisions.

You have to judge which type of wine to buy—American, French, or even wines from Italy, Spain, or Germany. Then you must choose among red, white, or rose. On top of that you have to buy a good year, wine from a crop that will improve as time goes by. Once you have chosen the wine, you have to decide how to buy it and store it.

The reason to invest in wines, despite all these choices, is that the profit potential is tremendous. Terry Robards of the *New York Times* cites the example of a red Bordeaux that he bought for $12 a bottle a few years before. When he wrote, the price had gone up to $125 a bottle, a rise of nearly 1,000 percent.

Such a sizable increase is unlikely in any other commodity. Soybeans were the glamor futures of the early 1970s because their price went from $3 a bushel to $12. That was a 300 percent rise, and it was huge for the commodity markets.

Investment in American wines is a fairly new business, so the scope of the possible profits is not as clear. However, a case of Inglenook vineyard wine, made before 1900 and stored in the John Daniel cellar, brought $5,000 at auction. A cask (about thirty gallons) of Pinot Noir 1970 has been sold for $2100 — although the wine of a current year is available for from $2 to $5 a bottle. In one recent wine auction, a case of Cabernet Sauvignon 1968 was sold for $210, although the wine from 1969 was selling for less than $5 a bottle or $60 a case.

One major difference in investment between California and French wines is that French vintages — a certain wine from a certain grower in a certain year — are smaller. That means that a well-heeled investor might easily buy up an entire vintage from that one vineyard. If it turned out to be a great year, he would have a virtual corner on that particular kind of wine and could charge his own price for it.

Sherry-Lehmann, a New York liquor importer and dealer bought 800 cases of Chateau Lafite-Rothschild 1959 at $2.37 a bottle and sold it for $3.70 a bottle. Fourteen years later, when the company could buy the wine at all it had to pay $83 a bottle. The vintage retailed for about $120 per bottle. If the company had held on to those 800 cases and not sold any, Robards says, it would probably have a corner on the wine and would be able to set its own price. Nobody else would have enough to make a major sale.

In addition to big potential profits, there are other advantages to investing in wine. One is that there is comparatively little competition — not many people are competing with you for the same wine. If you are a good judge and can tell early in the game when a vintage is going to turn out to be great, you should be able to buy it without too many other bidders against you.

A born wheeler-dealer will also get some pleasure from the sheer complexity of investing in wine. Unlike wheat or corn or copper, wine is not traded on a regular exchange. A good vintage is not even easy to buy. The best California vineyards are small, and not all of them ship wines out of the state. You might have to go to the vineyard itself to taste a new vintage and then take delivery at a California liquor store.

Then there are the problems of storing the wine once you've bought it and selling it once you have a profit. There are three ways of buying wine now and selling it later without having to take out a dealer's license — the license costs around $500 in most states and that would eat up some of your profits.

The first way is to arrange with the winery to deliver your purchase at some time in the future. That is how the cask of Pinot Noir was bought — although it was the 1970 vintage, it would not be delivered to the purchaser until about the middle of the decade. That was to give it time to mature in the cask, after which the winery was to bottle it and ship it to the buyer.

The second way of handling a wine investment is to have your dealer buy it for you and store it himself. You lend him the money to buy the wine, with a mortgage on it so it cannot be sold until you agree.

This is a deal that has to be worked out with the aid of a savvy lawyer, since you are not supposed to own the wine without a license but you must be able to get the profit when there is one. Some states have legal restrictions on who can lend money to liquor dealers, so this method won't work everywhere.

Either of these schemes, though, solves the problem of wine storage. Wine is highly sensitive to moisture, light, and temperature, so you can't just stack the cases in a dusty barn somewhere.

There's a third possibility that makes you face up to the storage problem. That is to buy the wine, take delivery, and then rely on having a regular wine auctioneer sell it for you. The only regular wine auctions in the United States so far are held by Heublein, Incorporated, Box 936T, Hartford, Connecticut 06101. The man to talk to is the manager of the international wine department. Incidentally, Heublein might be willing to buy your collection outright instead of auctioning it off. Make your own deal.

Heublein can be useful in another way, too. The firm publishes an auction catalog of wines, which gives a review of prices over the past five years of the rarest vintages that have been sold at the company's auctions and also indicates what may be available next time. The catalog costs $4 and serves as your free entry passport to the Heublein preview wine tastings and to the auction itself, held yearly in different United States cities. At the 1974 sale in Chicago, 30,000 bottles were auctioned, the most expensive being a jeroboam of Chateau Lafite, which was knocked down for $9,000.

One thing that will simplify your choice of what wine to invest in is the fact that not all of them improve with age. White wines, for instance, get better for only a few years after they are bottled. Since they would have to be sold before they deteriorate, they are not a good investment for long-term profits. Over a short term, though, they could make you some good money.

Says Vernon L. Singleton, professor of oenology (the science of wine) at the Davis campus of the University of California:

> There is no simple way to test wine's potential for improvement during aging and no opinion can be guaranteed. In general, the best one can say is that only initially good and relatively rich wines will profit from long bottle aging. Light wines which have freshness and grape aroma as their main desirable features will tend to lose these features during long aging. They will be different, certainly, after

aging, but more complex wines may be a more reasonable choice in expectation of the benefits of aging.

I have yet to see a pink wine (rosé) which was improved by long bottle storage, but both white and red wines can benefit. The grape varieties and wine types noted for producing agreeable wines are certainly to be recommended in that, not only are you more certain of a favorable response of the wine to aging, but also, if the object is resale, more certain of a favorable response by potential buyers.

You may get some helpful material on wine types and choices available from the Wine Institute, 717 Market Street, San Francisco, California 94103. As Dr. Singleton points out, nobody can tell you what wine to buy, although you can take expert advice.

According to a wine study made by experts assembled at the behest of *Time* magazine, a 1969 Cabernet Sauvignon from the Mondavi vineyard in California ranked higher than any of the French wines tasted by the group. When only California wines were tried, a Cabernet Sauvignon 1969 again was the winner. This time it came from the Beaulieu winery. The good results of the Cabernet Sauvignon are confirmed by independent wine experts. Robards says that "our best Cabernet Sauvignons, which can be quite competitive with French Bordeaux on a quality level, now reach the East Coast at $7 a bottle and up—if they get here at all."

This comment brings up another problem with wine as an investment—you can't always get and store the wine you want. You could sample whatever takes your fancy among the good wines and then write to the vineyard telling them you are in the market for so many cases, either for future delivery or for storage on your own premises, and asking whether the quantity is available.

Storage is a key factor in protecting your investment if you try to keep your wine yourself. Dr. Singleton says storage "should be limited to bottled wines because of the greater attention, risks, and know-how required for barrel or cask storage." He suggested a fixed temperature of 50 to 55 degrees F., low humidity so labels will not mildew, and low lighting if the cellar cannot be kept dark. The Wine Institute has a booklet with suggestions for storing wines when a cellar is not available.

From an investor's point of view, there are factors indicating that the price of wine is likely to go up.

For one thing, American consumption of wine is increasing—it doubled between 1968 and 1972, in just four years. Yet wine production cannot increase greatly because of lack of new land for vineyards in the California valleys. In one, Napa, people are planting vines on their front lawns because of lack of space for formal vineyards. The soaring price for wine grapes make the home grape arbor financially attractive—Cabernet Sauvignon grapes have gone up from $300 a ton to $1,000 in four years as demand increased.

The rising price for grapes is another indication that future wines will cost more than present ones, thereby widening the profit margin of the person who invests in wine now. And, if you think California can meet this demand, you can always invest in foreign wines. Early in 1973, there was a chance to buy some 1871 port that was more than 100 years old, through a British firm. The price was $170 a case. The company was the Hambleton Brewery Company Limited, Ornhams Hall, Boroughbridge, Yorkshire, England. The minimum investment they would accept was $2,500, but they also offered to store and resell the wine.

Another firm in the business is Wine Investments Limited, 51 Coxwell Street, Cirencester, Gloucester, England. This wine broker deals in Bordeaux, port and other vintages. It recommends what it considers best buys, handles all the details, and claims it has made an average 30 percent profit for its clients in some years. The minimum investment is 500 pounds (about $1,200).

On the London stock exchange you can buy shares in Sandeman and other wine companies which you will find listed in the London *Financial Times* stock table in a section headed "Beers, Wines and Spirits."

In the United States you could buy shares in such publicly

owned American wine producers as Almaden Vineyards, Tiburon Vintners and the Taylor Wine Company.

18

The Peculiar Case of
Scotch Whisky

I F YOU sip Scotch whisky by the glass and invest in it by the barrel, it would seem you would stack the odds high in your favor for both pleasure and profit. Yes, you *can* invest in Scotch whisky—trust the canny Scots to produce the world's most popular liquor and then figure out a way of making money on it on the side. The question is: Can *you* make money on it too?

Here is the plus side of the story. You buy whisky barrels—not just barrels in general, but specific, identified barrels, with serial numbers on them and registered in your name. They are kept for you in bonded warehouses in Great Britain, under the watchful eye of a uniformed British government inspector, who actually *lives* in the warehouse. You can insure your barrels with Lloyd's of London against all risks, including atomic radiation.

At times, investing in Scotch apparently has other advantages. In what other investment in the whole world are you offered insurance guaranteeing you against the risk of selling at a loss? Such insurance was offered in 1972 by a London whisky broker who had a United States office in New York. The London broker said the policy "holds the insured indemnified against the risk of sales prices being lower than purchase prices. Cover is taken out for four years at a premium of 6 percent total."

"This is an absolutely unique type of insurance," the broker added, "which to the best of our knowledge has never before been available and which shows clearly the faith of the insurance companies of this country (Great Britain) in the capital growth aspect of the Scotch Whisky industry."

Note that wording carefully. It says *four years*. Evidently we are dealing here with a long-term investment. It is obvious, therefore, that you must plan to use money that you can keep invested in Scotch for that length of time, that no emergency or unforeseen financial difficulty will force you to sell against your will before the four years are up. You might note also that on being queried in 1974 the broker's New York office said the insurance against loss "is no longer being offered."

A fairly large number of Scotch whisky brokers are available—about twenty of them in Great Britain and a smaller number in the United States. One of these, Accrued Equities of 122 East 42nd Street, New York 10017, among the earliest firms in the business in the United States, requires a minimum investment of about $2,400. Haffenden Whisky Blenders Limited, of Maidstone House, 25-27 Berners Street, London W1, England, has a £1,000 minimum, about $2,400. Accrued Equities says Haffenden is one of its sources of whisky for both purchase and sale.

What about your potential profit? Estimates from different sources in the trade vary, but they are invariably high. Accrued Equities has taken the average price of raw Scotch or "fillings" (which you buy) from 1954 to 1970 and the price of the four-year-old Scotch (which you sell) over the same period, to figure out the average return on a four-year investment.

In this calculation you have the essence of the Scotch whisky deal. You are buying raw spirits, which nobody can drink without gagging, and four years later you are selling a smooth, matured liquor that will tickle a connoisseur's palate. So here is the unique character of a Scotch whisky investment — it is one of the few commodities that improves and becomes more valuable as time goes by. The profit, Accrued Equities says, works out *on the average* to 93 percent in four years — that is, 23.5 percent a year.

Very interesting. But there are some nasty snags along the way. For one thing, Scotch, like many commodities, goes through boom-and-bust cycles. It goes like this: World War II interferes with Scotch production and causes a scarcity. Prices rise spectacularly. This attracts more production, exaggerated optimism, over-production. Then prices collapse. The problem now is excessive gloom because everyone involved in whisky got burned at the same time. Production is cut back. A new scarcity develops, prices rise spectacularly, and here we go again on the roller coaster.

In 1973 the Scotch industry was on the rocks. Peter Wright, managing director of Tomatin Distillers, the leading independent malt whisky producer in Scotland, predicted that about 100 million gallons of grain whisky would have to be poured down the drain because there was just too much of it around. There was a surplus of 200 million gallons, he claimed, and half of it would never be used. The whisky market is expanding, Wright conceded, but the trouble is that production expanded even faster during the 1960s.

Obviously, if you bought on the boom then and sold on the bust in 1973 you would not have done well at all. There are still other snags, but let's try to get around this one first. You do this by playing the averages, through a technique called *turnover*. You buy 1,000 gallons of grain whisky fillings, the zero age of newly distilled whisky. It might cost you $1.30 a gallon, or a total of $1,300. You buy another 1,000 gallons every year for four years.

After four years, the original whisky might be worth, say, $4 a gallon, or $4,000. You sell it and spend $1,300 of the proceeds to buy another 1,000 gallons of fillings. That gives you a $2,700 profit, and you are still the owner of 1,000 gallons of whisky maturing for sale in another four years. The next year you sell the second batch of 1,000 gallons, now four years old, buy 1,000 gallons of new fillings and take your profit, if any, again. In this way you average out the ups and downs of the whisky price every year and constantly renew your investment.

Your costs are warehouse charges, insurance, and brokerage fees. Warehouse fees would come to about 7 cents a gallon per year. For less than 1 percent a year you can insure your whisky against all risks, and brokerage fees may amount to 5 percent of the cost of the whisky. The insurance *does not* include the insurance against loss from lower prices that was mentioned above.

The second snag in this whisky barrel deal is that at least up to early 1974 there was nothing resembling an official whisky market. Most buying and selling is done by private negotiations within the trade. Blenders have their own secret formulas to produce their particular brands of whisky, and if they are short of one type they make a swap arrangement with another blender who has too much of it. Since all this is done in private and blenders are highly secretive anyway about their formulas, it is very hard to establish prices for different types and ages of whisky.

"As a result, " the *Financial Times* of London stated, "the prices charged to private investors in new whisky tend to be well above the normal price charged in the industry itself. Naturally, when insurance and storage costs are added, it is a very lucky investor who can make a worthwhile profit."

In February, 1974, a new organization was founded with the aim of solving this problem. The Whisky Exchange Limited went into business on Queen Victoria Street, London. It intended to introduce some order into a chaotic market by offering advisory services to Scotch whisky investors, providing statistical data and regulating brokerage activities. The Exchange's Chairman Keith St. John-Foster said he expected the exchange to evolve in time into a major commodity market. At the time of writing this it was too early to evaluate the exchange's effectiveness.

Meanwhile all this whisky that Mr. Wright of Tomatin Distillers says is going to be poured down the drain in fact "is nearly all owned by private investors who often paid ridiculously high prices for it," according to the *Financial Times*.

Many of them live outside the United Kingdom. . . the fraud squad has had a man specially briefed about the workings of the Scotch whisky business in the hope that he might be able to head off some future troubles. Irate investors from the States have written in protest to Prime Minister Edward Heath. . .one American has written he had been trying to sell some Scotch for more than a year. . . many U.S. investors seem to have paid in the mid-1960s up to $3 a gallon for whisky that has a maximum current value (in April 1973) of 50 pence ($1.25). . .Mr. Wright of Tomatin suggested that when investors find they can't sell the Scotch they will stop paying the warehousing charges. Then the warehouse owner will have a go at selling it—again without success—so it will be poured down the drain.

In the United States, at the same time the Securities and Exchange Commission (SEC) had been cracking down on some shady dealers who operated as brokers in the American market. It took several of them to court on charges that they failed to register with the SEC, stated falsely that such whisky investments always went up, assured their clients that they were completely insured against fraud or loss, and failed to reveal that the contracts were being sold for about double the price they were being sold for in Britain.

So what about all those luscious 25 percent yearly profits private investors were supposed to be making? It is not beyond the bounds of possibility that in some cases they were achieved by a "pyramid sales" effect. By this is meant that the original

United States investors, having paid an inflated price for their whisky to start, may possibly have been bailed out by subsequent American investors, who bought them out at even more inflated prices. These investors, in turn, were bailed out by yet other investors—until the bubble finally burst when no new investors were forthcoming.

Contributing to the growth in the number of investors have been favorable or at least uncritical commentaries on whisky barrel investments in American periodicals and financial publications. All of this publicity has been reinforced by the constant advertising of British and American whisky brokers.

Now, how can you get around all these dangers? First, you must deal in the United States only with firms that have registered and filed a prospectus with the SEC. Accrued Equities is one of these (it complied voluntarily even before the SEC required registration by whisky brokers), and its prospectus spells out clearly what some of the dangers are. Among other things, the prospectus states that "the registrant stands ready to perform services such as furnishing market letters, advising the investor as to the relative merits in investing in various types of malts and grains, advising the investor as to market conditions in resales. . . . .The registrant disclaims any contractual liability to perform such services."

Second, you must have your own disinterested source of information about prevailing prices for different types of whisky. You could protect yourself partially by comparing the prices quoted by different brokers. You could also keep up with prices through Harpers Wine & Spirit Gazette, Harpers Trade Journals Limited, Southbank House, Blank Prince Road, London.

But in the end, your only true protection against loss and your only real road to profit is by making yourself an expert You have to know the difference between grain and malt whiskies. You must be aware that the Scotch you buy in a bottle is a blend of both types, each different brand having its secret formula for combining them. Grain whisky is a standard type of product—it tastes very much the same wherever it comes from. Malt whisky, on the other hand, is highly individual—its taste and aroma is quite different if it is produced in the Highlands of Scotland, the Lowlands, the Isle of Islay, or the Mull of Kintyre. And it is the varying blends of malts that give each brand its distinctive flavor.

According to *Financial Times* writer Kenneth Gooding,

> Grain whisky is more easily produced, there will always be plenty of capacity in Scotland for producing it, and prices will never show more than a modest increase. Malt whiskies in the top category, which covers only a dozen or so distilleries, are always in demand, but since these distilleries have no spare capacity, their whisky is virtually never available to the general public. The whiskies offered to the private investor tend to come from distilleries—both grain and malt—which can't sell all they produce to the blenders, and it is unlikely that the blenders will change their minds even when the whisky matures.

Andrew MacDonald Limited, Scotch Whisky Brokers, 19-20 Bolton Street, London, England, says it supplies investors with some of the top-quality malt whiskies, including Mosstowie, Benriach, Aberlour, Glen Keith, Milton Duff, Strathisla, and Tamnavulin of the Glenlivet variety, as well as Dalmore, Caperdonich, Milburn, Glenugie, Glen Mohr, Inchgower, Glenfiddich, Bowmore, and others. Do you know anything about these varieties, with their smoky Gaelic names? If you are going to invest in them perhaps you should.

One possible source of information on the varieties of Scotch malt whiskies is the Scottish Council of Development and Industry, 1 Castle Street, Edinburgh, Scotland. Gordon & McPhail, an old established whisky firm of Elgin, Scotland, runs an exhaustive catalog of malt whiskies, their ages, strengths, distilleries, and prices. A similar catalog is put out by another whisky firm, William Cadenhead of Aberdeen, Scotland. Gordon & McPhail will sell you at retail, bottles of thirty-three different kinds of malt whisky. George Strachan of

Aboyne, Aberdeenshire, offers forty-three different kinds of malt whisky at retail, which it claims is every single kind available in Scotland.

If you have the time, the taste, and inclination a Scotch whisky pilgrimage to these places might be highly rewarding in pleasure and perhaps even profit as well. Turning yourself into a Scotch whisky expert could be a fascinating hobby. At the very least, you would soon have a unique collection of whisky bottles and labels of all shapes and sizes.

These numerous varieties of malts are what one might consider the genuine original whisky that Scotsmen drank for centuries. Blended whiskies, with an admixture of grain spirits, are a fairly recent development. Up to the turn of the century people drank pure malt whiskies — and now it seems that malts are coming back into favor. There are about 100 malt distilleries in Scotland, but nearly all their production still goes into the blends. Perhaps 3 percent of all Scotch whisky is sold in 1974 as a pure malt variety, but this percentage may well rise if the taste for distinctive malt flavors continues to spread.

Once you know your malts from A to Z you may confidently rely on your own judgment to buy a particularly outstanding variety for your own consumption and pleasure — or perhaps by the barrel, too, if you know the demand for this type is growing, or that it is in short supply and needed urgently by the blenders.

For the present let's just say that Scotch whisky is a great drink, but that bought by the cask in a warehouse without any special expertise on your part it may easily turn out to be a very bad investment. Remember that if you are unable to sell your casks in the British warehouse you cannot even take them with you to the United States. You have to get an importer's license to do that. So you will probably do much better for yourself just buying the varieties of Scotch you like by the bottle, for your own pleasure and to entertain your friends.

How to Invest in Scotch Whisky Companies

And while you are sitting back sipping the golden nectar of the Glens, rolling it around on your tongue, with the ice clinking in the glass, you might reflect that millions of people around the world like to do just that. That is the reason for the steady growth of Scotch sales around the globe, from Scotland and the United States to Venezuela and Japan, at a steady 10 percent a year. Basically, Scotch whisky *is* a good growth business, and there *is* a way you can profit by it.

Turn to the *Financial Times* of London and look up on the back pages the list of stocks quoted on the London Stock Exchange. They are classified in sections, one of which is headed *"Beers, Wines, and Spirits."* It contains about thirty stocks, including breweries and wine merchants as well as Scotch and other liquor companies. Here you will find names such as Tomatin, Distillers Company, Glenlivet, Highland Distilleries, Invergordon, Long John, Scottish & Newcastle Breweries, and Teacher's.

These are the people who know the Scotch business inside out. To a large extent they *are* the Scotch whisky industry. If Scotch whisky sales continue to expand at 10 percent a year, they are the firms that are going to achieve that growth and benefit by it. Their shares are a highly liquid investment you can buy or sell at any time at a publicly quoted and published price. So if you want to make money out of Scotch, you will probably do well to buy their shares and let the experts run the business for your profit. A portfolio of these stocks will probably give you far better results in the long run than a few barrels in a warehouse that you may or may not be able to sell at a fair price four years later.

Shares of Distillers Company, may be bought in the United States through any American stockbroker. The other whisky stocks could be purchased through a British bank, perhaps one of those mentioned in Chapter One in connection with British premium savings bonds. These banks will either get a London stockbroker's recommendation on a particular stock to buy or put you in touch with a broker. Many will also keep your shares in safe custody and collect your dividends.

Scottish & Newcastle Breweries produces beer as well as Mackinlay's Scotch Whisky, MacPherson's Cluny Scotch, and other marks, and it has a captive market in the 1,700 hotels, restaurants and pubs that it keeps under its direct management.

Distillers Company not only produces such famous blends as Vat 69, Dewars, Haig, Johnnie Walker, Black & White, King George IV, and White Horse, but it is also a major supplier of gin and vodka. If public taste should ever turn to these drinks and away from Scotch you would be well protected.

Another possibility to keep an eye on is Suntory, a giant Japanese firm that owns the world's largest malt distillery and controls about 70 percent of the Japanese whisky market. In 1972, the Japanese downed 16 million cases of whisky. In the same year only 9 million cases were consumed in all of Great Britain. A Suntory spokesman thinks the Japanese whisky market might well double in five years. The firm is also selling whisky in the United States. Suntory is privately owned and you cannot invest in it right now. But if it should ever go public, it might well be worth investigating. It might even turn out that the best place to invest in Scotch whisky is in Japan.

19

Race Horses

RACE horses, like diamonds, have always been considered the exclusive playthings of rich men and women. But they can also make money for a comparatively small investor.

True, you can't go into race horses on a contract of $40 a month, as you can with stocks. But your initial investment can be as low as $1,000 — and you can't even buy a bond for much less than that. In fact, it is even possible to take a chance in the racing business by buying stock for as little as $17 a share. A share won't make you rich, but it will keep up your interest in horse racing longer than a parimutuel ticket will.

However, the big ticket items like race horses should be adopted as an investment only by people who can afford to lose their thousand dollars. And, of course, if they don't lose, they can always invest more from their winnings. Race horse syndicate shares can run up to $250,000 or more.

There are different ways to invest in race horses, with the

possible profits keyed to the amount of money you put in. You can spend a quarter of a million dollars and join a syndicate that owns a horse of the caliber of Secretariat, winner of the Triple Crown of Racing in 1973. Or, you can spend $17 and buy a share in the San Juan Racing Association of Puerto Rico, which runs the El Comandante race track and pays a 10-cent stock dividend.

The ideal everybody dreams about is owning his own horse. But even before you buy your horse you should pick your trainer. He will not only prepare and run your horse for you, he will also handle the details of training and choosing a jockey, entering the horse in the race, and picking which race to run him in. In fact, the choice of a trainer is probably more important than the choice of a horse, because a trainer can steer you on to a good horse or steer you off a poor one.

Perhaps the best way to find a good trainer is to hang around the track kitchen, the track restaurant where the trainers and jockeys eat, and listen to the conversation. Useful — in fact, essential — advice to the beginner appears in a pamphlet published by the Cromwell Bloodstock Agency, P.O. Box 4218, Lexington, Kentucky 40504. Called "How to Buy a Race Horse," the pamphlet sells for $2.50 and is well worth the price.

One way to get a horse is to find a likely looking one that is already running and buy him. This class of horse usually runs in the so-called "claiming race," where every horse entered is offered for sale at the claiming price. The owner has to sell at this price, usually from $1500 to $5000, if he is entered.

The problem with claiming is that you must already own a horse running at that meeting at that track before you can claim another animal. Even then you can only claim a horse in the same price range as the one you already own. So the claiming route is good to enlarge your stable, but no good to start one.

However, you can use the claiming price as an idea of how much the owner will want for the horse you want to buy. Allow a few thousand dollars extra over the claiming price, however, because the owner will have to pay capital gains tax on his price. The Cromwell booklet explains all this in quite simple language.

The great advantage of buying a claiming race horse is that he is already racing and you have an idea of how he can do. And some of them do very well: one owner bought Stymie for $1,500 in a claiming race and then won $918,000 with him.

A second way of getting a horse is to attend the auctions of yearlings and bid on one after studying his pedigree. He won't be ready to race for a year, but it will take that long to train him and bring him up to his maximum potential. The auctions are held in various parts of the country several times a year, usually July through October.

A yearling will cost anywhere from $5,000 to as much as $200,000 for the offspring of a good sire and dam. The higher prices (and the better colts) appear at the summer sales. At the fall sale in Keeneland, Kentucky, the prices run a little lower

A third way of getting a horse is the syndicate route. Joining a syndicate is a good idea, since you will be associated with people who already know a lot about racing. The disadvantage is that a good syndicate, like a good man, is hard to find, and the prices can be high.

The Fasig-Tipton Company of Elmont, New York, which runs some sales at Saratoga, New York, says that it is possible occasionally to find a syndicate with shares as low as $1,000. However, Larry Ensor of Fasig-Tipton says this would be "unusual" and the more likely price would be $20,000 to $25,000.

Horse people say that if a syndicate is looking for partners, Fasig-Tipton, Cromwell, or some of the other bloodstock agencies would likely know about it. Your trainer would probably hear, too. Most of the really big syndicates, like the one that bought Secretariat for stud, run to around $175,000 to $200,000 per share. Membership in those is generally by invitation, since the kind of people who have that kind of money all know each other.

However, there is one man who in 1973 was reported by the Thoroughbred Breeders of Kentucky as being interested in forming small, limited partnerships or syndicates. He is Wells Hardesty, Investco Associates, P.O. Box 298, Winnetka, Illinois 60093.

The Breeders warn against "putting all one's eggs in one basket, in other words, in one horse."

> Therefore in order to have the proper quality stock to have a chance at racing or breeding success, it is advisable to spread the investment out among 5 or 6 horses as a minimum, through an investment of $100,000 or more.
>
> An alternative, and these are only beginning to take shape, would be to invest in a limited partnership in racing and/or breeding at a minimum cost of $15,000. This would be a private placement situation. A word of caution, though: there are not many private situations and the chances of a new investor being exposed to one are relatively small.

You may get further information by writing to Thoroughbred Breeders of Kentucky, P.O. Box 4158, Lexington, Kentucky 40504.

A fourth way to get into the horse business is to run your own breeding farm. That way you pick your own stallions and you own the mares you mate them to. The foal resulting — you don't pay a stud fee if your mare doesn't catch — can be either raced or sold. Starting a breeding farm is made easy, if not cheap, by an offer from a Louisiana firm. Rosalie Plantation at Alexandria, Louisiana, offered in 1973 a miniature breeding farm, complete with six mares already bred, for $125,000. You could even take up this offer on the installment plan, paying $35,000 down and the rest in five years, with interest at 7.5 percent on the balance.

The plantation — its address is Route 2, Box 83C, Alexandria, Louisiana 71301 — offered such support facilities for the breeding farm as an exercise track, veterinarian, and breaking and training people. In addition, you could breed your mares to the Rosalie stallions at half their usual fee.

The offer gives you twelve acres of land with a six-stall barn, the six mares ready to produce colts in the spring, management help, and a guaranteed market for the colts. Rosalie buys them at weaning time at a valuation put on them by two independent appraisers.

The plantation's brochure estimates that one mare, bred to a good-quality Kentucky stallion, should produce a colt worth $12,500 and the other five mares should produce colts averaging $5,500 per year. The cost of maintaining each mare is calculated at $125 per month, or $1,500 per year plus $300 veterinarian fees per mare.

Rosalie Plantation says its plan is "the easiest way an investor can own his own thoroughbred horse farm, get all the tax advantages and still have a chance at possible lucrative profits without management worries."

And finally there are always race-track shares such as the San Juan race track company. Its price-earnings ratio—the earnings compared to the price of the stock—at the time of writing is 15. That means that each share earns each year one-fifteenth of what the share costs. However, note that one-fifteenth is earnings, not dividends. The dividend near the middle 1970s was only 2/3 of 1 percent.

The stock has had wide swings up and down. From 1960 to 1974 it has been as high as 33 and as low as 3, so you could win or lose heavily on stock prices. The stock is listed on the New York Stock Exchange so it would be easy to keep track of it.

Operation of a breeding farm or ownership of a stallion requires some pretty intimate prying into the sex life of your horse. It is not, however, as active as you might think when you use the phrase "as happy as a stud horse." A stallion's sex life comes only during three or four months of the year. The rest of the time his owners keep him away from mares, who might kick him and hurt him, and they even truss up his genitals so he can't masturbate.

Stallions are used for stud only from the latter part of February through May. This is due to a peculiar racing rule that says all colts are a year old on January 1 after their birth, no matter when they were actually born (*foaled* is the technical term). That means a colt foaled on December 31 would be expected to race, two years later, against a colt foaled on January 2 of that year. The older animal, obviously, would be stronger and better developed than one born later.

Thus the breeder tries to have his colts dropped, or foaled, as early in the year as possible to give them more development time. And that, in view of the horse's eleven-month gestation period, means breeding only in the spring.

During the summer, the stud horse gets a plain diet and not too much work. But, beginning in October, he will get more and better food and regular exercise. That's to get him in shape for his real work of producing more race horses.

Once this real work starts, late in February, he will be mated, each time with a different mare, a couple of times a day, about the middle of the morning and again in the middle of the afternoon. Occasionally there may be an evening assignation for the cheaper stallions. However, Secretariat, the big horse of 1973, goes only once a day as a rule and gets a day off if he goes twice.

The actual coupling itself is quick, businesslike, and public. The mare is held by three or four men while the stallion, who is always ready for business, does his job. It's usually over in less than five minutes.

The mare is kept at the breeding farm for a few days to make sure she has conceived. If she hasn't, she gets a second chance. In fact, she gets five chances. After that, if she hasn't done her part, she goes home. Stud fees are payable at service, but in some cases they are returned if the mare doesn't produce a live foal strong enough to stand up and nurse immediately after birth.

Operation of a syndicate owning a stallion usually means that each owner of a share gets a chance to breed one of his own mares per year to the stallion. This means a good sire gets a chance to father some thirty-two to thirty-eight colts per year. Not all of these are successful, though, and one British publication has estimated that the owner of a share has only a 3.5 percent chance of making any money from his investment.

Horses are a risky business, whether you buy them, breed them, race them, or just bet on them. But there is always a long-shot chance of making a lot of money as well as getting all that fun out of a fascinating hobby. Remember the man who spent $1,500 on Stymie, a horse that gave him winnings of $918,000.

Remember also that horse racing and betting produce big tax revenues, and as a result many states are eager to encourage you as a horse owner or breeder. New York, for example, offers you financial incentives through breeders' awards if you raise horses in that state. For further details write to the New York State Thoroughbred Breeders Service Bureau, 598 Madison Avenue, New York, N.Y. 10022.

Index